Post-Traumatic Art in the City

New Encounters

Arts, Cultures, Concepts

Series Editor: Griselda Pollock

Conceptual Odysseys: Passages to Cultural Analysis
Ed. Griselda Pollock, 2007
The Sacred and the Feminine: Imagination and Sexual Difference
Ed. Griselda Pollock and Victoria Turvey Sauron, 2007
Bluebeard's Legacy: Death and Secrets from Bartók to Hitchcock
Ed. Griselda Pollock and Victoria Anderson, 2009
Digital and Other Virtualities: Renegotiating the Image
Ed. Antony Bryant and Griselda Pollock, 2010
Visual Politics of Psychoanalysis: Art and the Image in Post-Traumatic Cultures
Ed. Griselda Pollock, 2013
Visioning Israel-Palestine: Encounters at the Cultural Boundaries of Conflict
Ed. Gil Pasternak, 2020

New Encounters Monographs

Helen Frankenthaler: Painting History, Writing Painting
Alison Rowley, 2007
Eva Hesse: Longing, Belonging and Displacement
Vanessa Corby, 2010
Auschwitz and Afterimages: Abjection, Witnessing and Representation
Nicholas Chare, 2011
Crossmappings: On Visual Culture
Elisabeth Bronfen, 2018
Post-Traumatic Art in the City: Between War and Cultural Memory in Sarajevo and Beirut
Isabelle de le Court, 2020

Concentrationary Memories: The Politics of Representations

Concentrationary Memories: Totalitarian Terror and Cultural Resistance
Edited by Griselda Pollock and Max Silverman, 2012
Concentrationary Imaginaries: Tracing Totalitarian Violence in Popular Culture
Edited by Griselda Pollock and Max Silverman, 2015

Forthcoming

Between Holocaust Memory and Racism: Belonging and Culture in Germany
Annette Seidel-Arpachi
Voices of Art, Belonging and Resistance: In Conversation with Sutapa Biswas, Sonia Boyce, Lubaina Himid, Claudette Johnson and Ingrid Pollard
Ella S. Mills

Post-Traumatic Art in the City

Between War and Cultural Memory in Sarajevo and Beirut

Isabelle de le Court

BLOOMSBURY VISUAL ARTS
LONDON • NEW YORK • OXFORD • NEW DELHI • SYDNEY

BLOOMSBURY VISUAL ARTS
Bloomsbury Publishing Plc
50 Bedford Square, London, WC1B 3DP, UK
1385 Broadway, New York, NY 10018, USA
29 Earlsfort Terrace, Dublin 2, Ireland

BLOOMSBURY, BLOOMSBURY VISUAL ARTS and the Diana logo are trademarks of Bloomsbury Publishing Plc

First published in Great Britain 2020
Paperback edition first published 2022

A catalogue record for this book is available from the British Library.

Library of Congress Cataloging-in-Publication Data
Names: De le Court, Isabelle, author.
Title: Post-traumatic art in the city: between war and cultural memory in Sarajevo and Beirut / Isabelle de le Court.
Other titles: Tale of two cities
Description: London; New York: Bloomsbury Visual Arts, 2020. | Series: New encounters: arts, cultures, concepts | Revision of the author's thesis (Ph.D.), University of Leeds, 2012, under the title: Tale of two cities: post-traumatic art in post-war Sarajevo and Beirut in cross-cultural perspectives. | Includes bibliographical references and index.
Identifiers: LCCN 2020036394 (print) | LCCN 2020036395 (ebook) | ISBN 9781350194359 (hardback) | ISBN 9781350194366 (pdf) | ISBN 9781350194373 (epub)
Subjects: LCSH: Art and society–Bosnia and Herzegovina–Sarajevo. | Art and society–Lebanon–Beirut. | Sarajevo (Bosnia and Herzegovina)–Social conditions–20th century. | Beirut (Lebanon)–Social conditions–20th century. | Art and war.
Classification: LCC N72.S6 D457 2020 (print) | LCC N72.S6 (ebook) | DDC 700.1/03–dc23
LC record available at https://lccn.loc.gov/2020036394
LC ebook record available at https://lccn.loc.gov/2020036395

ISBN: HB: 978-1-3501-9435-9
PB: 978-1-3501-9439-7
ePDF: 978-1-3501-9436-6
eBook: 978-1-3501-9437-3

Series: New Encounters: Arts, Cultures, Concepts

Typeset by Deanta Global Publishing Services, Chennai, India

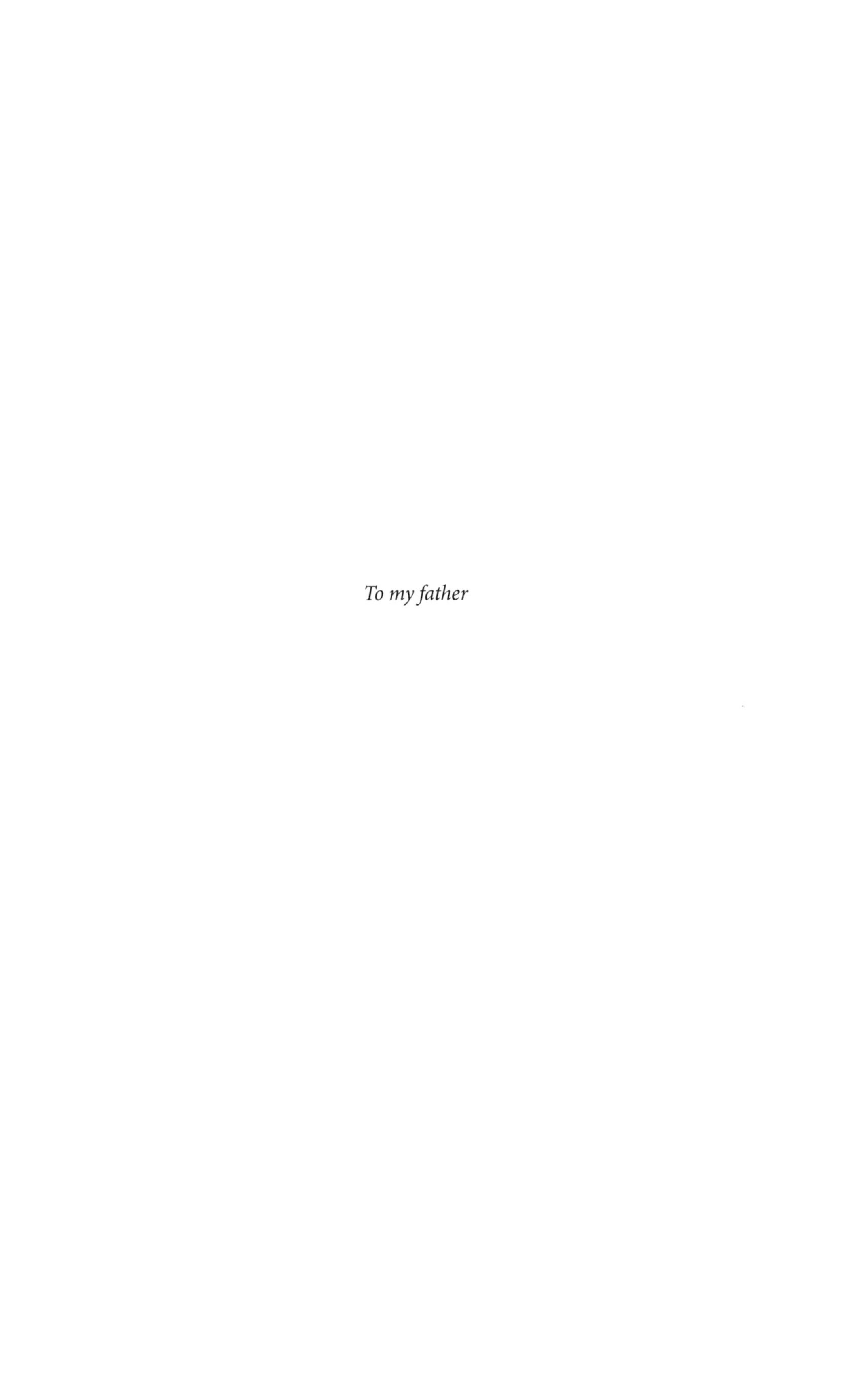

To my father

Contents

List of Figures

Acknowledgements

Many people have enabled me to complete this book.

Special thanks go to Griselda Pollock for her invaluable guidance and encouragement during the research stage and to Danica Dakić, Maja Bajević, Lamia Joreige and Paola Yacoub for their outstanding collaboration and openness.

For their help and support in different ways I am grateful to Michel Abou Khalil, François Barras, Stefanie Baumann, André Bekhazi, Dunja Blažević, Gregory Buchakjian, Yvana Enzler, Benjamin Hannavy-Cousen, Valerie Mainz, Alexandra Parigoris, Arvid Posse, Edin Numankadić and Francesco Ventrella.

For the editorial advice during the publication stage, I wish to thank Philippa Brewster, Margaret Michniewicz, April Peake, Arun Rajakumar and James Thompson.

Ultimately, I would like to thank my family for their continuous and loving support.

Series Editor's Preface

New Encounters: Arts, Cultures, Concepts

Griselda Pollock

> *How do we think about visual art these days? What is happening to art history? Is visual culture taking its place? What is the status of Cultural Studies, in itself or in relation to its possible neighbours – art, art history, visual studies? What is going on? What are the new directions? To what should be remain loyal?*

NEW ENCOUNTERS: Arts, Cultures, Concepts proposes some possible ways of thinking through these questions. First, the series introduces and works with the concept of the *transdisciplinary initiative*. This is not a synonym for the interdisciplinary combination that has become de rigueur. It is related to a second concept: research as *encounter*. Conjoined, *transdisciplinary* and *encounter* mark the interaction between ways of thinking, doing and making in the arts and humanities. Each of these modes retains distinctive features associated with their own disciplinary practices and objects: art, history, culture, film, photography and practice. Yet new knowledge is produced when these different ways of doing, making and thinking encounter each other across – and this is the third intervention – *concepts*. Concepts circulate between different intellectual or aesthetic discourses and cultures, inflecting them, sharing common questions but approaching them in distinctively articulated practices. The aim is to place these different practices in productive relation to each other, mediated by the circulation of concepts.

We stand at several crossroads at the moment in relation to the visual arts and cultures, historical and contemporary, and to theories and methods of analysis. The *Centre for Cultural Analysis, Theory and History* (CentreCATH) was founded as one experiment in thinking about how to maintain the momentum of the intellectual cultural revolution in the arts and humanities that characterized the last quarter of the twentieth century while adjusting to the different field of analysis created by it and to the constantly shifting economic, political and social ground on which we precariously stand in conditions of globalization and liquid modernity dominated by neoliberal reason.

In the 1970s–90s, the necessity, or the intrusion, according to your position, was Theory: a mythic concept with a capital T that homogenized vastly different intellectual undertakings. Over those decades, research and practice in the arts and humanities were undoubtedly reconfigured by the engagement with structuralist and poststructuralist theories of the sign, the social, the text, the letter, the image, the subject, the postcolonial and, above all, difference. Old disciplines were deeply challenged and new inter-disciplines – called studies – emerged to contest the long-established academic divisions of knowledge production. These changes were wrought through specific engagements with Marxist, feminist, deconstructionist, psychoanalytical, queer and postcolonial theory. Texts and authors were branded according to their theoretical alignments. Mapping produced divisions between the proliferating models. Could one be a Marxist and a feminist while drawing on psychoanalysis queerly?

A deeper split, however, emerged between those who, in general, were theoretically oriented and those who apparently did without theory: a position that the theoretically minded easily critiqued. Being positivist is, of course, also a theoretical position. It simply did not carry a novel identity associated with the intellectual shifts of the post-1968 university.

The impact of 'the theoretical turn' was creative; it has radically reshaped work in the arts and humanities in terms of what is studied (content, topics, groups, questions) and also how it is studied (theories and methods). Yet some scholars came to argue that work done under such overt theoretical rubrics was becoming tired; theory constrained the creativity of the new generation of scholars familiar, perhaps too familiar, with the legacies of the preceding intellectual revolution that can too easily be reduced to Theory 101 slogans (the author is dead, the gaze is male, the subject is split, there is nothing but text, etc.). The enormity of the initial struggles – the paradigm shifting – to be able to speak of sexual difference, subjectivity, the image, representation, sexuality, power, the gaze, postcoloniality, textuality, difference, queerness fades before a new phase of normalization in which every student seems to bandy around terms that were once, and in fact still are, challengingly difficult and provocative. Or worse. It is clear that bandying indicated that at least something of this intellectual and theoretical revolution was still – even in an etiolated form – part of public discourse.

Recent events have shown how the terms of critical thinking from feminist to postcolonial theory are not part of general discussion, even as they reappear on the media stage in the wake of new scandals or sexism and racism. Outrageous acts of sexual harassment and abuse are greeted, however, not with knowing acknowledgement of their structural place in a patriarchal culture of asymmetrical power relations but as the signs of a surprising number of 'badly behaved' individual men. Where is the sense that facing revelations of such an order necessitated a political-critical analysis rather than surprise and celebrity 'outing'?

Theory, of course, just means thinking about things, puzzling over what is going on, reflecting on the process of that puzzling and thinking. A reactive turn away from active engagement with theoretical inquiries in the arts and humanities is increasingly evident in our area of academe. It is, however, dangerous and misleading to talk of a post-theory moment, as if we can relax after so much intellectual gymnastics and once again become unthinking couch potatoes. The job of *thinking critically* is even more urgent as the issues we confront are so complex, and we now have extended means of analysis that make us appreciate even more the complexity of language, subjectivity, symbolic practices, affects and aesthetics. So how to continue the creative and critical enterprise fostered by the theoretical turn of the late twentieth century beyond the initial engagement determined by specific theoretical paradigms? How does it translate into *a practice of analysis that can be constantly productive and critically self-reflexive?*

The *New Encounters* series argues that we can go forward, with and beyond, *by transdisciplinary encounters with and through travelling concepts.* The notion of 'travelling concepts' was proposed by Mieke Bal, the leading feminist narratologist and semiotician, who launched an inclusive, interdisciplinary project of cultural analysis in the 1990s with the books: *The Point of Theory: Practices of Cultural Analysis* (Amsterdam and New York: University of Amsterdam Press, 1994) and *The Practice of Cultural Analysis: Exposing Interdisciplinary Interpretation* (Stanford, CA: Stanford University Press, 1999). In founding the Amsterdam School of Cultural Analysis (ASCA), Bal turned the focus from our accumulating theoretical resources to the work – *the practice of interpretation* – we do on cultural practices, informed not only by major bodies of theory (that we still need to study and extend) but also by the concepts generated within those theories that now travel across disciplines, creating an extended field of contemporary cultural thinking. Cultural analysis is theoretically informed, critically situated, ethically oriented to 'cultural memory in the present' (Bal, 1999: 1). Cultural analysis thus works with 'travelling concepts' to produce new readings of images, texts, objects, buildings, practices, gestures, actions.

In *Travelling Concepts in the Humanities: A Rough Guide* (Toronto: University of Toronto Press, 2002), Bal argues that concepts, formed within specific theoretical projects, move out of – *travel from* – their own originating site to become tools in the larger domain of cultural analysis. Their interplay produces a process that seeks to create a space of encounter between the many distinctive and even still disciplinary practices that constitute the arts and humanities: the fields of thought that puzzle over what we are and what it is that we do, think, feel, say, understand and live.

In 2001, a CentreCATH was founded at the University of Leeds, with initial funding from the Arts and Humanities Research Council, to undertake what we defined as a transdisciplinary initiative. We brought together, to advance research in and between, distinct but interrelating areas of fine art, social, feminist, queer and postcolonial histories of art and critical cultural studies – three areas that seem close and yet can be divided from each other through their distinguishing commitments to practice, history and theory respectively. CentreCATH was founded when visual studies/visual culture were contesting art history and inventing a new field. It was a moment of intense questioning about what constitutes the *historical* analysis of art practices as the increasing interest in the contemporary moment seemed to eclipse historical consciousness. It was a moment of puzzling over the nature of research through art practice, and of reassessing the status of the now institutionalized Cultural Studies.

CentreCATH responded to Mieke Bal's ASCA, therefore, with its own exploration of the relations between history, practice and theory in art and visual culture through engagement with transdisciplinary cultural analysis. This concept took its inspiration from the renewed studies of the unfinished project of *Kulturwissenschaft* proposed by Jewish German art historian Aby Warburg at the beginning of the twentieth century. Identifying five urgent but expanding research strands that are at the same time concepts – a) social hospitality, class and alienation; b) musicality/aurality/textuality; c) architecture of philosophy/philosophy of architecture; d) indexicality and virtuality; and e) memory/amnesia/history – CentreCATH initiated a series of encounters (salons, seminars, conferences, events) between artists, art historians, musicologists, musicians, architects, writers, performers, psychoanalysts, philosophers, sociologists and cultural theorists (see http://www.centrecath.leeds.ac.uk: especially Archive).

Each encounter explores a range of differences: feminist, Jewish, postcolonial, ethnic, sexual, politico-geographical, historical. Each acknowledges different ways of thinking and knowing in creative practice and critical thought. Each book in this new series is the outcome of this transformative and transdisciplinary research laboratory. Transdisciplinary means that each author or artist enters the forum with and from their own specific sets of practices, resources and objectives whose own rigours provide the necessary basis for a specific practice of making or analysis. While each writer attends to a different archive – photography, literature, exhibitions, manuscripts, images, bodies, trauma, sound, space and so forth – they share a set of concerns that defy disciplinary definition, concerns with the production of meaning, with the production of subjectivities in relation to meanings, narratives, situations, with the questions of power and resistance.

The form of the books in this series is itself a demonstration of such a transdisciplinary intellectual community at work. The reader becomes the locus of the weaving of these linked but distinctive contributions to the analysis of culture(s). The form is also a response to teaching, taken up and processed by younger scholars, a teaching that itself is a creative translation and explication of a massive and challenging body of later twentieth-century thought, which, transformed by the encounter, enables new scholars to produce their own innovatory and powerfully engaged readings of contemporary and historical cultural practices and systems of meaning. The model offered here is a creative covenant that utterly rejects the typically Oedipal, destructive relation between old and young, old and new, while equally resisting academic adulation. An ethics of intellectual respect – Spivak's critical intimacy is one of Bal's useful concepts – is actively performed in engagement between generations of scholars, all concerned with the challenge of reading the complexities of culture (see Gayatri Spivak, *A Critique of Postcolonial Reason: Toward a History of the Vanishing Present* (Cambridge, MA: Harvard University Press, 1999)).

One of the five key research areas that form the theoretical plait of the *New Encounters* series is *Memory, History, Amnesia*. This explores the issues of cultural repression, forgetting, recovering and reshaping memory within the multiple historical conditions of the oblivion and the need to process the past that is, if unprocessed, a traumatic pressure on the present and a deformation of possible futures. Isabelle de le Court's monograph, *Post-Traumatic Art in the City: Between War and Cultural Memory in Sarajevo and Beirut* contributes specifically to this complex area through a detailed contextual study of the conditions, and indeed the damaged and rebuilt infrastructure, for any artistic practice in societies devastated by civil war. She offers close readings of key artworks that create post-traumatic transformation through diverse artistic strategies that emerged from, and contribute to the understanding of, the site-specific tragedies and sociocultural traumas caused by civil war in a specific locus – two historic cities: Beirut in Lebanon and Sarajevo in Bosnia Herzegovina, now politically distanced but once part of one Empire. Both cities are of ancient origin and have witnessed the coming and decline of multiple empires and transient political formations. As capitals of modern nation states, they are distinctive for their layered histories, with many religious traditions and linguistic communities meeting over centuries in both cultural co-existence and co-creation, and, at times, in bitter political conflict. Both cities have suffered untold material and psychological damage from the unleashing of violence in civil war in the later twentieth century. Isabelle de le Court's research involved close and personal contact with the artists and art organizations emerging in both cities. She has lived and taught in Beirut for many years, experiencing on the ground the fractured fabric of the redevelopment of a still wounded city. As this book was going to press, Beirut suffered a devastating explosion that caused both terrible loss of life among its citizens and fearful damage to the buildings and homes of hundreds of thousands. This book's exploration of the recent past of both cities works through the lens of the works of four artists, each deeply affected by their relations with their cultural communities and historical legacies, each with a distinct practice and a singular perspective on the relations of place, fabric, affect and fidelity. The book offers its contribution to the larger field of the study of art and war and delivers a model for reading and engagement with the contemporary art that the author explores as *post-traumatic*.

There are cities all around the world whose population and fabric bear the wounds – both physical and psychic traumas – of war and civil conflict. Artists do not merely register them. Their work shapes and preserves a memory for the sites of pain while offering aesthetic transformation through which both their immediate audiences and viewers in general may encounter these legacies and reflect on what the artists seek to bring into visibility. Focussing on the later twentieth and early twenty-first century, *Post-Traumatic Art in the City: Between War and Cultural Memory in Sarajevo and Beirut* develops a model for contemporary art history that will tragically be profoundly relevant in the braiding of memory, history and amnesia with conflict and political dereliction. It is also a reminder of the people who bear the burden and carry the scars of their suffering, to which artists bring their transformative witness.

Centre for Cultural Analysis, Theory and History,
University of Leeds 2020

Preface

4 August 2020. I am working on the proofs of *Post-Traumatic Art in the City.* I hear about the deadly Beirut explosion through Twitter. A friend of mine sends me pictures of his damaged apartment, telling me he is safe because he was on the other side of the house. I feel numbed, shocked, while images of the explosion and of the deadly blast a few seconds later are on loop. I am seized by sadness and anxiety for all my friends and acquaintances in Beirut, a city I used to call home for four years.

The explosion in the port of Beirut – the largest urban explosion in the world since Hiroshima and Nagasaki, though fortunately not nuclear – destroyed in a mere fifteen seconds what it would have taken many years of war to inflict. In that instant, 190 people lost their lives, while 6,500 people have been injured and 300,000 are left homeless. My former home in Gemmayze has suffered massive damage. One of my past colleagues at the university where I was teaching was, however, among the casualties. He had been filming the fire at the port just moments before the second and more deadly explosion. Images sent by friends, or that I see on social media and the media, are overwhelming in their devastation and human suffering. So are the messages: 'We are fine. . . . Luckily, we are suffering only material damage to our house.' In the images, I see former students, armed with brooms, helping people to clean their homes and the streets from the shards of shattered glass lying everywhere.

In this book, I do not treat cities as only physical places or geographical locations. They are sites of political and artistic life; they are imaginative locations, steeped in histories of pain, conflict and memories. Beirut has again been deeply hurt not only in its urban fabric but in its very flesh. No longer a resident of Beirut, I shall never know the experience of being a witness to such an event. This reminds me of a comment I often heard while Lebanese were talking to me about the war, stating that 'You never fully understand when you have not experienced it.' Language falls apart in the face of such a traumatic event. Words cannot help us to verbalize what cannot be described: feelings of desolation as much as of anger that this unbearable tragedy and material destruction could happen in the midst of an unprecedented economic crisis and a deadly pandemic. Despite my powerlessness in the face of these events and of such immense psychological and material suffering, I can only, with my book, pay tribute to a city and its inhabitants dear to my heart.

Isabelle de le Court
Swiss Alps, August 2020

Introduction

This book is a tale of two cities, Sarajevo and Beirut, 2,000 kilometres apart, yet joined by the fact of having experienced prolonged trauma at the end of the twentieth century. What happened then and there in Beirut and Sarajevo, the capital cities of Lebanon and Bosnia and Herzegovina, respectively, turned them into some of the darkest places on earth. Fragmented by recent wars and even violence, the urban, social and cultural fabric of these cities were radically disrupted by their being the front lines of prolonged war.

This book is also about art created in the aftermath of the violent wars that ravaged both cities at the end of the twentieth century. How can art engage with violent histories when their consequences often involved the destruction of the economies, the cultural institutions, and basic conditions for making and showing art?

These two cities, one in Europe and the other on the Mediterranean coast of what is known as the Middle East, were both once part of the Ottoman Empire (1229–1923).[1] The historical trajectories of these two cities, however, followed different paths during the nineteenth century. Reaffirming the principle of nationalism in the Balkans, the Treaty of Berlin (1878) attached Sarajevo to the Austro-Hungarian Empire.[2] In the aftermath of the First World War, in which the Ottoman Empire had been militarily defeated and politically weakened, Lebanon was placed under French Mandate in 1920 from which it only gained independence in 1943.[3]

The purpose of this book is to place the historical, political and social histories of these two cities in the later twentieth century in critical relation to artistic practices that explore the diverse legacies of violence, instability, memory, loss and fragmentation created in Beirut and Sarajevo as a result of conflict. My aim is not to compare and contrast two cities. Instead, I want to use their distinctive historical experiences of war and the cultural responses that followed as a method to elaborate an argument about art in post-traumatic urban spaces and places.

Exposed to the ravages of war, both countries could be represented as victims either of sectarianism – Lebanon – or of exacerbated nationalisms –

Bosnia and Herzegovina.[4] Yet such interpretations are locally contested. The Lebanese Civil War(s) (1975 to the beginning of the 1990s) and the war in Bosnia and Herzegovina (1992–5) were of unequal length. The cause of each was diametrically opposite, as political scientist Florian Bieber asserts, 'The temporary dissolution of central control in Lebanon was the result of competing groups trying to dominate the state, while in Bosnia it was not dominance that was the bone of contention, but rather the very existence of the state.'[5]

The General Framework Agreement for Peace, signed on 14 December 1995 in Dayton, Ohio, brought the Bosnian conflict to an end. The west road into Sarajevo was reopened on 26 February 1996. The signing of the Taif Agreement on 22 October 1989 was such a precarious ending to the Lebanese conflict that it left the country unstable and incapable of enjoying real peace. The blurred boundaries of the Lebanese conflict created a permanent feeling of unfinished business, which has been reflected in political instability as well as vulnerability to external aggression from neighbouring countries.

Under the pressure of war, the economic, social and political systems of Beirut and Sarajevo simultaneously collapsed. In the case of Sarajevo, the rebuilding of a war-torn society was inflected by the larger issue of post-communist Eastern Europe. Both cities were subject to an internationally monitored establishment of democracy in their countries, Bosnia and Herzegovina, although Lebanon was, in addition, deeply shaped by its double postcolonial condition.

Extended war and its long-lasting after-effects had massive effects on artistic production in both cities. After mass violence, the role of artists, those living locally and abroad – while maintaining strong links with the city – lay in finding an appropriate language with which to tell a story embedded in pain. They would be called upon to use and to respond to their own experiences in the context of a cultural experience of trauma permeating their entire societies. In the ever-shifting conditions of daily strife and violence, artists had, therefore, to negotiate exceptional conditions for living, let alone making art. Thus, I shall explore the ways in which what I am calling *the post-traumatic* shaped a range of artistic practices in very specific ways as artists sought to formulate works capable of touching or transforming the affective legacies of the traumatic experiences both in and of the cities in question.

Before I began this book, I had analysed the long-standing relationship between war and art. War has been a recurring theme in art history. We are familiar with the historically established genres that celebrate military conflict and conquest while also inciting pathos towards the suffering of the victims. It was, however, the shifts in representation and interpretation of war in the nineteenth and twentieth centuries that initially aroused my special interest. Classical and allegorical representations of triumph or romanticized realism gave way to increasing focus on the devastation of war and the killing of innocents. The tradition of glorifying war and its heroes gave way to the denunciation and criticism of war and violence.

The vast painting created by Pablo Picasso (1881–1973), *Guernica* (1937, Madrid, Museo Reina Sofia), is perhaps the embodiment of such twentieth century turns in the representation of war, notably in his decrying in visual terms a war targeting civilians and soldiers alike. The chaos of contorted figures and animals did not specifically allude to the dramatic fate of the city of Gernika. The Basque capital was bombed on 26 April 1937 with Franco's permission by sixty German and Italian planes dropping incendiary bombs of ECB1. When first exhibited in Paris at the 1937 *Exposition Internationale des Arts et Techniques dans la Vie Moderne* at the Spanish Pavilion, Picasso's agonized reaction to the tragedy was, however, coldly received, even among the Basque delegation.

Yet, as art historian Gijs van Hensbergen claims, 'Picasso had resorted to employing images whose simplicity and meaning could travel across every cultural divide.'[6] Thus, it was only during the Second World War that the painting began to acquire iconic status, particularly after the bombing by Japanese forces of the American naval base of Pearl Harbour in December 1941 and the repeated shelling of numerous cities across Europe. By then, the language Picasso had created in *Guernica* had perhaps become familiar and recognizable. It is very much my intention, throughout this study, to examine how specific artworks linked to the Sarajevi or Beiruti context might themselves achieve this ability to speak both within and beyond their local contexts. How are works of art deeply and affectively rooted in powerful feelings about locality and nation able to engage viewers outside of Lebanon and Bosnia and Herzegovina without becoming part of the lingua franca of international art that risks abstracting them from the specific conditions of their creation? The works of art I shall be analysing, therefore, take their place within the frame of contemporary art with its international audiences. Nevertheless, any reading of the works made in response to specific historical and cultural intensities demands careful historical decipherment and attentiveness to their singular conditions of artistic production.

On war and history

Since I am examining these specific artworks linked to post-conflict cities, it is not my purpose to reopen the generic debate of 'What is war?' especially in the aftermath of what Jean Baudrillard identified as new virtual wars.[7] In the nineteenth century, the influential theorist of war, Carl von Clausewitz (1780–1831), famously argued that war should be grasped as the calculated use of violence for rational political ends.[8] A Prussian officer, Clausewitz understood how the qualities of the soldier could turn the unpredictable chaos of war into an ordered sociopolitical event, thus producing his principle that war is the continuation of politics by other means. In the twentieth century, in a lecture at the Collège de France, Michel Foucault (1926–84) reversed Clausewitz's principle:

> At this point, we can invert Clausewitz's proposition and say that politics is the continuation of war by other means. [. . .] According to this hypothesis, the role of political power is perpetually to use a sort of silent war to reinscribe that relationship of force, and to reinscribe it in institutions, economic inequalities, language, and even the bodies of individuals. This is the initial meaning of our inversion of Clausewitz's aphorism – politics is the continuation of war by other means. Politics in other words, sanctions and reproduces the disequilibrium of faces manifested in war.[9]

Foucault's inversion can be largely observed in both capital cities where this perpetual relationship between war and politics resembles *a state of confrontation*. Since war is researched in further fields than history, anthropologists Bettina Schmidt and Ingo Schröder have pointed out how war is made by 'those who hold power in the society':

> The concept of war describes a state of confrontation in which the possibility of violence is always present and deemed legitimate by the perpetrating party, and in which actual violent encounters occur on a regular basis. It also means a relationship of political collectivities above the family level, ranging from bands or segmentary lineages to states (or even multiple-state alliances). In none of these collectivities, even in the most egalitarian band societies, is the decision to go to war reached unanimously by all group members. It is made by those who hold power in the society.[10]

Schmidt and Schröder's definition corresponds to numerous attempts at historical acknowledgement in my two case studies, such as the causes of the war in Bosnia and Herzegovina and the Lebanese Civil War(s), in times when both countries, due to their fragile political balance, could slide back into war and political struggle.

Two different issues arise when considering this relation of politics and war in the Bosnian and the Lebanese conflicts. On the one hand, the conflict(s) in

Lebanon (1975–91, summer 2006) is a fifteen-year Civil War, which is still an ongoing process – if you refer to the war with Israel in the summer of 2006, the political instability in terms of electing either a president or a prime minister in the last years and the assassinations that dominated the international headlines at the end of the first decade of the twenty-first century. Moreover, Lebanon was under Syrian domination until the Cedar Revolution, also called Beirut Spring in 2005, following the assassination of former prime minister Rafik Hariri on 14 February 2005.

A tragic incident marks the starting point of the Civil War in Lebanon, and is officially acknowledged as such: on 13 April 1975, a bus full of Palestinian passengers was attacked by right-wing Christian militants in Ain El-Rammaneh, a Christian district in East Beirut. According to sociologist Samir Khalaf, twenty-eight people were killed.[11] On the contrary, a consensus on the exact date of the conclusion of the conflict is still lacking. Should its ending be marked by the signature of the Taif Agreement, in the city of the same name in Saudi Arabia on 22 October 1989? Known as the 'National Reconciliation Agreement', this treaty was not approved by any of the militias. Some say the conflict ended in 1990, with the implementation of the Taif Agreement, while other civilians would most likely place the end of the fighting in 1991.

In her introductory chapter to *Lebanese Cinema: Imagining the Civil War and Beyond*, film theorist Lina Khatib simply states, 'The Lebanese Civil War started in 1975 and ended in the early 1990s.'[12] Her answer to this problem of dating illustrates the general feeling about the inconclusiveness of the ending of the war. Despite the cessation of open conflict around the early 1990s, the south of the country had been a constant battlefield between Israel and the Hezbollah up to 25 May 2000, when Israel totally withdrew its troops from Lebanon. The Lebanese still refer to this period as *the events – al hawadith* – to evoke a war that destroyed both the physical and psychological fabric of the city and their country.[13]

On the other hand, Bosnia and Herzegovina was fighting for its own independence between 6 April 1992 and 14 December 1995. Sarajevo, its capital, due to its location in a valley basin, was the scene of an agonizing siege. Its population was trapped for 1,395 days, the longest siege in modern history (6 April 1992 to 26 February 1996), as the city was surrounded by Serbian Bosnian forces.[14] The population's survival mainly depended on the UN humanitarian airlift, which could not take place on a regular basis. After the war, this country had radically to reorganize itself as a society in a now post-communist era while rebuilding new infrastructures to sustain an independent nation.

In both cases, the long-negotiated and well-integrated multiculturalism enjoyed for centuries broke down. Former neighbours who had lived side by side in relative peace now turned against each other in intercommunal strife.

My purpose is not purely a historical reconstruction of the events. This book offers a study of cultural responses to the post-conflict conditions. I will not, therefore, in the following pages, give a critical account of the different conflicts that shaped these two countries. I refer the reader to the extended literature that arose during or after these events, particularly in the field of history, political science and conflict management.

On art

As an art historian researching post-traumatic art in these two cities, I investigate the conditions for making art itself, which along with other infrastructural elements of society as a whole were undermined by prolonged violent conflict. The *art scenes* of these cities, at least directly after the war, were extremely fragile with virtually no funding available for culture in their respective states. I would like to address the new conditions in which artistic practices coincidentally appeared in the mid-1990s in both cities, confronting war, peace, memory and cultural trauma. At the end of their respective wars, these two cities became sites of re-emerging artistic practices reflecting on the experience of the siege and the war in Sarajevo, and on the cleavages between past and future in Beirut, through local and global perspectives. War operated as a disruption of the natural flow of history. Yet its aftermath was rich in artistic responses. Sometimes, artworks emerged out of ideas and concepts conceived during the war but which, materially speaking, could only be created in the aftermath of the war. The artworks produced after the conflict are wide-ranging, as the infrastructure was deeply marked by the impoverishment of cultural support during the conflicts.[15]

At the same time my encounter with specific artworks arrested me and unsettled my art-historical approach. As a result, I decided not to use the model of the synoptic survey but to adopt a model of close reading of specific works or practices, since it seemed impossible to make generalizations. It was also necessary to address the question by such detailed examination of a range of different practices in terms of media and form, and in terms of the self-positioning of the artists in relation to the larger historical events in which they had been variously caught up. Dealing with a situation of fracture, the engagement with fragments might better register the conditions for making art and the conditions about which the art was being made.

In the second part of this book, therefore, I wish to think about highly specific elements, by offering a close reading of these artworks. Each work calls to be read in its own terms, but each reading depends on the relevance of specific elements. In their resonance they seem to catch themes – such as language, the fabric of the city, the belonging – or not – to a specific diaspora – that I found important in the way they intertwine and are present in these artworks. My choice, therefore, particularly focuses on four cases, artworks or series of artworks by the following artists: Danica Dakić (*b.* 1962), Maja Bajević (*b.* 1967), Lamia Joreige (*b.* 1972) and Paola Yacoub (*b.* 1966). This choice is a result of a long and critical process based on the strength, aesthetic formulation, criticality and contemporaneity of their work in relation to the phenomena of post-war and post-trauma artistic practice. Moreover, these artists are more than inside reporters; they live or travel abroad, while maintaining a strong bond with their city. Hence, it was necessary, prior to these separate chapters, to give an indication of the cultural institutions as well as the state of the art scenes following the end of the two conflicts.

Language has also played a role in this study. This question of multilingual forms of access, communication and dissemination touches on both the historical contexts for the artworks I am studying and the context for all contemporary art mediated by the legacies of colonial relations, past empires and contemporary forms of cultural hegemony that shape the international art world into which the internationally active but locally engaged artists are operating. Thus, Dakić and Yacoub both live in Germany while Bajević lives in Paris and Joreige in Beirut. They inhabit different languages. I speak German with Dakić, French with Bajević – who lived in Paris for a long time – with Joreige and Yacoub, for whom French is an inherited effect of the French Mandate in Lebanon and of the extended Lebanese diasporic impact on the way Arabic, French and English are still spoken interchangeably at home in the Lebanese upper class.

As I do not intend to display a comprehensive survey of cultural production in the aftermath of the war in Bosnia and Herzegovina and Lebanon, I had to impose a certain number of limitations to my research. First, I am dealing with art produced in or directly related to the cities of Sarajevo and Beirut, and not to the art that emerged in the two countries at large. Even if the art scenes in both countries are mostly concentrated in the capital city, I cannot ascertain that art produced in Sarajevo and Beirut is representative of artistic production in smaller cities and villages throughout the country. In Bosnia and Herzegovina, for example, Banja Luka, the second city of the country and capital of the Republika Srpska (RS), became in the past few years the site of emergence for a new art scene, through which a younger generation who grew up during the war reflects on war, power and politics, in a similar movement that took place in Sarajevo after 1996.[16]

On fragments

Preceding the four separate chapters, the first part of this book is an attempt to keep both cities in dialogue. It is, therefore, structured from the perspective of the two cities and not their countries at large – while setting political, demographical, religious, sociological and juridical powers together with artistic expression. Second, I wish to provide the reader with an understanding of Sarajevo and Beirut, as unique and differentiated geographical spaces during the conflict and after, including brief notes on the political reshaping through the Dayton and Taif agreements. I begin with Sarajevo, a decision that could be judged as a chronological inaccuracy because the events in Lebanon were officially concluded before the outbreak of violence in Bosnia. This order reflects the process of the research as I encountered post-war Sarajevo before I experienced Beirut's spatiality.

The series of snapshots of different aspects of the history and fabric of the two cities that I offer in the first part of the book are conceived as fragments. This mirrors Bosnia and Herzegovina and Lebanon as fragmented states, while their capitals can be understood as symbols of this fragmentation. I am drawing, therefore, on Walter Benjamin's methodology for his *Passagen-Werk* (*Arcades Project*) that still resists fully comprehensive reconstruction from his notes and fragmentary references. While examining the prehistory of modernity through the city of Paris – and especially the Parisian arcades in the nineteenth century – Benjamin was confronted with the issue of the discontinuity of experience. How would he find the most appropriate literary form to write on the object(s) of his investigation? In his collection of essays about cities, *Einbahnstrasse* (*One-Way Street*, 1928), Benjamin gives an idea of this process of fragmentation used as a literary form:

> [It] must nurture the inconspicuous forms that better fit its influence in active communities than does the pretentious, universal gesture of the book – in leaflets, brochures, articles and placards. Only this prompt language shows itself actively equal to the moment.[17]

Benjamin's choice of the fragment is based on his will to do justice to things by setting them in a new context, destroying the world of what he considers false images. His starting point is, therefore, the fragment, and not the totality of an element. Benjamin seeks to distance himself from the continuity of history:

> The price of any dialectical account of history is abandonment of the contemplative approach characteristic of historicism. The historical materialist must sacrifice the epic dimension of history. The past for him becomes the subject of a construction whose locus is not empty time, but the particular epoch, the particular life, the particular work. He breaks the epoch away from its reified *historical continuity*, and the life from the epoch, and the work from the life's work. But the result of his construction is that in the life's work the epoch, and in the epoch the cause of history are suspended and preserved.[18]

Benjamin is, therefore, working on what he named *Jetztzeit*, on how the presence of the now is filling the time of history: to him, 'history is the subject of a structure whose site is not homogeneous, empty time, but time filled by the presence of the now [Jetztzeit]'.[19] The histories I am dealing with are far from being homogeneous, and I was inspired by reading Benjamin's *Einbahnstrasse*, on the one hand, and, on the other hand, Jean Said Makdisi's personal memoir and first-hand account of the 1982 Israeli invasion in Lebanon and the Civil War published under the title *Beirut Fragments: A War Memoir* (1990). Makdisi adopts a comparable form of narrative. By not approaching the war in Lebanon as a whole entity, her memoir consists of a collection of fragments. Makdisi's reflection starts with the question of how to write about the events she experienced, as an inhabitant of Beirut during the war, but also as a woman, a wife, a mother and a teacher of English literature.[20] Makdisi explains how she tried different forms of narratives, first trying to keep a diary of the war. She raises the issue of writing about the experience of war:

> I tried to force the experience into a comprehensible shape. I searched for a form to fit it into, for some implement to help me impose my need for order on the chaos around me, and I found instead that the chaos imposed itself on me. Clarity, reason, justice, symmetry, tradition, decorum – those were the tools I brought and they were as easily defeated as if I had tried to contain a pool of blood with a picket fence. Forms defaulted one by one as I held them up for trial against a crumbling reality. I wanted something uniform to hold it all, for I am one person – am I not? – and my need for unity and exactness grew in proportion as the country about me fell further and further apart.[21]

My own attempt to provide the reader with a comprehensive survey of historical events was doomed from the beginning. Due to the fragility of this task –

trying to describe the reality of war and its aftermath in a large overview – it could only fail, considering the anarchy of the events reflected in scholarly literature. There is no unified, right and true universality of war but a plurality of experiences and interpretations of the same events. It appeared, therefore, that finding a new narrative structure might be more challenging. Yet it could present a clearer and more meaningful representation of the historical, social, political, anthropological, urban and artistic aspects embedded in the cities of Sarajevo and Beirut. The narrative Makdisi finally adopts in her book mixes, on one hand, so-called vignettes, an aspect that, according to the author, 'tell more about the realities of Beirut life than the reams of newspaper articles with their interminable political analyses and predictions, most of which prove, sooner or later, to be quite wrong.'[22] On the other hand, she chooses to adjust her narrative to the image of a kaleidoscope.

Note on the post-traumatic

Despite its contested interpretations, I decided to use the term 'post-traumatic' in the title of this book to qualify the kind of art which I am analysing. The word itself calls on the instance of trauma, regarded both as a clinical concept and a research concept in recent literary studies, cinema studies and art history since the 1990s.[23] First of all, I would like to stress that the presence of the 'post' in front of the term 'traumatic' signals the sense of temporality: thus I am, therefore, looking at artworks produced in the aftermath of the war, in the years following the end of the conflicts in Sarajevo and Beirut. The 'post' here refers to a given period of time and characterizes the re-emergence of the art scenes of Sarajevo and Beirut in the second half of the 1990s. 'Traumatic' refers to the highly disruptive events produced through acts of violence in both cities. Drawing on the post-traumatic, therefore, involves touching upon the issue of trauma which has been primarily described as an affect of war, to later open up to a trauma theory based on other instances of possible traumatic experiences.[24]

I am outlining here two definitions of the post-traumatic in order to reinforce my argument of the temporal afterness of a traumatic event. The first one is the definition of the Post-Traumatic Stress Disorder (PTSD); the idea of a delayed effect of a profound shock derives from what was identified during the First World War as shell shock. In the aftermath of subsequent wars during the twentieth century, more particularly, the Vietnam War, a clinical diagnosis of post-traumatic shock came into psychiatric discourse in 1980.[25] Whereas PTSD was used to diagnose 35 per cent of the American veterans of the Vietnam War (1955–75), the American Psychiatric Association only adopted it in 1980, defining it as,

> The development of characteristic symptoms following exposure to an extreme traumatic stressor involving direct personal experience of an event that involves actual or threatened death or serious injury, or other threat to one's physical integrity; or witnessing an event that involves death, injury, or other threat to the physical integrity to another person; or learning about unexpected or violent death, serious harm, or threat of death or injury experienced by a family member or other close associate.[26]

Although being more related to its possible causes than symptoms, this definition of the PTSD gives us a sense of how a condition affecting mostly military personnel has had increasing consequences on civilians throughout the twentieth century, an importance underlined by Mary Kaldor's observation that the ratio of casualties between military and civilian shifted from 8:1 at the beginning of the twentieth century to 1:8 during the 1990s wars.[27] PTSD is linked to traumatic events in the sense that it causes alterations in somatic and psychological functioning. The traumatically shocked individual has experienced a traumatic 'stressor', namely, an experience outside the range of usual human experience. Not surprisingly, such an affect of post-traumatic shock within a *civilian* population was widely reported in Sarajevo, where the conditions of the siege were so extreme. Mentioning a Sarajevi psychiatrist who worked with veterans of the Bosnian War, anthropologist Peter Locke confirms the hypothesis that post-traumatic symptoms in Sarajevo are so widespread that this issue becomes banal, almost irrelevant.[28] This statement joins the opinion of Slobodan Loga, another psychiatrist from the University of Sarajevo, who declared in 2003 that the entire population of Sarajevo suffered from PTSD.[29]

A non-medical definition of the post-traumatic, as an effect registered and created in cultural forms, is provided by film theorist Joshuah Hirsch. Hirsch's definition helps me to frame what I am studying in the field of artistic practices, where trauma was, until recently, little explored in film studies and even less in visual arts. We need, therefore, to acknowledge two levels. First, populations can suffer post-traumatic stress from the events they endure during a prolonged Civil War or siege. Second, the effects of such extremity of experience can shape the forms and affects of artworks created out of these experiences or to give forms to the trauma itself.

In his book *Afterimage: Film, Trauma and the Holocaust*, Hirsch uses the term of 'post-traumatic'. It describes the way in which a film-maker, or artist, 'enables the spectator to encounter historical events as trauma, *i.e.* as a crisis of representation or of representability, that is, although grounded in personal experience, able to operate in the space of public discourse by means of an artwork'.[30] Hirsch defines the post-traumatic as either referring to particular traumatic events or producing in the spectator a vicarious trauma – through seeing images of it:

> A trauma is less a particular experiential content than a form of experience, so posttraumatic cinema is defined less by a particular image content – a documentary image of atrocity, a fictional image of atrocity or the absence of an image of atrocity – than by the attempt to discover a form for presenting that content that mimics some aspects of posttraumatic consciousness itself, the attempt to formally reproduce for the spectator an experience of suddenly seeing the unthinkable.[31]

Although Hirsch poses the idea of post-traumatic art, particularly cinema, through the notion of vicarious trauma produced by encountering a representation of an event, the case studies I am working on are different. The latter do not intend to give the viewers a vicarious sense of the horror, represented or not. Hirsch's notion, which derives from the Caruthian model of the belatedness of trauma and the delayed, uncontrolled re-enactment of the past as its significant markers, underlines my sense that the works at which I am looking are being made in the aftermath of events that are traumatic.[32] The case studies I am examining are rather about the afterness of trauma, about the affective charge of exile, of the way different elements, such as amnesia and displacement, are being brought to the surface by specific forms of aesthetic formulation.

Like Hirsch, art historian Ernst van Alphen examines vicarious trauma in the framework of his studies of post-Holocaust art and imaginative literature.[33] While challenging our conception of life, death, mourning *and* recovering from a horrific event, van Alphen is reflecting not only on witnessing or testifying to the actual experience but also on the more general post-conflict effect expressed through/in specific artworks. Van Alphen writes about the artistic process producing a re-enactment and the way art thus positions its audience not as witness but as subjects who can be affected by the artistic work:

> We are no longer listening to the factual account of a witness, to the story of an objectified past. Rather, we are placed in the position of being the subject of that history. We are subjectively living it.[34]

Van Alphen extends this vicarious effect to a post–Civil War effect through this sense that the art is actually producing some of the effects and ravages of history instead of representing them. Van Alphen proposes a framework of the re-enactment effect to which the art at stake in this book can be linked. Trauma is not, and indeed cannot be, represented and does not produce in the viewer a vicarious trauma through this specific art, but it can affect the intimated otherness. Elusively encountered, the displaced encounter with a traumatic event or experience becomes a *possibility* through artistic practice. In my particular case studies, the specificity lies in the accumulated pain of a destroyed city and the affect aesthetic practice can generate in an afterness of reflection or investigation. As Griselda Pollock has argued in her book *After-affects | After-images*, it is the encounter with traces of trauma which she calls *after-affects*, 'which might be processed aesthetically'.[35]

Before outlining further this possibility of an aesthetic encounter with a traumatic experience or traces of it through an art practice, I would like to briefly sketch out, as an excursus into anthropology, Veena Das's insight on looking at historical violence and the way it affects everyday life. Das underlines the experience of coping with everyday life, during and after the traumatic events. While exploring paradoxes of violence and trauma theory – such as the Partition of India in 1947 and the massacre of the Sikhs in 1984 following the assassination of Prime Minister Indira Gandhi – Das remarks that the specificity of her own case studies, in terms of personal and cultural histories, required other means of analysis than the trauma theory developed around the Holocaust as its paradigmatic case.[36] Das suggests that a trauma is rooted in the specific location of suffering and the connection of this suffering to everyday life in ways that must be studied without psychologizing the victims.[37] Thus, the act of witnessing becomes a fragile equilibrium between the engaging with everyday life and containing the traumatic wound and seeking to prevent its effects from leaking into this everyday life:

> I have argued elsewhere that witnessing is not a matter of all of nothing, and I trust that the previous chapters have shown a different picture of witnessing – as in engaging everyday life while holding the poisonous knowledge of violation, betrayal, and the wounded self from seeping into the sociality of everyday life. [. . .] I have suggested that the idea that the reenactment of the past at the collective level is [*sic*] *a compulsion to repeat* seems to short-circuit the complex ways in which we might understand how particular regions of the past are actualized through mediums of rumor, or in the singularity of individual lives as they knit together relations that have become frayed.

Das, therefore, rejects the concept of the re-enactment of the past in order to focus on the specificities of the context(s) at stake, either collective or individual. This allows her to pay attention to the issue of life going on and being lived while traces of the trauma co-inhabit those living on after 'poisonous' events.

Sarajevo and Beirut are two cities that, at the turn of the twenty-first century, were either recovering from or coping with the consequences of disruptive strife. Thus I am engaging here with the way everyday life both during and after the conflict has been registered as individual or collective lived experiences, particularly through the work of the artist – as an active witness – and the way these experiences, often connected to a political or social context, are conveyed in his/her artworks. In those artworks the traumatic load, without being recognized as such by audience unfamiliar with the exact context of the trauma, may still arouse an affected response in the viewer.

In her study of this complex relay of art, trauma and time, *Empathic Vision: Affect, Trauma and Contemporary Art*, art historian Jill Bennett theorizes this particular effect as 'empathic vision'. In the cases she studies, the historical or actual trauma is not recognizable as such in the artists' work. The events are not represented in any way. Bennett observes, however, how the traumatic is nonetheless at work in an internal dynamic within the forms and aesthetics of these artworks. With her statement 'art can capture and transmit real experience', Bennett privileges form over the meanings that she considers 'ill served by a theoretical framework'.[38] What Bennett suggests here is that confining art to being about trauma is to reduce the diversity of signifying potentialities in each artwork to a single concept of what trauma is – in her case she is referring to the psychoanalytical definition of the traumatic. She is arguing that the works to which she refers are merely symptomatic registrations of trauma. They seek to find forms through which to engage the viewers in registering affectively the force of political violence in different areas in the world but without offering an overt political analysis or critique. Bennett carefully looks at artworks by Sandra Johnston (*b.* 1968), Doris Salcedo (*b.* 1958), William Kentridge (*b.* 1955) and Willie Doherty (*b.* 1959), whose works arise from and speak to conflict and the effects of political violence in Colombia, South Africa and Northern Ireland.

Bennet's interest and argument lies in the fact that these artworks, produced in a diversity of political and violent contexts, have a shared history, which is traumatic. It is, however, the way they articulate this history and its effects without producing the sense that either trauma is unknowable or it can be vicariously represented that is remarkable. The artists have the ability to articulate something that, though being owned by them, speaks to the larger community that has shared these traumatic events. Bennett's intention, therefore, is more 'to show, then, how, by realizing a way of seeing and feeling, this art makes a particular kind of contribution to thought, and to politics specifically: how certain conjunctions of affective and critical operations might constitute the basis for something we can call *empathic vision*'.[39]

Let me clarify. Art might register the impact of trauma by bearing witness to an event that so overwhelms its subject; it cannot be described, or imaged or represented. As a void in experience, it registers negatively. Art might also bear witness to events, standing a little to a side, but seeking to convey the overwhelming horror or pain. This might be called creating the space for vicarious experience of an extreme suffering or shock. But if the events that created the pain, shock or extremity arise out of what is profoundly political, the artist is positioned at once inside and outside, that is to say, affected and thus moved to make the work but also responsible for making works that can engage non-participant viewers to grasp the trauma of political violence and the politics of the violence that is traumatic. Thus, Bennett reads the artworks, not their ostensible topics, for how they might solicit a viewer's response through as viewers to experiences of others and of this order.

I have chosen to study artworks that concern a reality of the traumatic event as it is *owned* by someone, and how the artwork invites the audience in a way to take part in this experience through the raising of an affective/empathic encounter that engages the viewers by aesthetic means: not aestheticizing but intensifying senses of sight, feeling, space, memory, affects. This reality of a traumatic event can originate from what Mieke Bal has named a 'traumatogenic' event – an event that is not necessarily traumatic in itself but can generate traumatic effects. Mieke Bal develops this analysis in her publication on Colombian artist Doris Salcedo.[40] In *Of What One Cannot Speak*, Mieke Bal emphasizes the entwining of art and politics in her approach to violence registered through art. While looking at a specific piece by Doris Salcedo (*b.* 1958), *Noviembre 6 y 7* (2002), which commemorates a mass killing that took place eighteen years earlier in Columbia, on 6 November 1985, Bal does not pose the question whether the artist is traumatized or not by the events she witnessed. Bal neither attributes a trauma to the artist nor does she deny its possibility. Bal's argument concerns the ways in which the issue of memory is connected to the traumatogenic event. An artwork emerges from a violent event, either collective or cultural, that has the status of a traumatogenic one: one that could generate trauma. Since the traumatogenic event stands for a frozen moment in memory, the art piece gives to this event a kind of treatment that cures the traumatic nature of its anonymity.

Through the artistic practice, the perception becomes, therefore, about giving a colour, warmth to the frozen moment of the traumatogenic event through a thawing of frozen, arrested, namely traumatic, memory. Bal, therefore, explains how Salcedo's *Noviembre 6 y 7* becomes then a 'perception subjectivized':

> She [Salcedo] subjectivized the objective, cold perception with the help of memory, that memory that remained inaccessible. For this thawing of cold perception, memory must be 'heated' out of its grave. [. . .] The result is a perception subjectivized by memory; a perception that is possible, accessible, 'warm'. That thawing itself, rather than the resulting memory, is the artist's *act* of memory.[41]

Hence, it is because of the specific articulation of the artwork that the artwork makes a perception become memory. The traumatogenic event is entombed but haunting. Being given the vividness of aesthetic warmth and structuring, the event no longer traumatizes, that is, freezes, deadens, but enters the circuits of living and thinking as an active memory, which can have effects, politically, in the present.

Bal's reading of Salcedo's *Noviembre 6 y 7* contributes to the analysis of my case studies in the following ways. There are violent events, which happened somewhere, distant or not from the artists. The artworks awaken memory, while this enlivened memory makes the artworks active. These performative interventions create moments for encounter with legacies of violence that need forms for their processing and working through. And through the aesthetics, the artist's artworks have some sense (in the double meaning of perception and understanding) of these events. They aesthetically generate an affect that is not merely a representation of the event, or even a formal mode of remembering. They work with and through the traumatic charge to open up the past to reflections on the many threads fractured and woven by the return to these often painful events. As art historian Kristine Stiles has recently argued while discussing visual language wrought by destruction, violence and trauma, 'something has happened to someone in life, from whose consequences a sequence of events and questions of value have unfolded and through which an artist translated pain into art.'[42] Kristine Stiles argues that there are risks involved if we fail to acknowledge the traumatic events to which an artist has attended. Nonetheless, for Stiles, it is not so much the actual events as their *consequences* and the resulting pain that the artist translates into art. Neither documentary nor reactive nor therapeutic, the artistic process is active and creative. It is performative in the way that it both recreates the traumatic and contains it through creating forms for its effects.

If each artistic practice analysed in the four separate chapters is singled out in terms of its distinctive patterns relating to the use of specific media and formal or narrative devices – the alienated self-portrait, the performance, the journey, the landscape – nonetheless their artistic modes share the same field of exploring trauma and memory across time and space.

Structure

Chapter 1 examines historical symptoms and social features as fragments. It also examines the stake of cultural institutions – existing and emerging – after the wars in Sarajevo and Beirut, including some aspects of art produced in the conditions of war out of a movement of artistic and intellectual resistance. It addresses the phenomenon of a culture of resistance experienced during the siege of Sarajevo and the crucial aspects of cultural life in the face of a conflict. I am taking as the most powerful example the series of exhibitions *Witnesses of Existence* (1992–3). Held in half-destroyed buildings and organized by the Obala Gallery, the project initiated an unprecedented artistic movement that would soon be exhibited abroad, among others at the forty-fifth Venice Biennale in 1993.

The nature of trauma and its consequent dislocations had a direct impact on the writing about the Beiruti art scene during the Civil War. If it has been attested, that, like in Sarajevo, artists were still active throughout the conflict and that exhibitions were taking place on a regular basis, no research on this subject has been undertaken to this day. Therefore, this aspect of the city stays out of reach, producing a disruption which is part of the nature of trauma. Trauma disrupts the flow of history, leaving gaps and holes that are not retrievable. This structural lack is peculiar when it comes to cultural and historical specificity.

In the aftermath of such destructive conflicts, the cultural institutions in both cities found themselves in fragile situations and their lack of respective funding could not support contemporary experimental practices. New cultural actors came into existence, mostly through international and private funding – public funding being invested in the reconstruction process almost in its totality. Two of these new institutions are the Soros Center for Contemporary Art in Sarajevo (SCCA, later Sarajevo Center for Contemporary Art, established in 1997) and the Lebanese Association for Plastic Arts, Ashkal Alwan in Beirut (established in 1994). In terms of artistic production, the length of the conflicts produced a gap in both cities between artists active before the war and a new generation of fine arts students during the war, who became active in its aftermath. In Sarajevo, these two generations exhibited together at the end of the 1990s, whereas in Beirut the gap was more profound due to the more-than-sixteen-year Civil War.

Chapter 2 focuses on *Autoportrait* (1999), a video work by Bosnian artist Danica Dakić, in which the artist represented herself as endowed with a second mouth in place of her eyes. To each mouth belongs a specific narrative: one in Bosnian, the other in German. These are about the mystery of voices, and the way voices can be heard in absence of people or can be imitated. As is Dakić, I am dealing with the issue of language, of the notion of voice and the re-voicing, a re-articulating that challenges presumptions and authority of other voices and silences disrupting this authority. The apparent prevalence of autobiography does not always mean an assertion of subjectivity; in the case of *Autoportrait* it reveals rather a withdrawn subjectivity. Whereas Dakić was not living in Bosnia and Herzegovina during the war, she engages with the historical events of the city of Sarajevo by blinding herself and endowing her face with this second mouth in lieu of her eyes. Dakić, therefore, focuses on a particular issue of migrancy and a concomitant life experienced through multiple languages and cultures that draw largely from beyond her own experience, touching issues such as translations of languages and subjects as well as colonialism.

Chapter 3 looks at *Women at Work* (1999–2001), three performances set up by Bosnian artist Maja Bajević together with a group of refugee women from the Srebrenica area. For anyone living in that region – and in Bosnia and Herzegovina and the Balkans – the name Srebrenica carries the same atrocious weight as Auschwitz does for the history of the Holocaust. Bajević's intention, however, is not to commemorate the events of July 1995 but to catch the traumatic resonance of what it means for those who, having lived the consequences of the massacre of Srebrenica, having been estranged from their men, sons, brothers and expelled from their houses, sent to an area far from the one where they used to live, become, through artistic expression, visible again. Using public venues for her performances, Bajević works on the notion of (re-)giving a home to women who had been estranged from their own space and emplacement. By transposing domestic activities such as embroidery – *Under Construction*, Sarajevo, 1999; *The Observers*, Ferney-Voltaire, 2000 – and laundry – *Washing Up*, Istanbul, 2001 – outside the intimacy of the household, Bajević and her co-performers took over the public space, reaffirming it as a substitute for the lost home or even a metaphor of the lost country – Yugoslavia. Through the use of textile, the artist builds an interaction between the intimate, private and the social, public realms.

Chapter 4 analyses *A Journey* (2006), a 41-minute video by Lebanese artist Lamia Joreige, that investigates the artist's family past through the eyes of three generations of women: the artist's grandmother, her mother and her own position in contemporary Lebanon. Building on a long-standing engagement, Joreige shares her own relationship with the fabric of the city of Beirut, widening it to a mapping of the Middle East before and after 1948. Joreige particularly focuses on the geographic distance separating Beirut from Jaffa (Yaffa), the city where the artist's grandmother, Rose Kettaneh, grew up in the 1920s. Overlaying that past with another more recent traumatic event in the family's history, Joreige draws attention to specific elements of the war in Lebanon, such as the kidnapping of civilians for the purpose of exchange with war prisoners. This phenomenon left its indelible mark on Joreige's family, as the artist's uncle fell victim of this practice in the 1980s and has never been found since his abduction. These elements deal with mediating family history, memory, family narratives and the archive. Yet, they have to find their articulation within the more generic background of the nation, diaspora and the Middle East. Finally, Joreige's *Journey* is an observation of the relationship between the artist, her mother and grandmother, about the way the different generations consider or live through traumatic experiences, while the inexorable elusiveness of the past continuously escapes them, leaving them in their haunted contemporary present. The crisis of transmissibility is shown by how past elements diverge and fail to fully touch. Thus, *A Journey* is an example of how memories of the past impinge on the present.

Chapter 5 analyses a series of photographs in Beirut and in Southern Lebanon by Lebanese artist Paola Yacoub. In her photographic practice, Yacoub confronts a certain sense of what is a palimpsest – in a Huyssenian sense in the urban and landscape fabric in the aftermath of this long, everlasting conflict. Yacoub deals with the fabric of the city of Beirut, pushing its boundaries to the Lebanese territory and the cities where she has either lived or studied: Paris, London and Berlin. Yacoub works on the relationship between the city and post-war landscapes, and the way the two are linked through the circulation of architectural elements. Through a photographic careful consideration of this circulation of territory, the artist intends to let her camera display what cannot be talked about: the war. Because of a Lebanese official politics of amnesia, the continuing conflict and its subsequent Syrian occupation are generally repressed. Hence, Yacoub works out a way of not having to describe the suffering resulting from such traumatic circumstances on an individual level. The artist refers to Wittgenstein's notion that one cannot express the suffering of the hair and develops a theoretical strategy, which can be read in her photographs. The latter seem haunted by a certain uncanny and therefore resist conventional visual representations.

1

Setting the (art) scenes

A comparative approach to site-specific discourses in post-conflict cities

The city as a site and symbol of struggle

In his definition of the city, urban historian Lewis Mumford proposes that the city is more than a purely physical entity; it is also a social institution – or a collective anthropoid body – generating a site of identification for its inhabitants. He writes,

> The city is a related collection of primary groups and purposive associations: the first, like family and neighborhood, are common to all communities, while the second are especially characteristic of city life. These varied groups support themselves through economic organizations that are likewise of a more or less corporate, or at least publicly regulated, character; and they are all housed in permanent structures, within a relatively limited area. The essential physical means of a city's existence are the fixed site, the durable shelter, the permanent facilities for assembly, interchange, and storage; the essential social means are the social division of labor, which serves not merely the economic life but the cultural processes. The city in its complete sense, then, is a geographic plexus, an economic organization, an institutional process, a theatre of social action, and an aesthetic symbol of collective unity.[1]

Cities have political, cultural and physical significance in proportion to their size and density of population. As a result we could argue that the conditions of war have a greater impact in and on cities than in rural areas. Fighting in urban areas is an operationally challenging military action and casualties among civilians are usually higher because of the sheer concentration of population, who are often trapped in crowded spaces. Moreover, capital cities may be conflict-prone because they embody the very *idea* of a state and are the seats of government and hence symbolic as well as actual authority and power.

Ethnographers Ida Susser and Jane Schneider developed the concept of 'wounded cities' – a concept that can be applied usefully to both the cities of Sarajevo and Beirut after they suffered extreme violence in and damage to their urban and social fabric. Although Susser and Schneider's research focuses partly on the impact of the globalization process in cities around the world, they dedicate a chapter to cities that have experienced prolonged fighting, such as Belfast or Beirut. Both ethnographers acknowledge the difficulties of reclaiming space after extraordinary violence: 'The difficulties of reclaiming a city damaged by widespread killing, and of projecting a new image of healthy restoration, are shown to be considerable, the more so because reclamation processes can themselves have destructive spin-offs.'[2]

In the case of Sarajevo and Beirut studied in this book, the shifts of population and the level of physical destruction in the wake of siege and division have worked to disrupt the integrity and coherence of each city. Instead of being single and united, both cities became *pluralities* for their different communities of inhabitants, ladened with, or split by, varying allegiances. Both cities became physically dislocated. A front line cut Sarajevo off from its suburbs. In Beirut the city was split between West and East, turning the city centre into an inaccessible no-man's land.

Reconstruction normally provides a conclusion to war and its destruction. It signifies a positive change in direction to rebuild after the wounds of war. In Sarajevo, however, it initiated a long and complicated process for the restitution of ownership for those returning home from abroad.[3] In Beirut there was widespread criticism of the reconstruction policies, particularly of those overseeing the reconstruction of the Beirut Central District (BCD); long and expensive reconstruction processes have not allowed a return to the normality of previous urban life. Solidere's decision to reconstruct Beirut as 'the ancient city of the future' has, in its modernist and highly nostalgic drive, left many individuals behind failing to address psychological and emotional freight associated with past and present sites and spaces.

In order to approach the complex history and the new – or the extension of old – sociopolitical structures of two cities torn asunder by war, I will use the model of the vignette to elucidate some of the key historical and sociopolitical dimensions of the war in both cities. The vignette is necessarily brief and must, of course, simplify the immensely complex effects of continual war on the cities and their inhabitants. But my purpose is not urban history. I need to draw a picture of several aspects of war and these cities so as to provide the necessary ground for understanding of the subjectivity of the artist-resident or artist-exile and for the analysis of the specificity of each of the works I shall be studying in detail. This is not a sketch of the background against which art is made. It is an evocation of the sites to whose 'woundedness' the artists sought to give a form or an image.

Trying to describe a reality of war that has been both collectively and individually experienced requires a different form of narrative rather than legitimating the fragile task of undertaking an accurate historical account. Thus, we need to outline the lines of conflict, the movement of peoples, the impact of political initiatives to resolve the conflict, and the reconstruction processes and the formation of memory. This 'historical' analysis of the situation in each city throws up a question rarely asked: How could and did any kind of cultural life, any form of artistic practice, survive such profound disruption and devastating destruction? Furthermore, if the conditions for even bare life have been systematically eroded, how was the institutional fabric necessary for any art practice – art centres, archives, exhibition spaces, sites of debate and education – rebuilt in the aftermath? What are the current conditions that enable and sustain artistic practice and culture in these cities: an exploration from which we can learn a great deal about the underpinnings of art and cities normally invisible to our inquiring gaze because they seem exactly that, normal. It is to art made in the abnormal and the recreated in its wake that we can then turn.

Lines of conflict

Sarajevo

In Sarajevo, the siege line maintained by the Serbian army was positioned on the surrounding hills and stretched for 64 kilometres, totally encircling the city.[4] From June 1992, UN troops held the airport for humanitarian aid purposes, and thus prevented civilians and soldiers from getting in and out of the city. The two zones around the airport were held by the ARBiH (Armija Republike Bosne I Hercegovine, Army of the Republic of Bosnia and Herzegovina). In early 1993, compelled by the decreasing amount of munitions and the hardships facing civilians, the ARBiH dug a kilometre-long tunnel beneath the airport towards Butmir. Called Objekt D-B ('Object Dobrinja-Butmir'), the tunnel resembled a horizontal mineshaft, through which ran electrical cables, a light rail system and a pumping system to prevent it from flooding. From July 1993, the tunnel was used as a conduit for arms, munitions, essential supplies and people (Figure 1.1).[5]

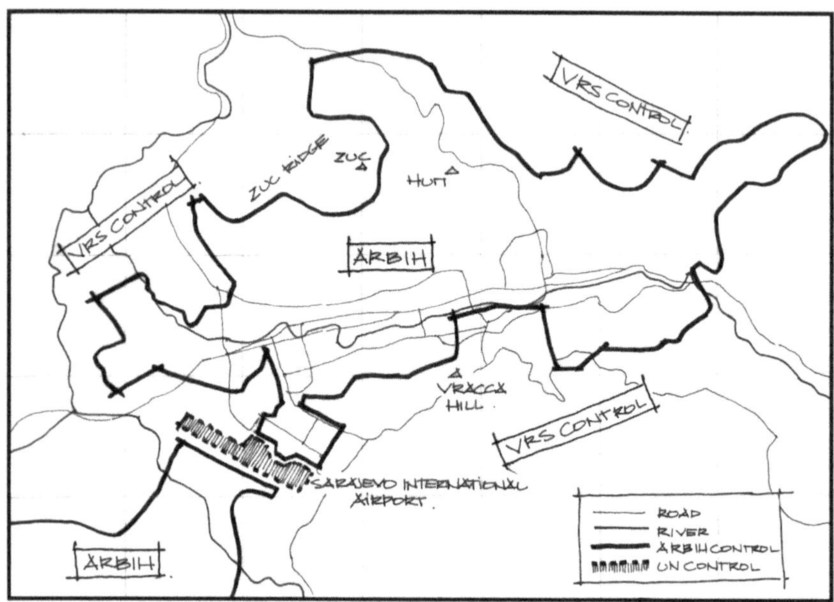

Figure 1.1 *Front Lines in the Siege of Sarajevo*, June 1992. © Michael Kassatly.

The siege of the city has been defined by urban analyst Martin Coward as 'urbicide', this being 'the destruction of the urban insofar as it is the arena in which an encounter with difference occurs'.[6] In the case of Sarajevo, the city centre kept its unity although it was estranged from some of its suburbs and was targeted by external assailants as well as snipers who never hesitated to shoot at anyone coming into range. Sarajevans tried, at any cost, to stick to their pre-war routine to preserve a certain way of life. In Ivana Maček's words, 'the imitation of life that appeared in war-torn Sarajevo was central to the changes of normality, because it allowed for sociocultural continuity in circumstances that unravelled the social fabric as well as disrupting material existence.'[7] Each passing month brought it lots of further strain. The frustration of living under siege grew and became almost unmanageable, expressed in impulsive acts of recklessness erupting against the cautious daily routines established earlier. In their study on violence and survival, Antonius Robben and Carolyn Nordstrom reflect on violence and particularly on the everydayness of conflict, on how few people are indeed prepared to adapt to these new living conditions but nonetheless cope with them as best they can:

> The everydayness of war is a never-ending stream of worries about the next meal, the next move, and the next assault. [. . .] But such life-threatening violence

> demonstrates the paralysis as well as the creativity of people coping with duress, a duress for which few are prepared.[8]

The conditions of living in the city deteriorated so much that it evoked images from daily life centuries ago; everything had to be done manually: fetching water, laundry, food, scrounging for firewood. Hope for a better future and a return to reality kept people coping with the siege, in a city where nobody had believed a war could ever break out.

During the war, ethno-nationalistic politics specifically targeted the cultural symbols of Sarajevo, and more generally of Bosnia and Herzegovina, in order to eradicate difference and create the idea of separate, sovereign territorial entities. Writing on the meaning of this destruction of cultural heritage in urban Bosnia and Herzegovina, Andras Riedlmayer emphasizes its targeting of the memory of a successfully shared past which was embodied in a material testimony to former cultural and ethnic, religious and political, coexistence:

> Rubble in Bosnia and Herzegovina signifies national extremists hard at work to eliminate not only the human beings and living cities, but also the memory of the past [. . .] The museums, libraries, mosques, churches and monuments speak eloquently of centuries of pluralism. It is this evidence of a successfully shared past that the nationalists seek to destroy.[9]

Because of Sarajevo's long history of coexistence between different ethnic groups, the destruction of interstitial areas of common cultural heritage was systematically undertaken in order to effect ethnic cleansing in this particular territory.[10]

Beirut

In 1975, the front line, commonly named 'the Green Line', divided the city of Beirut between East and West. The Green Line was named after the belt of greenery that emerged when grass and trees grew in this area. It ran along the Damascus Road on a north–south axis and was guarded by ever-shifting militias. The PLO/Lebanese coalition had effective control of the predominantly Muslim West, while the Lebanese army and the Christian parties were in control of the predominantly Christian East. In October 1976, the Arab Deterrent Force was established by the Arab League. Hence, Beirut was reunified, but this unification lasted only until July 1980, when the city was again divided (Figure 1.2).

The *Bourj* area, the heart of the city situated around Martyrs' Square, was transformed into a no-man's land. Throughout the conflict, it lost its identity

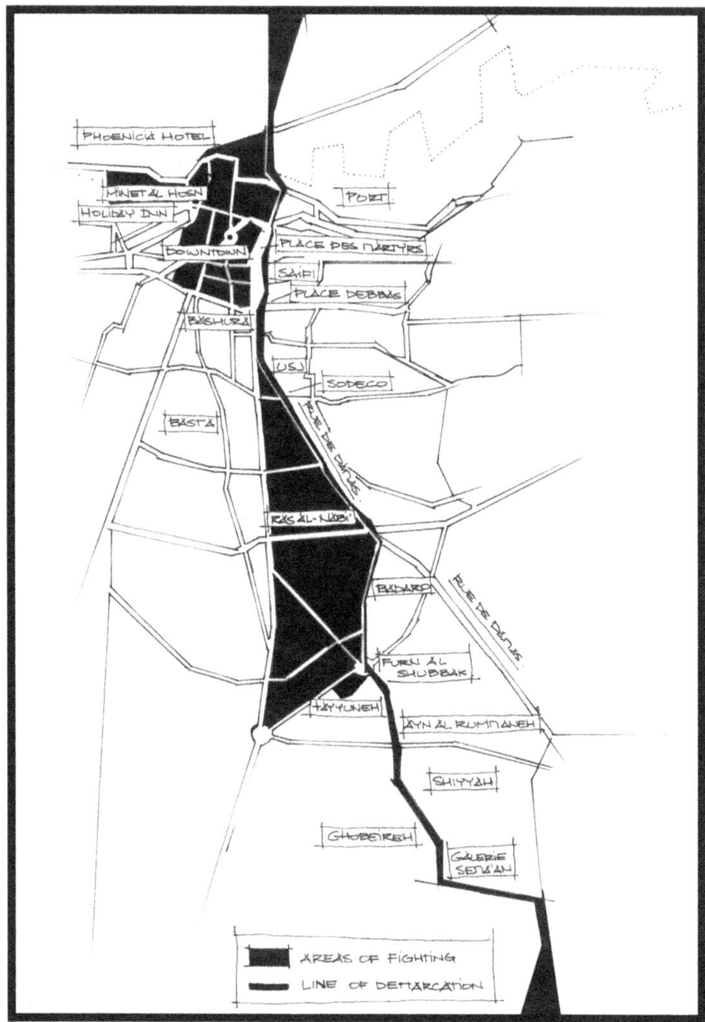

Figure 1.2 *Beirut, The Line of Demarcation during the War.* © Michael Kassatly.

as the city's central point and its architectural features. People used to refer to the Green Line in Arabic as *al mahawir al taqlidiya* (the traditional lines of confrontation).[11] Similarly, the museum – in Arabic *al Mathaf* – did not refer to its role of cultural and historical institution but as one of the rare passages across the Green Line, where queues of people waited to cross it in order to reach the other part of the city. For the inhabitants of Beirut, the Green Line radically impacted on their urban environment and living space.

Beiruti also had to adapt to survival schemes and be put at risk in their everyday lives, shifting from ordinary times to extreme situations. Aseel

Sawahlha designates the city during the war as 'an icon of destruction'.[12] Shelling and violence could be followed by times of relative peace, when people recovered a kind of normality of life, carrying on with their pre-war daily tasks. One had to adapt to a double life: one with a normal appearance and the other endangered with the risk and violence of civil strife.

A whole generation grew up during the war, and whenever they could, young people went out to dinner, to nightclubs, to the beaches or to the ski resorts. A number of them were sent to school abroad by their families due to the war's lengthy duration. Because violence progressively escalated and contaminated new areas of Beirut and the country, experience of war could greatly vary. Artist Walid Sadek confessed in a 2002 documentary *Voices Off* that he had in fact pleasant memories of the Civil War. During the first months of the conflict, his family relocated to their summer residence in the north, where the young Sadek spent hours learning to swim and playing tennis. For Sadek, this 'dubious effect of not carrying the war' struck back during his time abroad, in a moment of political awakening.[13]

Casualties and population movements

Sarajevo

The war in Bosnia and Herzegovina was the most deadly conflict in Europe since the Second World War. According to a 1991 census, Bosnia's population was estimated at over 4.3 million. During the conflict, 200,000 Bosnian civilians and 60,000 soldiers died, 174,000 were injured and approximately 2.5 million citizens were displaced; 1 million of these went abroad. By the end of the war, Bosnia and Herzegovina's population had shrunk by 1 million from its pre-war total, and had increased again to 3.5 million by 2001, of which approximately one-third resides in RS.[14]

In Sarajevo alone there were 10,541 casualties and 60,000 wounded during the siege. War-related displacements also brought to the city a cultural change, as at least 90,000 people arrived from other parts of Bosnia and Herzegovina and 240,000 pre-war inhabitants had left it.[15] The population of the city decreased from 510,000 in 1991 to 360,000 in 1999. The majority of Bosnian Serbs left the city, and the Bosnian part of local population represented 87 per cent of its inhabitants by 1997.

Due to the visibility of its concomitant humanitarian crisis, the Bosnian conflict was associated with issues of humanitarian aid like no other war before. More than 100,000 foreigners, a dozen UN agencies and over 200 non-governmental organizations were estimated to be part of the humanitarian operation in the country.[16]

In Sarajevo, the pre-war inhabitants, commonly named *Sarajlije*, complained about the erosion of culture because of the massive exodus which took place on the one hand and the displacement of estranged people to the city on the other hand; they started to portray themselves as cultural strangers within their own city. As Rada Iveković remarked, 'The countries of Ex-Yugoslavia have been *bled* of their youth and intellectuals.'[17]

Beirut

By the end of the Civil War at the beginning of the 1990s, half of the population of Beirut had left their homes temporarily or permanently, and the Lebanese diaspora is supposedly almost three times the population of Lebanon. The loss of human lives during the war is estimated over 144,000, that is, 5 per cent of the population. This figure does not include deaths that resulted from Israeli aerial attacks on Palestinian refugee camps, the fighting among Palestinian armed groups or armed clashes between Amal and Fatah in and around these camps. In addition, over 184,000 people were injured, over 13,000 maimed and over 17,000 disappeared (mostly kidnapped and killed).[18] The Lebanese government gave the following figures for the 33-day war in the summer of 2006: 1,183 civilians were killed, 4,054 wounded, 262,174 civilians permanently displaced and 1,000,000 temporarily displaced.[19]

The cleavage between rural areas and city is also found in Beirut, where many inhabitants moved from the mountains to the city during the war. Many did not return to their pre-war homes, which lacked basic services and employment opportunities, even when offered compensation for their status of internally displaced persons (IDPs).[20] The Lebanese Ministry of the Displaced was established in 1992 to deal with this conflictual situation opposing present squatters and former owners of housing units. Its figures and statistics about the displaced population are articulated as follows:

> 9,000 families had been displaced, with an average of 5.7 persons in each family. 18,000 homes were completely destroyed, and many seriously damaged. 45,000 families illegally occupied the homes of other families. 12,000 families lived in dwellings not designated for human habitation, such as commercial buildings, industrial centers, and buildings liable to collapse.[21]

The resettlement of IDPs and refugees is among some of the most difficult post-conflict issues. Christopher Moore and Gary Brown give the following reasons for it:

> Return is frequently hindered or blocked by total or partial destruction of homes, land, and property; illegal occupation or encroachments by other parties; non existent, unclear or contested ownership documents; lack of resources to help returnees rebuild their lives; and renewal of on-going tensions or outright conflict between those coming home and those who never left their communities.[22]

Community reintegration and return to a state of normality are necessary requirements for peace, reconciliation and economic development. The prospect of an economic miracle as a pacification process returned to the country never materialized, mainly due to the government's monetary, financial and economic policies. These different policies plunged the country into stagnation and recession with social, demographic and political consequences.[23]

State and political structures before and after Dayton and Taif

Sarajevo

The eleven articles of the Dayton Peace Agreement (DPA), initiated in Dayton in November 1995 and signed in Paris on 14 December, aimed to provide Bosnia and Herzegovina with a structural and institutional framework for the reconstruction and reorganization.[24] Although the DPA recognized Bosnia and Herzegovina as a multi-ethnic country, in practice it is composed of two distinct entities: the Federation – largely Muslim and Croatian – and the RS – largely Serbian and a neutral, self-administrative unit, the Brčko District, which is formally part of both entities.

Even if this partition is uneasy, as no stable border exists between the Federation and the RS as well as no official frontier exists between the Muslim and Croat within the Federation, however, these two distinct entities were forced after the war to operate in close proximity to each other and to deal with common issues together.

A three-person presidency, based on national and territorial exigencies, was established. This presidency consists of one Serb elected by the RS, a Bosnian Muslim (Bosniak) and a Bosnian Croat directly elected by the citizens of the Federation. Decisions by the presidency are supposedly by majority, but disapproval within the presidency would de facto block a decision. A two-chamber parliamentary system was also created. As for the judicial system, this latter was compromised by the fact that many of the country's qualified jurists emigrated during the war; their positions were taken by political appointees with few qualifications. This led the UN Security Council to establish an international monitoring board in July 1998. A heavy international military presence, the IFOR, was already in place since it replaced UNPROFOR on 20 December 1995.[25] Its main tasks consisted of assisting the UNHCR; rebuilding infrastructure such as roads, railways, bridges and airports; and demining. Apart from this military implementation of the DPA, the civil implementation of the agreement involved some international institutions (UN, the EU, OSCE, NATO etc.) to create the Office of the High Representative (OHR), which was established by Annex 10 of the DPA. The High Representative's mandate was to monitor the implementation of the DPA and promote full compliance by all parties, and to coordinate the international community's contributions to civil implementation. This led the High Representative to interpret in the last resort on the DPA's civilian provision and to represent the liaison with the IFOR.[26] Through the OHR, the UN and the OSCE, the international community secured ultimate control over political, economic and social developments.

The establishment of the International Criminal Tribunal for Former Yugoslavia (ICTY) in The Hague in May 1993 was the last important implementation agreed in the DPA regarding the prosecution of war criminals. The ICTY would become the first international court prosecuting and trying individuals for violation of humanitarian laws since the end of the Second World War, resurrecting the principles of Nuremberg. Although supporters of the court hoped for a role of the ICTY in social reconstruction, ambivalence about its work and results had been expressed by various parties even before its formation.

Bosniak judges viewed the eventual trial of major war criminals such as Slobodan Milosević (1941–2006) and Radovan Karadžić (*b.* 1945) as possibly contributing to social reconstruction, whereas Bosnian Serb judges held mixed opinions about the impact of these trials on the rebuilding of the country. Moreover, various Bosnian legal professionals shared the opinion that the ICTY was working in isolation in The Hague, and not in tandem with local judicial institutions.[27] The ICTY mandate lasted until November 2017, and the International Residual Mechanism for Criminal Tribunals (IRMCT) has been handling residual functions of the ICTY since.

Despite these numerous international monitoring measures, re-establishing a fragile and resilient order in the country at large and in Sarajevo was not a success. Sarajevo did not emerge as such a strictly divided city as Beirut, but the emergent order was built on ethnic, nationalist and religious issues. Many Serbs, fearing the consequences of the Dayton Agreement implementation, fled the city after its signing, while Muslim refugees from the former Eastern Bosnia – now RS – moved to Sarajevo.

Beirut

According to the National Pact, built on the relative power of each sect prior to Lebanon's independence in 1943, the post of president is reserved for Maronites, the prime minister for Sunnis, the speaker of the Chamber of Deputies for Shiites and its vice-speaker for Christian orthodoxies. Article 95 of the Constitution amended that civil service positions were to be distributed so that each community was proportionally represented, and seats in parliament were distributed six to five in favour of the Christian community, reflecting their slight numerical advantage among the population at that time.[28] Thus, Lebanon's political institutions are balanced according to the 'Rule of Sixes', as they have been designed to ensure this equitable repartition of the six most powerful confessional communities. Sectarianism in Lebanon is based on eighteen recognized sects, forming a framework favouring people's loyalties more than national affiliation. The absence of civil rights gives more power to sectarianism, as birth, marriage and death have to be certified by religious authorities. Mixed marriages are not possible in Lebanon; one of the partners must either convert or the couple has to marry abroad, usually in Cyprus. Likewise, atheism is not officially allowed, as religious affiliation is obligatory for official records.

As Youssef M. Choueiri argues, Lebanon's political system, based on religious differences and known as confessionalism,

> [. . .] generates civil wars as a result of its confessional structures and their contradictory interests. In this sense, one could explain the various civil wars in Lebanon in terms of the uneven development of the social, economic and cultural structures of the various sects in their co-existence within a certain political arrangement. This friction is an inbuilt mechanism that is triggered into violent confrontations whenever a certain sect feels itself capable of tipping the balance of power in its favour.[29]

After several failed attempts at peace agreements, the best known being the Geneva Conference (31 October to 4 November 1983), the Lausanne Conference (12–20 March 1984) and the Damascus Tripartite Agreement (28 December 1985), sixty surviving MPs of the 1972 elections were sent to the city of Taif in Saudi Arabia (22 October 1989). All negotiations resulted in one document, composed of four distinct parts, the Taif Agreement, also known under the names of 'National Reconciliation Accord' or 'Document of National Understanding'.[30] The country's identity was stipulated as 'Arab by affiliation and identity'.[31]

The Taif Agreement altered the formula of power-sharing between Christian and Muslim communities, enabling an equal representation in parliament. Allowance was given for the temporary presence of Syrian troops to help Lebanon. These had to withdraw within a two-year deadline, but this withdrawal had to be mutually agreed upon by the two countries. Consequently, Syria exercised substantial political influence in Lebanon until the spring of 2005. The real difficulty of the Taif Agreement was, rather than its structure, its implementation, as Samir Makdisi notes,

> Still, no matter how imperfect its implementation, the accord was the means for ending the civil war, and thus served an important objective. It is an open question whether it can constitute the ultimate political framework for ensuring political stability in the long run, which proved to be right.[32]

Even if the Taif Agreement succeeded in silencing the guns and containing sectarian violence, it reinforced sectarianism as a consequence. The legalization of Syrian suzerainty was achieved in May 1991 through the Treaty of Brotherhood, Cooperation and Coordination.[33]

International intervention and monitoring did not succeed in its implementation in Lebanon. The international community did deploy its United Nations Interim Force in Lebanon (UNIFIL) in 1978 in the south of the country, yet its mandate involved preventing incursions along the Israeli border.

In 1991, instead of initiating investigations of human-rights violations during the conflict, the Lebanese government passed a General Amnesty Law (Law 94/91) which granted amnesty for all crimes committed by militias and armed groups – except Palestinian ones – before 28 March 1991. All legal actions against war criminals were abandoned and militia leaders could resume their posts in parliament or ministries.

This impunity of the Lebanese judicial system did not allow the country to enter a process of societal healing through a process of restorative justice, as seen in the ICTY attempts in former Yugoslavia and with the Truth Reconciliation Commission (TRC) in South Africa. This importance of societal healing triggered by justice is stated by Harvey M. Weinstein and Eric Stover:

> It is often argued that trials and truth commissions promote reconciliation by forcing societies emerging from war or periods of political violence to 'come to

> terms' with the past, achieve 'closure' and stability, and rebuild a new system of governance based on democratic principles.[34]

Instead, Lebanon as a state, more than being corrupted, ignored the fate of the 17,000 people who disappeared and were abducted during the conflict. Considering this environment of impunity, Prime Minister Fouad Siniora's request to the UN Security Council to adopt Resolution 1664 on 29 March 2005 appeared contradictory to the system in force. This resolution drove the set-up of a quasi-international court investigating the assassination of former prime minister Rafiq Hariri, opening a 'one-time exception to the rule' of unlawful solutions and corruption prevailing until then, hence worsening a pre-existing crisis. In his request, Siniora asked for the establishment of a 'tribunal of an international character to try all those who are found responsible for this terrorist crime'.[35]

Reconstruction and memory process

Sarajevo

In the spring of 1994, a UN team estimated that 60 per cent of the buildings in Sarajevo had been severely damaged or destroyed: the cost of restoring the city to its pre-war state would be in the region of $4 billion.[36] There was a strong sense of relief that the war ended, yet this situation devoid of victory brought a sense of uncertainty about the future. The country's infrastructure was in a devastated state, too: all the railroad lines, seventy bridges, 2,000 kilometres of roadways, airports, gas and electricity, and communication lines were cut. More than two-thirds of the total housing, as well as infrastructure for social services (hospitals, schools, etc.) were either destroyed or damaged. The per capita income dropped to below $500, industry operated at 5 to 10 per cent of its pre-war capacity, not to mention the devastating effect of landmines on agricultural land and that approximately 80 per cent of the population was dependent upon international food assistance at the end of the war.[37]

Due to the total reconfiguration of the country, people had to claim property and there was privatization of previously socially owned apartments. As the Dayton Peace Agreement had guaranteed the right of return to all refugees and displaced people, expelling and re-accommodating occupants and determining who held the right of occupancy of any given property became a lengthy and difficult process.[38] The attempt to create a new form of strong nationalism among the Serbian population also made use of the opportunity left by the collapse of communism in 1989–91 to intensify divisions within the Yugoslav Federation.

Psychiatrist Vamik D. Volkan suggests in a study on ethnic violence that the creation of socialist Yugoslavia after the Second World War jeopardized people's attempts to resolve their past conflicts and war trauma and this meant that these were inherited by later generations.[39] Volkan's suggestion of a 'chosen trauma' has been countered by numerous voices, of which I would quote Harvey M. Weinstein and Eric Stover, who in their book *My Neighbor My Enemy: Justice and Community in the Aftermath of Mass Atrocity* linked the situation in former Yugoslavia to the Rwandan tragedy:

> These wars were not clashes between cultures or civilizations, nor were they the result of ancient ethnic or tribal hatreds. They were fabricated wars, forged out of the raw opportunism of political extremists who inculcated and exploited paranoia and nationalist myths to stoke the fires of ethnic hatred.[40]

Beirut

In 1992, a confiscation law was passed, expropriating private properties in a delineated area known as Beirut Central District (BCD). Confiscated property rights were compensated by shares in the Solidere company – a private for-profit organization founded in May 1994 and responsible for the development of BCD. Distinctions between private and public interests represent one of the most persistent criticisms of the Solidere project. As pointed out by Saree Makdisi,

> What Solidere and the new Lebanese government seem to represent is precisely the withering away of the state as well as whatever one might have called a public sphere or civil society, and their final and decisive colonization by capital. [. . .] In fact, the process of postwar reconstruction in Lebanon has been one of astonishing self-enrichment for the ruling elites, at tremendous public cost.[41]

In a post-war time with symptoms of retribalization and collective amnesia towards the civil strife, critics of Solidere's rehabilitation of Downtown accuse it of adopting a culture of disappearance.

Martyrs' Square is partly being reconstructed.[42] In an architectural study conducted by the American University of Beirut in 1990 on the mental image of Beirut, Martyrs' Square was rated by far the most important landmark in Downtown. As Samir Khalaf points out, 'Beirut's central square has always displayed curious historical features for its survival as a fairly open, pluralistic and cosmopolitan urban district.'[43] Martyrs' Square was considered because of its symbolic significance prior to the war, its recognizable spatial character due to its rectangular shape closed by buildings and its focal point, the statue, and finally as a strategic location.[44]

In his essay 'Ruins', Jalal Toufic narrates the excursion Dima al-Husayni, a fifth-year architecture student at the American University of Beirut, took with her class in the city centre before its reopening. To confront her mental map with the architectural reality of the buildings still standing in the city centre was entering in conflict with memories of these same places her parents had transmitted to her. Toufic recalls how, in the evening, when Dima thought again about this excursion, the different elements, her second-generation memories were mixed up with the places she had physically witnessed earlier that same day:

> Later, in her home, she tried to recall what she saw. Instead of the destroyed, deserted city center, it was the city center of the memories of her parents, the colourful, populated city center that sprang to her mind. It was with difficulty that she could recall the destroyed city center and superimpose it on the pre-war city center.[45]

In societies emerging from war, repression and colonialism, memory has a particular bearing on individual and political communities. In Beirut, the process of memory raises a central issue as a result of the Civil War and its subsequent reconstruction. Amnesia emerged out of the often-fractured nature of memory and is considered a subsequent effect of the Civil War. This phenomenon of amnesia has even been qualified as 'hypermnesia' by scholars like Jens-Peter Hanssen and Daniel Genberg:

> Particularly in the case of postwar Lebanon we witness an (over-) abundance of overlapping, conflicting and rivaling memories, a sort of 'collective hypermnesia', that have in common a celebratory conception of history. Indeed, the frequent public debates about collective forgetting seem only to amplify the phenomenon.[46]

Even the Lebanese history books used in schools today notably lack a section relating to the Civil War and beyond. The committee of historians entrusted with the delicate task of writing Lebanese official history repeatedly fails in its attempts to submit a narrative of the war, which would accommodate all the various communities. Lebanon still awaits an official written history beyond 1946, and it is de facto, therefore, a country without official history, even a compromised or negotiated one.[47] Historian and archaeologist Alfred

Naccache pushed the definition further, qualifying the reconstruction of Beirut a 'memorycide'.[48] Naccache elaborates on how the archaeological excavations of Beirut could have helped to reach a 'consensual national history'.[49] According to Naccache, this could have led to 'the writing of the much-sought-after unified Lebanese History Book'.[50]

Still, this state of amnesia, evidenced by the General Amnesty Law passed in 1991, has not yet convinced the different sectarian and political communities to form a consensus over a common vision upon the post-conflict condition. As this consensus about Lebanese history is lacking, each coalition of inhabitants promotes its own version of history. In this fractured view, a common history lies in the discourse of rupture and continuity in Beirut's reconstruction debate. Interpretations of the conflict(s) in Lebanon vary in official, academic or popular realms and therefore need to be negotiated. These different forms of memory all emanate from individual experiences, either socially constructed, imagined or represented.

In the first part of this chapter, I have tried to give historical evidence about the conditions of both cities, which intertwines with the four artistic interventions that register in aesthetic terms the impact of these major historical, economic, social, material and architectural conditions. Those were created by, during and after the violence of the conflicts that were enacted in and on these two cities. The purpose of assembling these fragments was to lay in the ground upon which any artistic practice in and about these cities operates. The issue at stake is not that the art is merely a reaction to historical events or conditions. Art negotiates these conditions in diverse aesthetic modes. Having 'set the scene', it is possible now to approach the conditions for art practice in such circumstances.

The artistic scene during the war

Sarajevo

War brought change not only to the daily, political and social life but also to the artistic situation in Sarajevo. In spite of the siege, Sarajevans got involved in artistic life, performing and attending performances, even if this artistic life was often restricted to the fact that it was actually taking place. The artists who stayed had difficulty in engaging in their vocation, due to the siege conditions and the lack of material. Consequently, art production was emphasized by more individual and unique features than in the pre-war period. Nonetheless, some cultural institutions such as theatres and art galleries functioned as such during the war. Hundreds of artistic activities such as theatre, concerts and exhibitions were organized, attended by thousands of inhabitants; for the exhibitions the figure of 300 is today commonly accepted though not verifiable.[51] Each exhibition was a proof of the interaction between the artists and the community. Due to safety concerns, however, anyone organizing an art exhibition would not release in advance the date and venue. Interviewed by Craig Mitchell Zelizer, an anonymous exhibition organizer active during the war says about this strategy he and his colleagues developed at the time:

> [We] could not announce in public as [we were] afraid of being targeted. We would usually just knock on people's doors and pass around leaflets a few hours before. Sometimes [we] would have to wait several days to have exhibits.[52]

The art of 'resistance' or 'survival' took place at different levels: the most visible example was the series of exhibitions *Witnesses of Existence*, held between December 1992 and March 1993. In December 1992, Nusret Pašić opened a one-day solo exhibition in the devastated Sutjeska Cinema. Following his initiative, seven other artists exhibited in the following months under the auspices of the Obala Gallery and its director Mirsad Purivatra: Zoran Bogdanović, Ante Jurić, Petar Waldegg, Mustafa Skopljak, Edin Numankadić, Sanjin Jukić and Radoslav Tadić. In March 1993, the eight artists exhibited together at the same location. Using for their artworks material found on the spot, ruins and half-destroyed objects, the *Witnesses of Existence* soon engaged an international audience with the state of destruction and urbicide of the city, at the same time bearing witness to the cultural resistance so important to the besieged city.

Following their common exhibition, these artists received an official invitation to exhibit at the 1993 Venice Biennale by its artistic director, Achille Bonito Oliva.[53] Unfortunately, none of them were able to leave the besieged city, and they were represented in Venice by video works, a documentary on this wartime exhibition and a catalogue presented by Izeta Građević, one of the directors of the Obala Gallery.[54] Following the Venice Biennale, *Witnesses of Existence* was shown in Biel (Switzerland) and Edinburgh. Invitations from Paris (Gallerie Nikki Diana Marquard in collaboration with Gallerie du Jour), Berlin and New York followed. For the exhibition in New York Kunsthalle in the East Village, UN officials based in Sarajevo, who had seen the exhibition and been impressed by the artworks, agreed to transport the artworks out of the country to Ancona, Italy. In his review of the New York exhibition for *Art in America*, art critic Jamey Gambrell notes on the way the artworks succeed in negotiating with the circumstances of war: 'As the title of the exhibition puts it, their works bear witness to existence, to human perseverance under extreme circumstances.'[55] *Witnesses of Existence*'s motto was to keep working at all costs and under any circumstances, to make the opposition between construction and destruction happen in the city, more than to create a sense of normality. This cultural resistance lies in the fact, as stressed by the painter Miroslav Bilać, 'we couldn't do anything about the destruction of the town but we could keep its pulse alive. If we let the town die spiritually then it truly would be dead. But thanks to people who left that spiritual need, that it must not die, for the whole period of the siege Sarajevo was very much alive.'[56]

Another expression of art as resistance was the war advertising campaign led by the group *Trio*, formed by Bojan and Dada Hadžihalilović and Lejla Mulabegović. By redesigning international advertising campaigns, replacing, for example, the slogan *Enjoy Coca-Cola* with *Enjoy Sarajevo*, these artists, more than presenting a criticism of the American culture and its infiltration in Bosnia and Herzegovina, integrated in them messages from Sarajevo. They also delivered a message warning the international community: Sarajevo, a victim and a place of resistance trying to defend fundamental rights of a civilized society, could also happen somewhere else.

In his dissertation 'The Role of Artistic Processes in Peacebuilding in Bosnia-Herzegovina', Craig Mitchell Zelizer formulates the hypothesis that by means of artistic activities during a conflict, people can temporarily forget the war raging outside their door. Zelizer grounds his argument on conflict analysis theory:

> Since the war caused a significant breakdown in society and isolation, the arts helped promote a means of community, even if it was only temporary. Although most arts activities took place under difficult circumstances, such as without heat and by candlelight, people who attended the performances could be transported to another reality for the duration of the performance.[57]

Ultimately, foreign artists, theatre directors, actors and other cultural workers lent their talent to the cultural life of Sarajevo: two examples being the musical *Hair* in the winter of 1992 or Beckett's *Waiting for Godot* directed by Susan Sontag.[58]

Meliha Husedžinović, director of the National Gallery of Bosnia and Herzegovina, stayed critical towards this international visibility of the Sarajevo artistic scene, stressing that

> Time is needed in order to judge with historical distance whether it was the war situation alone or the art that began in Sarajevo under siege – as if a catharsis

> for all the terror and fear – that provoked the interest of the world in our artistic situation.[59]

In the middle of dramatic events, the questions about the influence of social events on culture remain. So does the issue of artists' ability to change the world. In Sarajevo, the answer is clearly no, as art did not stop the bombs falling and provide nurture to its population, but their limited act proved that despite the lack of basic subsistence artists still kept their critical spirit.

Cultural institutions in the aftermath of the war

Whereas the war had seen emerge an art for resistance and survival, its aftermath initiated a kind of art oriented to peace-building and healing. So-called cultures of resistance strived to retain their traditional institutions, using them to control the extreme forces which had tried to annihilate them.[60] Yet, after the war ended, Sarajevi and Beiruti artists found themselves in a fragile situation, due to the absence of institutions supporting contemporary experimental practices, which had yet to be fully instrumentalized. This state led to the emergence of new institutions through private and international funding. Public funding was generally invested in its totality into the national reconstruction process. Thus, these new, non-profit organizations operated in isolation and the art they promoted could not be absorbed by an insufficient art market.

In Sarajevo, two generations of artists, one *pre-* and one *post*-generation, took part in the same exhibitions, reclaiming the space of the city for its inhabitants once the weapons had been definitely silenced by the DPA, whereas in Beirut, the lengthy duration of the war provoked a deeper generational rupture. A so-called post-war generation of artists developed media-archival practices over the last decade of the twentieth century.

Sarajevo

The situation of the cultural institutions after the war was quite alarming. In spite of a return to normal, war left a vacuum. Previous infrastructures like the Oriental Institute, The National and University Library and the Olympic Museum had been annihilated in the spring and summer of 1992. As Robert Donia stresses, 'Each of the three major institutions noted above was representative of the city's multi-ethnic life, and the Oriental Institute held the treasures of the Ottoman era so despised by the Serb nationalists.'[61]

Under the DPA, the different institutions fell under political units supporting culture and education. Mostly surviving through foreign donations, the state had almost no budget left for culture, considering the high costs of post-conflict emergencies such as reconstruction and the reorganization of the whole national infrastructure.

This general poor state of cultural institutions led to a privatization process of culture, through the creation of new organizations: the Ars Aevi Project, the Soros Center for Contemporary Arts – referred to as SCCA, which in 2002 became the Sarajevo Center for Contemporary Arts – and the Bosniak Institute.

The Ars Aevi Project

In the summer of 1992, on the night the Olympic Museum was in flames, Enver Hadžiomerspahić had the idea of inviting internationally renowned artists to react and protest against the intensive shelling and the situation of siege to which Sarajevo was subjected. Each artist was expected and encouraged to donate a work and help forming a collection for a future museum. First named Sarajevo 2000, the project was later renamed and is nowadays known as the Ars Aevi Project. Hadžiomerspahić was invited to present his project at the Venice Biennale in 1993. Prompted by the absence of Sarajevo artists, Hadžiomerspahić made this statement on getting out of Sarajevo:

> I arrived at the press conference in Venice from a besieged city, as a rare and strange live specimen, inviting the world's artists to become founders of the collection for their new museum in Sarajevo. [. . .] I decided to invite the directors of renowned contemporary art museums, foundations and centres from friendly cities in neighbouring countries to be the 'ambassadors' of the Ars Aevi idea; and I proposed that, through collective exhibition, they present the works of the artists-founders of the Sarajevo Collection, whom they invited and who responded to the invitation with enthusiasm. [. . .] I wanted the process of formation of the Collection to simultaneously become a powerful process of regional and international promotion and affirmation of our initiative.[62]

The project grew rapidly, thanks to the cooperation of European contemporary art institutions and collective donations of artworks. However, the war in Sarajevo prevented the display of the works in Sarajevo, and temporary centres were created abroad: first in Milan (1994/9), Prato (1996), Ljubljana (1996) and later in Venice (1997), Vienna (1998), Bolognano (1999/2003). The collection, which includes works by Michelangelo Pistolleto, Christian Boltanski, Sophie Calle, Anish Kapoor, Marina Abramović, Bill Viola, Mona Hatoum, Juan Muñoz,

Joseph Kosuth, 130 artworks in total, were first presented in Sarajevo in 1999. Despite its extensive and qualitative collection, the Ars Aevi Project struggles for its survival; in spite of a long-term collaboration with artists, museums, galleries, cities and architects to establish the Museum of Contemporary Art in Sarajevo, only the bridge designed by Renzo Piano outside the Depot where the artworks are kept was constructed over the Miljacka River in 2002. The Ars Aevi team even received in 2002 an eviction notice from the Ministry of Culture. Reflecting back on this painful incident, Edin Hajdarpašić bitterly states that 'the government's assurances of support often turned into a serious obstacle for the functioning of cultural institutions'.[63]

Soros Center for Contemporary Art, today Sarajevo Center for Contemporary Art

Another significant artistic institution, the Soros Center for Contemporary Art (SCCA), opened its door in Sarajevo at the end of 1996. SCCA Sarajevo was the last centre belonging to this SCCA network to be founded.

Hungarian born American philanthropist Georges Soros established in May 1985 in Budapest the Soros Foundation Fine Arts Documentation Center, which expanded its activities in 1991 under the new name of SCCA. Between 1992 and 1999, twenty new SCCAs opened in seventeen countries: through annual exhibitions of local contemporary art, the centres collected documentation on works by local artists and offered grants, while collaborating with each other from country to country. As observed by Nicolas Guilhot,

> These Soros networks were mostly outsiders of the former regime: individuals who occupied marginal institutional positions but occupied dominant positions on the intellectual or cultural scene, and who therefore belonged to a 'protected' opposition, strengthened by its international reputation and its contacts abroad.[64]

Curators David Elliott and Bojana Pejić resorted to the SCCA centres to select local works of art for their exhibition *After the Wall – Art and Culture in Post-Communist Europe* (Stockholm, Moderna Museet, 1999): this was one of the most visible of the SCCA network operations on an international level.

In 2000, Soros decided to phase out the Soros network by changing the centres' names and registering them as local, non-governmental and non-profit organizations. The Open Society Institute granted them financial independence, which meant that some of them would disappear if they failed with their fundraising strategy.[65] Nina Czegldedy and Andrea Szekeres pointed out the benefits and the difficulties of this granted independence of the SCCA centres from Soros' Open Society:

> The autonomous structure of SCCA, independent of state bureaucracy, however, allowed for flexibility in addressing topical issues and promoting new initiatives. Nonetheless the original aims of funding and presenting the most up-to-date projects were latterly often restricted by limited budgets.[66]

SCCA Sarajevo was devoid of any exhibition space, and was therefore a mobile art centre. It aimed to organize an annual exhibition and create an archive centre, providing databases on artists, completed with the formation of a library. Dunja Blažević, the director and main curator of the SCCA Sarajevo, stresses the importance of the role of such institutions in a post-war period, emphasizing its cultural activities:

> This center focuses on the most pressing problems of contemporary art in post-war time: overcoming the information gap and the relation center / periphery – re-establishing contacts to the outside world, exchanging information, establishing dynamic communication; overcoming discontinuity – repairing links in the chain of memory that runs from the pre-war years to the present; stimulating cooperation with the Bosnian artists in the Diaspora (particularly the young and middle generation); creating a new art scene – developing new projects and ideas in order to give coherence to scattered creative energies and providing financial and organizational help for new individual and collective initiatives which, on a local level and according to local criteria, are not recognized or accepted as art.[67]

The tasks listed above by Blažević were undertaken by SCCA since its opening, yet I would pay particular attention to the centre's first three yearly exhibitions later in this chapter; they are of greater significance as they involved two generations of artists in long-term and ambitious projects, yet they were organized at the time of SCCA's full functionality.

The Bosniak Institute

Finally, The Bosniak Institute, founded in Zurich in the 1970s by a wealthy Bosniak, Adil Zulfikarpašić, moved to Sarajevo in the late 1990s and took office in a building incorporating an Ottoman public bath in 2001. The Bosniak Institute aims to assemble all kind of references such as books, manuscripts, periodicals and artefacts related to the Bosniak past and focuses on supporting scientific research rather than artistic practices. The building it occupies embodies Eastern and Western influences traditionally characteristic of Bosniak national identification. This institute counts as an institution of written social memory in Bosnia and Herzegovina.

Beirut

In Lebanon, the Civil War acted like a tabula rasa process in the visual arts. The surviving or newly created cultural institutions supporting a small number of new artistic productions therefore were significant to a post-war generation of artists. Since the reopening of the Beirut Theater in 1992, its direction employed young actors and artists, many of them educated abroad. According to Arnaud Chabrol, its role is highly important, due to the presence of these young artists who found in the Beirut Theater their first support: it supported the emergence of a new generation of artists.[68] Through this first impulse, other cultural actors emerged, such as the Ayloul Festival, Ashkal Alwan, two institutions whose artistic festivals dominated the artistic scene of Beirut for many years. To these two institutions were later added the Arab Image Foundation and the Beirut Art Center (BAC).

The Ayloul Festival

Directed by curator Pascale Feghali and writer Elias Khoury, the Ayloul – meaning September in Arabic – Festival became an annual event between 1994 and 2001. This art festival took place in different locations in Beirut until 2001, at which point it was stopped and its two organizers, Elias Khoury and Pascale Feghali, were arrested as political dissidents – to be released immediately. The Ayloul Festival brought together Lebanese and foreign artists alike, composed of theatre, performances, conference and visual art. The festival got its inspiration from the work achieved by the Beirut Theater, active on progressive performances since the 1970s. According to Catherine David, the Ayloul Festival is said to have introduced the artists on the current Lebanese scene, including Walid Raad and Lamia Joreige.[69] The Ayloul Festival was a proclamation of art done and exhibited without the authorities' help, taking part in the expressiveness of the post-war city.[70]

The Lebanese Association for Plastic Arts, Ashkal Alwan

A similar institution to SCCA was founded in Beirut in 1994, Ashkal Alwan, directed by Christine Tohme and known as the Lebanese Association for Plastic Arts. Its first exhibitions took place in public spaces: in the Sanayeh Garden, a public garden, in West Beirut in 1995; the Sioufi Garden in 1996; the Corniche in 1999 and Hamra Street in 2000. Ashkal Alwan took over the formula of the Ayloul Festival, but contrary to this latter, organized its exhibitions along the main streets of the city. In an era dominated by phenomena of post-war amnesia, artists were asked to invest physical traces of the Civil War before they disappear, particularly critical towards the Solidere project. Since 2002, Ashkal Alwan has also held seven editions of a regular forum on cultural practices, *Home Works*, which functions during over a week as a platform for documentaries, exhibitions, films, lectures, videos, performances, book launches and other cultural events.[71]

In 2011, with the support of the Ford Foundation, Ashkal Alwan launched its Home Workspace, a facility dedicated to education and research. Every year, artists take part in a residency with an invited resident professor.

The Arab Image Foundation

Fouad Elkoury, Samar Mohdad and Akram Zaatari founded the Arab Image Foundation in 1997. The foundation is dedicated to collecting and preserving photography in the Middle East and North Africa through indexing, exhibiting and promoting it. The idea of the foundation emerged from collecting archives from commercial studios, not only in the Lebanese cities of Beirut, Saida and Tripoli but also in Damascus and Aleppo, in order to avoid their destruction when these studios were closing down. The FAI project reflects the history of photographic production from the advent of photography to nowadays.[72]

Beirut Art Center

January 2009 was marked by the opening of the BAC, founded by curator Sandra Dagher – who curated the first Lebanese Pavilion at the Venice Biennale in 2007 – and artist Lamia Joreige. The BAC represents a great achievement as a curatorial institution equipped with an exhibition space, an auditorium and screening room, a media centre and a bookshop. As stressed by its directors,

> The purpose of BAC is to serve as a catalyst for the realisation of contemporary art projects and for the interaction of local and international cultural players. In particular, the center supports local and regional contemporary artists, who face great difficulties due to the lack of financial and institutional support in this field.[73]

In the years following the end of the war, all these institutions were providing a platform for experimental and politically engaged artistic practices, in spite of more galleries having since then opened their doors. These institutions are founded by foreign international foundations, local private sponsorship and occasional funding from the Ministry of Culture in Lebanon.

It is in the framework of some of these institutions or through their networks that Danica Dakić, Maja Bajević, Lamia Joreige and Paola Yacoub produced part of or some of their projects discussed in this dissertation. There are, of course, other significant actors in both cities, like the Kamerni Teatar 55 in Sarajevo, very active in the war, Sfeir-Semmler Gallery, 98 Weeks, Mansion, Dawawine and Zico House in Beirut, which I would like to mention.

Post-war art scene

Sarajevo

The emigration abroad of many artists was felt as a great loss to the art scene. Yet, those who stayed were confronted a real challenge in engaging further with their artistic vocation. For the first three annual exhibitions of the Soros Center for Contemporary Art, its director, Dunja Blažević, chose to move these exhibitions from the usual museums' or galleries' exhibition spaces. Blažević, therefore, was taking into account the conditions of post-war Sarajevo and the use of new artistic forms:

> The creative energy manifested in the war produced completely new artistic phenomena (contextual, situational, reflexive, existential art). Artists are changing their behaviour (the artist-audience relation), working method, they are using new means. In this context, one must also analyse war video and photo production, created from the feverish need to record the moment between life and death. Meeting Point wants to collect and valorise a part of this precious material, and again 'gather' and guide the scattered creative energy, especially of young artists. The end of the war and return to normal life is disciplining art. Its need for socialising has been lost; it is returning to its 'natural place' – to schools, ateliers, galleries.[74]

In 1997, SCCA's first annual exhibition, *Meeting Point*, was held in the summer garden of the Ćulhan, located in the remains of a sixteenth-century Turkish bath stove-house in the Old Town. Similarly, through a process of reappropriation of public spaces by artistic life, the two following annual exhibitions, *Beyond the Mirror* (1998) and *Under Construction* (1999), took place in different locations in the city: *Beyond the Mirror* on Marsala Tita Street, on Obala Maka Dizdara Street, on the Miljacka River, in the bookstore Buybook and so forth and *Under Construction* on the facade of the National Gallery of Bosnia and Herzegovina, forming an unusual exhibition space.

Meeting Point, a fifty-day event series – between July and September 1997 – invited participants to take possession of this timeless, historical site and to interact with different relations: space and time, private and public. Among the thirty participants, two generations of artists displayed objects, installations, videos, rows of pictures and sculptures. The middle generation was constituted by artists born before 1965 who had a long artistic background and identifiable individual style. Among them were Jusuf Hadžifejzović, Edin Numankadić, Salim Obralić, Nusret Pašić and Gordana Anđelić-Galić. They were quite nostalgic about pre-war life and, having studied in Belgrade, Sarajevo or Zagreb, were concerned about the loss of Yugoslavia and its disintegration into different states. The young generation involved young artists born after 1965, whose studies had been interrupted by war. Most of them were at the time still studying at the Academy of Fine Arts. Others, like Nebojša Šerić Šoba, had fought during the war. Some of them, Anela Šabić, Suzana Cerić, Hamdija Pašić, Kurt & Plasto, Dejan Vekić, Rachel Rossner, Nebojša Šerić Šoba, Anja Zlatar, Zlatan Filipović, Damir Nikšić, Anur Hadžiomerspahić, Eldina Begić and Alma Fazlić, gathered together to create the group *Maxumim* in 1996. Active between 1997 and 2000, *Maxumim*'s artistic approach addressed issues of the war experience, from an individual and collective viewpoint, investigating the art of communication more than style. Their practice, therefore, was grounded on the use of symbols with clear readable meanings. Their second exhibition, for example, was about repainting the walls of the Collegium Artisticum in white – their contribution to the gallery which, then, exempted them from paying a fee for using this space.

The wide range of electronic technology used by Sarajevi artists after the war not only make it an easy and manipulable medium and cheap material but kept the artists' work into a critical approach; its virtuality was not operating as an annihilating property but as the means by which they could project their artworks outside real space and time, creating an art for every time.[75] As underlined by Meliha Husedžinović, art production became made of 'attempts at the so-called democratisation of art and their departure from traditional systems of representation'.[76] There lies no wonder in the fact that young artists, still in search of expressing their art, turned to new medias in order to find new forms of representation.

Beirut

The artistic scene in Beirut in the aftermath of the war is represented by a generation of artists born in the late 1960s or early 1970s. Most of them live and work in Beirut. Even if not locally feted by local audiences in the late 1990s and early 2000s, many of these artists – among them Lamia Joreige, Walid Raad and the Atlas Group, Khalil Joreige and Joana Hadjithomas, Tony Chakar, Akram Zaatari, Jalal Toufic, Rabih Mroué and Lina Saneh, Ziad Abillama, Paola Yacoub – have produced a strong international presence. Their art probes experimental art and critically engages with sociopolitical issues related to power, war, identity, production of knowledge and the writing of history. Even if most of them know each other, are closely related or befriended, and exhibited together on different venues, Catherine David refuses to present them as a group. In a lecture given on the occasion of the first forum *Home Works* in 2002, David described them as 'artists sharing a cultural project, even if one is able to discern that this project is far from being homogeneous or uniform, and that some of its cracks and fractures might deepen in the future, maybe even in the near future'.[77] David develops her argument further, considering Beirut's artistic body of work as 'excessively marginal', unfolding in a 'privileged context'.[78]

In the cosmopolitanism in force in Beirut, a number of artists were part of migration in the 1980s, a neglected effect of war. They were, therefore, trained in America or in Europe before returning to Beirut in the 1990s. They brought with them not only their knowledge acquired abroad but also an extended network through which they started to operate. As remarked by Sarah Rogers, the tradition for Lebanese artists to train in cities like Paris and New York was common practice throughout the twentieth century, but this phenomenon increased due to the Civil War. The absence of fully operative educational institutions in Beirut during the war partially explains the fact that many Lebanese artists sought their education abroad.[79] This question of cosmopolitanism is a recurrent one in Beirut. Sarah Rogers considers cosmopolitanism in Beirut's art scene as 'a set of networks and processes through which artistic languages and their accompanying values are continually appropriated and refashioned by artists and their critics'.[80] If in 1995 sustaining the art scene seemed a real challenge, by 2002 Beiruti contemporary art practices had become part of the mainstream international venues and art market. An extensive quote from Suzanne Cotter, curator of *Out of Beirut* at Modern Art Oxford 2006, illustrates this sustained effort to gain recognition on the international art scene:

> Politics tend to dominate discussions with artists in Beirut; as do attempts to wind one's way through the labyrinthine history of the civil war and the city's

> reconstruction in the post-war period. [. . .] In Beirut, there are no contemporary art museums, no major prizes, and no art fairs mobbed by huge crowds of people. In short, there is no real public for contemporary art to speak of; certainly not on any significant scale, with the exception of what appears to be the beginnings of a small group of collectors who frequent the recently opened gallery Sfeir Semler and the old Karantina area of the city. Instead, networks of artists, writers, performers, and film-makers run independent spaces and organize events and small festivals where work can be presented for short periods. Their approach is as much a response to the lack of dedicated spaces as it is to the strict censorship laws applied to all forms of public expression in Lebanon. The apparent urgency of work produced in this context reinforces the paradoxical sense of privilege for many artists who, while keeping their day jobs working in the universities, newspapers, television stations, remain unfettered by the cultural institutions and economic politics of public institutions and the market with which we are familiar elsewhere.[81]

Artists' works are meant to attract an academically sophisticated audience, which explains why there has long been an attempt to exhibit abroad rather than in Beirut. Beirut's post-war art scene is known for its archival aesthetics, crossing borders between fictional and historical narration. Grounded in individual experiences of the Civil War, Walid Raad's Atlas Project distorts this experience to a 'montage of stories', appearing though a little absurd yet historically plausible. Lamia Joreige and Akram Zaatari initiate an historical journey through documentary photographs. Confronting the historical specificities of the Civil War through individual experiences provokes a disruption in the narrative cohesion of the war, putting in question the complete understanding of its history. As Rogers puts it, 'The work's interdisciplinary approach and its related blurring of the boundaries between artistic illusionism and documentary realism is often read as symptomatic of post-war Beirut rather than as a strategic intervention playing off that context.'[82] Hence, most Lebanese artists do not frontally engage with the Civil War, rather choosing to work on its symptoms or traces, through fictionalized individual experiences.

In her study of the evolution of visual arts in Egypt, Lebanon and Iraq, Silvia Naef underlines the fact that Lebanese painters did not use their art as a political vehicle already during the French Mandate, qualifying this absence as part of 'national character precisely defined in Lebanese art prior to the war'.[83] In the time of the French Mandate, most artists, although being Maronites, were producing 'art for art'. It has been, therefore, difficult to know about their real political ideas or engagement with politics in the area. This internationalism is therefore not new in the Lebanese art scene, as recalled by Abbas Baydoun, 'that we call instinctive [. . .] for this art is open almost unconditionally to the world and is a direct inheritor of a century and a half of Western art'.[84] Nowadays, the country is suffering under a lack of expression, which rigorously suppresses remembrance of the war; the importing of this internationalism into Lebanese art provokes the Lebanese artists to use and challenge Western forms of art.

2

Past / present / here / there

Voicing loss and dislocating subjectivity in Danica Dakić's video installation *Autoportrait* (1999)

In 2000, a disfigured yellow human creature was displayed on the poster of the exhibition *Ich ist etwas Anderes: Kunst am Ende des 20. Jahrhunderts*, which translates as *I is an Other: Art at the end of the twentieth century*, held at Kunstsammlung Nordrhein-Westfalen, Düsseldorf, 19 February to 18 June 2000. The title of the exhibition was based on the famous avowal by French nineteenth-century poet, Arthur Rimbaud (1854–91): 'Je est un autre' – 'I is an Other'.[1] In her essay 'Strangers to Ourselves', as well as focusing on the experience of migrancy, French literary theorist Julia Kristeva makes the following observations on Rimbaud's words, *Je est un autre*:

> Rimbaud's *Je est un autre* ('I is an other') was not only the acknowledgement of the psychotic ghost that haunts poetry. The word foreshadowed the exile, the possibility or necessity to be foreign and to live in a foreign country, thus heralding the art of living of a modern era, the cosmopolitanism of those who have been flayed.[2]

Invited by the poster to the exhibition, visitors to the Kunstsammlung would then contemplate the video installation *Autoportrait* from which the creature on the poster originated, created by Danica Dakić (*b.* 1962, Sarajevo). In a darkened space, a large screen (280 × 210 cm) was positioned directly on the ground in the middle of the room. The screen could be seen from both the front and the back, allowing the viewers to interact with the piece by moving around it in space and engaging with it at eye level. The presentation of the installation consisted of a single shot of four and a half minutes that is created by the superimposition of two shots shown simultaneously and presented as looped videotape (Figure 2.1).

A large-scale yellow nude female body on a dark background represents the only point of light, of which only the head and shoulders are visible. They serve

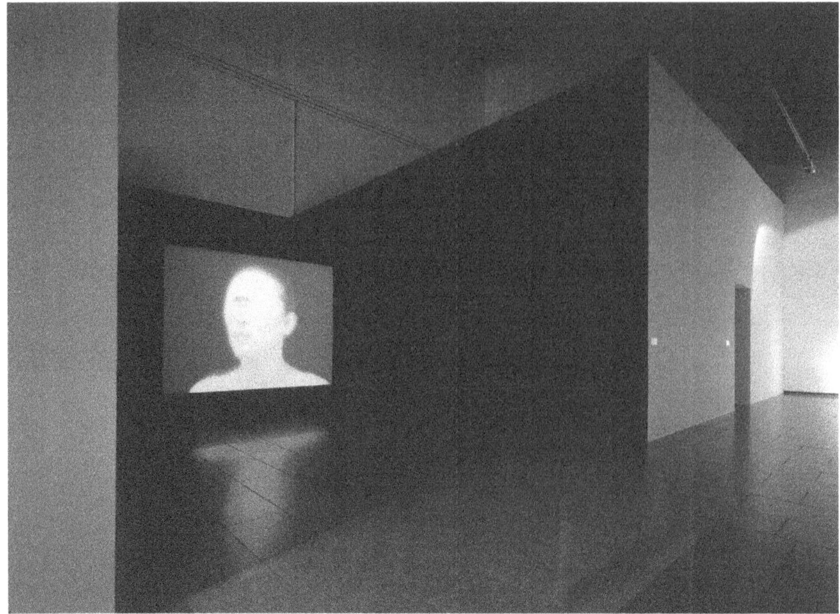

Figure 2.1 Danica Dakić, *Autoportrait*, 1999. Installation view: Düsseldorf, Kunstsammlung Nordrhein-Westfalen, 2000. © Egbert Trogemann, VG Bild-Kunst Bonn.

as the only point of light in the room. The three-quarter position of the face does not technically allow this figure to *look* directly at the visitors. Moreover, 'she' cannot *see* them. Resembling a terrible scar amid the harmonious facial features, a second mouth has taken the place of her eyes. The staging of a face-to-face encounter can produce a highly disturbing effect on the viewer. The two mouths of this sightless creature speak, however, and what they utter is a collage of two tales – two traditional narratives. The mouth in the correct anatomical position speaks first in Bosnian, the artist's mother tongue, and its words are followed shortly by those of the second mouth speaking in German, the language of her adopted country. The two narratives emanating acoustically from these two mouths form a soundtrack of the two voices working in both parallel and overlay (Figure 2.2).

The narrative in Bosnian speaks about an island that is inhabited by voices. The story is one the artist Danica Dakić had read as a child in a collection of 100 tales from all over the world. The version she uses in *Autoportrait* is as follows:

> The island where he was, was called the Isle of Voices; it belonged to the tribe, but they made their home upon another, three hours' sail to the southward. There they lived and had their permanent house, and it was a rich island [. . .]

As for the Isle of Voices, it lays solitary the most part of the year. [. . .] It had its name from a marvel, for it seemed the seaside of it was all beset with invisible devils; day and night you heard them talking one with another in strange tongues, day and night little fires blazed up and were extinguished on the beach; and what was the cause of these doings no man might conceive. [. . .]

This was a thing peculiar to the Isle of Voices.

These fires and voices were ever on the seaside and in the seaward fringes of the wood, and a man might dwell by the lagoon two thousand years and never be any way troubled; and even on the seaside the devils did not harm if let alone. Only once a chief had cast a spar at one of the voices, and the same night he fell out of a coconut palm and was killed. [. . .]

It was all bare in the strong sun; there was no sign of man, only the beach was trodden, and all about him as he went, the voices talked and whispered, and the

In den Tagen, die zu uns im Traum sprechen, lebte ein Mann, der mit dem Spottvogel verwandt war. Er baute Hütten aus trockenem Gras. Vor jeder Hütte zündete er ein Feuer an, damit es aussah, als ob dort jemand wohnte. So errichtete er ein ganzes Lager. Zuerst, ging er in eine Hütte hinein und weinte wie ein kleines Kind, dann in die nächste, wo er wie ein Kind lachte. Dann ging er an den übrigen Hütten vorbei und sang mit der Stimme eines Mädchens und dann sang er wie ein Mann. Ein Stückchen weiter sprach er mit der zittrigen Stimme eines Greises und der kreischenden einer alten Frau. So ahmte er alle Stimmen nach, die er je gehört hatte und der Lagerplatz schien bald voller Menschen zu sein. Einmal kam einer vorbei. Der Mann war neugierig, welcher Stamm hier wohl lebte und kam näher. Vor dem Lager jedoch stand nur der Spottvogel vor einem großen, brennenden Feuer und wartete bis der Mann in seiner Nähe war. Der Mann sagte: „Ich hörte viele Stimmen. Welcher Stamm wohnt hier?" Der Vogel sagte: „Ich bin alleine hier. Sieh' selbst nach, nur ich bin da." Der Mann war überrascht und fragte: „Wo sind denn alle hingekommen? Ich hörte deutlich das Weinen eines kleinen Kindes, ich hörte Männerstimmen und Frauenlachen. Viele Stimmen hörte ich, aber ich sehe nur dich." „Ich bin alleine. Ich weiß von keinem anderen Menschen hier." „Es müssen welche da sein," sagte der Mann. „Ich hörte Kindergeschrei, Frauenlachen und Männerstimmen; und nicht die Stimme nur eines Mannes, sondern das Gespräch vieler Männer." „Es ist wirklich niemand da außer mir," antwortete der Spottvogel. „Frage nicht deine Ohren, denn die ließen dich etwas anderes hören. Frag' lieber deine Augen, denn die täuschen dich nicht. Siehst du jemanden anderen als mich?"

Otok na kome se nalazio Keola nazivali su Otokom Glasova; pripadao je jednom plemenu čije je stalno boravište bilo na drugom otoku, udaljenom tri sata plovidbe prema jugu. Tamo su živjeli i tamo su im bile kuće, a bio je to bogat otok. O samom Otoku Glasova znalo se sljedeće; otok je veći dio godine pust, ime je dobio po jednom čudu, jer čini se da je cijela obala otoka opsjednuta nevidljivim vragovima. Noću i danju čuje se kako medjusobno razgovaraju nekim čudnim jezicima. Noću i danju male bi vatre plamsale i gasile se na obali i niko živ nije znao uzrok tih zbivanja. Bila je to osobitost Otoka Glasova. Vatre i glasovi javljali su se uvijek na morskoj strani otoka i na rubu tamošnje šume. Čovjek bi mogao boraviti kod lagune i 2000 godina a da nikad ne doživi nikakvih neprijatnosti. Vragovi nisu nikome činili ništa na žao ako ih se pustilo na miru. Obala je bila sasvim pusta. Posvuda su mogli da se čuju glasovi kako govore i šapuću, a male su se vatre pojavljivale i gasile. Tu se govorilo svim jezicima svijeta: francuski, holandski, ruski, tamil, kineski... Koja je god zemlja poznavala magiju, tu je bio poneko od njenog naroda. Sada je Keola postao najuplašeniji čovjek na sva četiri okeana. Bilo mu je jasno da se dogadja nešto neobično, jer glasovi su se motali po cijeloj obali, podižući se i zamirući, pretičući jedan drugoga. Po zvuku tih glasova činilo se da su čarobnjaci bijesni.

Figure 2.2 Danica Dakić, *Autoportrait*, 1999. Texts. © Danica Dakić.

> little fires sprang up and burned down. All tongues of the earth were spoken there; the French, the Dutch, the Russian, the Tamil, the Chinese. Whatever land knew sorcery, there were some of its people whispering.
>
> So now Keola was the most terrified man in the four oceans. [. . .]
>
> And it was plain to him it was something beyond ordinary, for the fires were not lighted nor the shells taken, but the bodiless voices kept posting up the beach, and hailing and dying away, and others following, and by the sound of them these wizards should be angry.

The other narrative, in German, tells the story of a mocking bird, a bird possessed of the ability to produce and imitate as many different voices as an entire village might contain. He uses this gift to trick strangers and passers-by:

> In those days, when they spoke to us in dream, lived a man who was related to a mocking bird.
>
> He had built himself a number of grass nyunnoos. He made fires before each, to make it look as if someone lived in the nyunnoos.
>
> First he would go into one nyunnoo and cry like a baby, then to another and laugh like a child, then in turn, as he went the round of the humpies he would sing like a maiden, corrobboree like a man, call out in a quavering voice like an old man, and in a shrill voice like an old woman; in fact, imitate any sort of voice he had ever heard, and imitate them so quickly in succession that anyone passing would think there was a great crowd in that camp.
>
> A fellow would hear the various voices and wonder what tribe could be there. Curiosity would induce him to come near. He would probably peer into the camp, and, only see the Mocking Bird standing alone, at a small distance from a big glowing fire.
>
> Then he would ask him what he wanted. The stranger would say he had heard many voices and had wondered what tribe it could be, so had come near to find out. The Mocking Bird would say 'But only I am here. See, look around, I am alone.'
>
> Bewildered, the stranger would look round and say in a puzzled tone of voice: 'Where are they all gone? As I came I heard babies crying, men calling, and women laughing; many voices I heard but you only I see.'
>
> 'And only I am here. I know of no people. I live alone.'
>
> 'But there should be someone. I heard babies crying, women laughing, and men talking, not one but many.'
>
> 'And I alone am here. Ask of your ears what trick they played you, perhaps your eyes fail you now. Can you see any but me?'

Hence, *Autoportrait* works on two axes: sight and sound. These can also be articulated as the tension between the image and language and correspondingly,

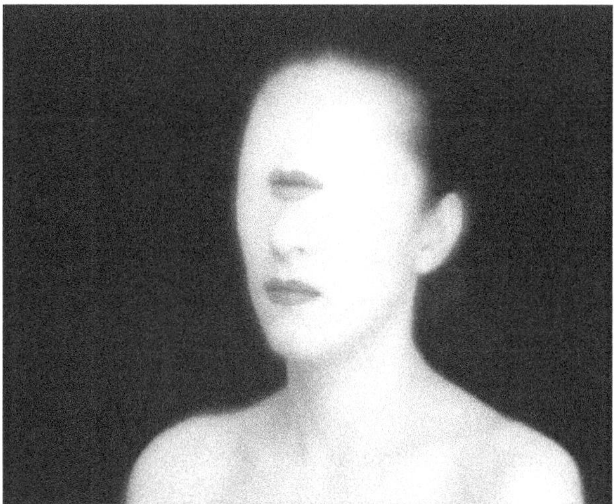

Figure 2.3 Danica Dakić, *Autoportrait*, 1999. Video still. © VG Bild-Kunst Bonn.

for a viewer the oscillation between seeing and listening. While the image contradicts the act of speaking and the power of speech, the act of hearing is also triggered by the three-quarter pose of the creature, which dramatically brings out one of its ears while at the same time it hides the other. Within this dualism, the treatment of the two axes presented together is reinforced by the two narratives, which revolve around the reality of voices and the transformation of individuals. Dakić positions herself as articulating her position in the differing cultures of Bosnia and Herzegovina and Germany, giving each an equal force retaining their linguistic autonomy and yet working side by side in the audiovisual space of the installation. By displaying this *double-identity*, Dakić therefore draws into view a particular dimension of migrancy and a concomitant life experienced through multiple languages and cultures (Figure 2.3).

Danica Dakić's artistic practice during the early 2000s was clearly shaped by her experience of migrancy. If her formulation of migrancy and its subsequent transitional spaces previously drew from the artist's own experience, the motif of migrancy in her work inscribed different levels in time. These all concur with Iain Chambers' description of that same concept:

> Migrancy involves a movement in which neither the points of departure nor those of arrival are immutable or certain. It calls for a dwelling in language, in histories, in identities that are constantly subject to mutation. [. . .] Living between worlds, caught on a frontier that runs through your tongue, religion, music, dress, appearance and life.[3]

Born in 1962 in Sarajevo, Danica Dakić graduated from the Academy of Fine Arts of Sarajevo (enrolled between 1981 and 1985) and the University of Arts in Belgrade (1985–8), where she trained as a painter. In 1988 she moved from Sarajevo to the West German city of Düsseldorf, where she eventually attended Nam June Paik's masterclass at the Kunstakademie Düsseldorf between 1988 and 1990.[4]

When war broke out in Sarajevo in the spring of 1992, Dakić remained in Germany. Soon after the beginning of the conflict, she was cut off from her family and friends, initiating a state of uncertainty about their fate and well-being that lasted for four years.

By the end of the war, her work reveals the extent to which Dakić's perception of reality had undergone change. In her work an individual experience of transitional identities and interstitial spaces becomes prominent as a theme. She was living – in mind and spirit as well as physically – between two localities. Sarajevo represented her *Heimat* (Home country) and Düsseldorf represented her actual *Heim* (Home). This tension sensitized her to the question of migrancy, together with the transposition of cross-cultural identities in a world of perpetual movement and mobility.

The work: Making and material

The production of *Autoportrait/Self Portrait* was a technically complicated and psychologically fraught process for Dakić. She was assisted by photographer and cameraman Egbert Trogemann. During the process a plaster mask was applied to Dakić's eyes and forehead, and the artist thus experienced a physical blinding (Figure 2.4).

Once applied, the mask would only hold on her face for a certain time, so Dakić had to repeatedly perform over two days of shooting which took place at an interval of several weeks. Dakić and Trogemann had decided to aim for achieving a single, continuous shot using mini DV, and not to retouch it more than necessary. The temporary blindness caused by the application of the mask made her lose her balance. Consequently, she faced the difficulties of maintaining her head in a straight position during the shooting. The most imperative requirement for the video's success relied on the fact that the two mouths should appear symmetrical on the final montage. Trogemann, who was behind the camera and responsible for the filming process, would make her start over again if her head wavered even slightly.[5]

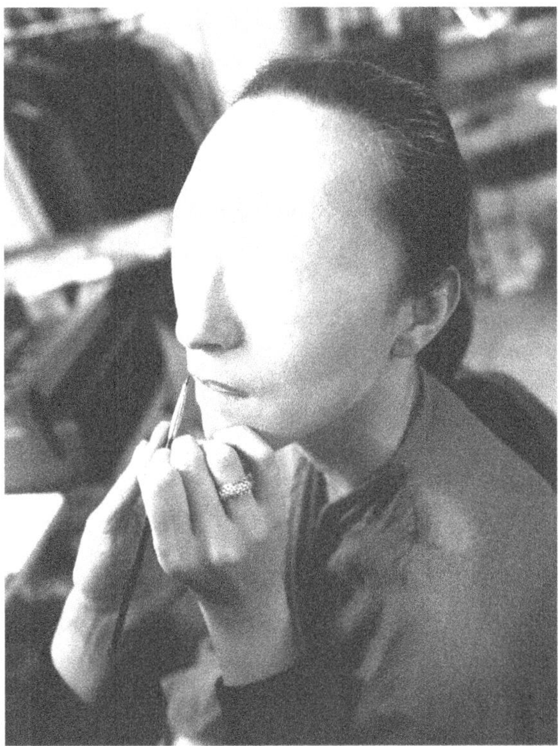

Figure 2.4 Danica Dakić, *Autoportrait*, 1999. Mask for the shooting. © VG Bild-Kunst Bonn.

During an interview, Dakić recounted to me the impotent feeling of being unable to direct the shooting, she being in the front and not behind the camera. Another aim of the piece that all involved were attempting to create was that the subject of *Autoportrait* should look beautiful in spite of the monstrosity of an eyeless face with two mouths.

In form and genre, *Autoportrait* emerges as a multi-layered collage. A technique borrowed from visual art, particularly from Braque and Picasso's Cubist experiments, collage is a mode of assembling pieces or fragments. In his essay of 1959, 'Collage', Clement Greenberg states the relevance of this method as being a turning point not only in cubism but in the evolution of the modernist art in the twentieth century. Referring to Braque and Picasso's works between 1907 and 1914, Greenberg contends that collage emerged as something implicit and inevitable in the course of their joint effort to give art that vision of a 'purer pictorial work'.[6] It has been argued that the proper term to apply to video should be montage; for example, Gregory Ulmer distinguishes the terms in the following definition: 'Collage is the transfer of materials from one context to another, and montage is the dissemination of these borrowings through the new settings.'[7] Nonetheless, I dismiss this convention while writing about Dakić's *Autoportrait*, and instead apply the notion of collage in the sense exemplified in Nam June Paik's *Global Groove* (1971), which was among the first video collages.[8] I am, therefore, considering Donald B. Kuspit's argument that relativity becomes inherent in art. In his essay 'Collage: The Organizing Principle of Art in the Age of Relativity of Art', Kuspit observes how

> In practice, the collage displays a situation of irreducible tension between a subjectivity eager to identify itself yet incapable of completely doing so, and an objectivity in the process of breaking-down objects in the process of losing their hold on subjects. [. . .] This is the relativistic message of collage: the keeping in play of the possibility of the entry of the many into the one, the fusion of the many into the one.[9]

Autoportrait is itself a visual and auditory collage of two sequences which together produce the disturbing face. The soundtrack appears to be a collage of two languages, which in themselves present a textual collage of narrative. From these collages result a certain disruption of the original meaning. The collage consisted of the different fragments mentioned previously, the image, the soundtrack and the autobiographical elements of dailyness transform the piece into a perpetual coming into being, or an almost unexpected encounter of these elements.

The French title introduces the etymology of the term 'autos' from Greek *αυτός* and 'portrait' from the French *portraire* – to portray. The term 'self-portrait' now conventionally refers for obvious reasons to a portrait made by an artist of her/himself. That is typically achievable only when the artist paints from her/his own reflection in a mirror.

I am thus invited by the title to consider the work not only as a portrait/portrayal of one person but as the portrait of a particular person, the artist. In what sense can such an aesthetic collage created through filming the masked face of the artist by another produce the effect of a *self-portrait*? The title is in this case not self-explanatory, but still, the artist is in the image, and this is her voice speaking on the soundtrack. The self-portrait represents a shape-shifting subject; although representing the artist as a subject, it is nonetheless an image and as such an object, a representation of her body. It keeps in play a balance between subjectivity and objectivity through subject and object, enabling what Amelia Jones calls tensions: 'image versus the thing itself: the subject constituted by culture versus the subject constituting culture'[10] putting emphasis on the fact that we are dealing here with an act of interpretation. Whereas art is often conceived as a manifestation of the artist, interpretation exists between the work and its reception. Artists have the capacity to blur or exacerbate the tensions between the artwork and its subject, and in their own way they can counter the tendency in modern times to conflate the artist with his work.[11] When analysing a self-portrait, we have to ask how far the biographical account can explain the complex effects of the work. Taking this on within a cultural and historical framework, art historian and curator Bojana Pejić situates the motif of the two mouths in terms of time, a past versus a present moment:

> When, in the video *Self Portrait* (1999), we see and hear Danica Dakić's mouth telling a fairytale in her mother tongue, while another mouth in place of her eyes tells a different story, in German, it is not a split identity or a divided self that we are witnessing here, but a self that oscillates between the past and the present.[12]

According to Pejić, therefore, the artist locates herself between a past associated with a country and its language on the one hand and a shifting, dislocated, and uncertain present on the other.

The narratives in *Autoportrait* are fictional. Biographical events rarely find a direct expression in Dakić's work. *Autoportrait* is her only work to date specifically labelled as a self-portrait, but it is not the only one that represents her as sole protagonist. Of the work the artist states, 'It is so depersonalized that it is no longer important that this is me.'[13] Moreover, she distances herself further from her two self-representations by giving them the titles *Autoportrait* and *Madame X* in a third language, French.

By conveying the narratives through her own vocal *organon*, she speaks in the first person and she is using the word 'I', which is found in the narratives of the piece. At some point, in the German reported narrative, the Mocking Bird tells the stranger, 'I am alone here. See, look around, I am alone.' The 'I' refers therefore to the infinity of subjects present in the narratives.

The eighteenth-century Scottish philosopher Adam Smith offers the following commentary on the common sense of the word 'I' and how, by being spoken by a particular individual, the 'I' links the predicate to the predicated:

> I differs, however, from all other general words in this respect: that the objects of which it may be predicated, do not form any particular species of objects distinguished from all others. [. . .] It is far from being the name of a species, but, on the contrary, whenever it is made use of, it always denotes a precise individual, the particular person who then speaks. It may be said to be, at once,

> both what the logicians call, a singular, and what they call, a common term. [. . .] The work of art falls in the range of expressive forms, considered as something which is neither expressive projection nor description.[14]

As Smith argued, the 'I' demonstrates a particular singularity, belonging to the speaker. On the other hand, in the twentieth century, in his famous essay 'Shifters, Verbal Categories, and the Russian Verb' (1957), Russian-American linguist Roman Jakobson describes the first person pronoun as a shifter between the sender and the receiver. Jakobson reflects on how 'the general meaning of a shifter cannot be defined without a reference to the message'.[15] Examining Burke, Beneviste, Husserl and Russell's position on the personal pronoun 'I', Jacobson finally states that 'shifters are distinguished from all other constituents of the linguistic code solely by their compulsory reference to the given message'.[16] For this prominent linguist, personal pronouns belong to a complex category, where code and message overlap.

Dakić's distancing demonstrates the ambivalence towards taking the 'I' too autobiographically and triggers the question of the relation between the subjective and objective in this particular piece. *Autoportrait* might then be read as an ambivalent form of autobiography creating a third category by mixing personal elements with fictional and imagined ones. Instead of being a faithful reproduction, the piece suggests the artistic creation of a new form of autobiographical language, which then performs an interpenetration of public elements with the sphere of a singular, specific person.

Autoportrait creates a visual language for the experience of loss. It formulates the emptiness of vision in the artist's experience that counterbalanced by inner perceptions of the events. What I am suggesting is conveyed by what the art historian Jill Bennett, writing of a range of trauma-related artworks, observed as their shared characteristic: 'Their contribution tended to lie in the endeavour to find a communicable language of sensation and affect with which to register something of the experience of traumatic memory – and this, in a manner of formal innovation.'[17]

Three years before the making of *Autoportrait*, during her first stay in Sarajevo after the war in the spring of 1996, Dakić felt estranged from her home town as she contemplated a city utterly altered by the war. That which previously made her feel at home had disappeared. She was seized by a feeling of being cut off. Loneliness resonates in the narrative of the *Mocking Bird*: 'I am alone here, can you see anyone but me?'[18] In reaction to this profound change and feeling that she had to be publicly active as an artist in Sarajevo, she started working on *Madame X: Passing By* (1997) – a work in which her mouth already played a central role. Filmed in Hi8, the video shows the artist's speaking mouth displayed in black and white. The video was placed on a screen in a small passage off the main street in the old town of Sarajevo. The mouth speaks yet the video is devoid of soundtrack. *Madame X* is at the same time active and speechless; the passers-by are unable to hear her. When asked what *Madame X* is trying to tell the Sarajevans, Dakić answered that 'she speaks about the fact that one only hears when one wants to and also only what one wants to hear' (Figure 2.5).[19]

Even so, a *complete* understanding of the soundtrack of *Autoportrait* presupposes linguistic knowledge of both Serbo-Croatian and German. The audience does hear two voices; it sees, however, only one face. Since *Autoportrait* has been exhibited mainly in German or Serbo-Croatian speaking countries, there is an expectation of at least a partial understanding of the soundtrack by its audiences. The viewers become listeners and are taken into a witnessing position. They cannot understand the meaning of both narratives delivered but grasp, instead, their nature in accordance with Jill Bennett's argument that traumatic art is not a faithful translation of testimony but a vehicle for the interpersonal transmission of experience.[20] The installation works as an overwhelming sound and image event. The video projection produces a highly charged body, affecting an audience that stands face to face with this haunting disfigured face.

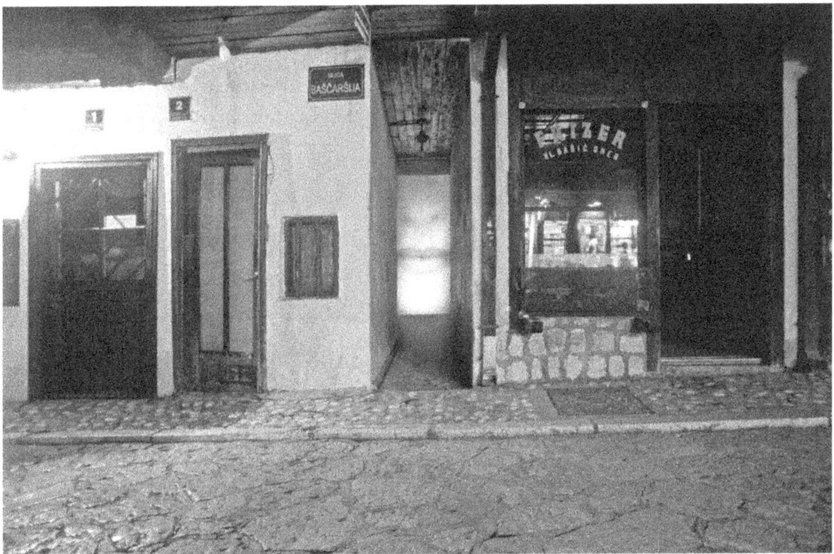

Figure 2.5 Danica Dakić, *Madame X*, 1997. Installation view: Ćulhan, Sarajevo, 1997. © VG Bild-Kunst Bonn.

A second visual feature that catches the audience's gaze but registers with a lesser impact than the second mouth is the skin tone of this unclothed body, which appears unnatural because of its luminous dimension. Through the editing of the videotape, colourization was used to obtain the yellowish skin tone.

Skin represents a bodily envelope that provides a spatial limit to the body. The sensory organ of skin provides the self with its physical boundary. This transitional surface protects an individual from outside attacks and at the same time enables one to interact with others. In his book *The Skin Ego*, French psychoanalyst Didier Anzieu emphasizes the sensorial dominance of the skin occupying as it does a surface of about 18,000 square centimetres for an adult. The skin also has the capacity to judge time and space, supplementing to a lesser degree the sensory capabilities of the ear and the eye.[21]

In the Renaissance sight and touch were regarded respectively as the highest and the lowest senses. This tendency shifted in the eighteenth century, when terminology designated *face* for sight and *feeling* for touch. A whole new dimension has arisen for such perception in the age of virtuality and the immateriality of web-related technologies and tactility.[22] In her book *Skin as a Cultural Border between Self and the World*, German cultural theorist Claudia Benthien states how, in the beginning of the nineteenth century, there was a clear distinction between corporeal feeling and an internal form of feeling. Drawing on the Grimm Brothers' *Wörterbuch* (1826), Benthien states that although being placed under the same entry, *feeling* (*Fühlen*) and *emotion* (*Empfindung*) are discussed in separate sections.[23]

The emphasis on the skin in *Autoportrait* is linked both to the absence of sight in the subject and how *sight* and *touch* are conveyed in the audience's *feeling* of the piece. The five external senses differ in nature and form from the inner emotions that exist and emanate – when they do – from within the body's physical boundaries. The skin becomes first a site of self-consciousness that arouses psychic and unconscious processes, as argued again by Benthien: 'The corporeal feeling is proclaimed as a model, as a precision on the level of individual history, of what are now inner feelings, as in Anzieu's psychoanalytical conception whereby skin sensations serve merely as analogies for psychic, unconscious processes.'[24]

In *Autoportrait*, the yellowness of the body, which also resembles the colour of the cadaver in death, can immerse the viewer. The audience encounters and engages with the yellowed but luminously coloured woman's body and face while the image activates a consciousness of their own boundaries as viewing and experiencing subjects. A cognitive language establishes itself through these direct physiological vectors mediated by the artwork. Moreover, the skin's ability to produce auditory sensations when sounds are made means that the skin, as a cultural and biological liminality, becomes a reflexive surface on which the two narratives reflect. *Autoportrait* does not simulate the touching sense but instead creates a new experiment of touch that visually and psychologically seeks to produce a bodily reflex within the audience.

Language: Stevenson versus Nyoongar culture

On these two foundations, linguistic aspects of the work become pertinent in regard to an individual's personal experience of displacement and exile. *Autoportrait* was mostly shown in areas where the audience could understand at least one of the narratives, the Bosnian or the German, while elsewhere the viewers or listeners would be themselves dislocated by lack of understanding of any words. Thus *Autoportrait* might be placed in conversation with the work of Czech-Canadian artist Vera Frenkel, . . . *from the Transit Bar*, first shown at *Documenta IX* in Kassel (1992), a work which also draws on the experience of displacement, of being *between cultures*, by staging images whose words have been dubbed into languages, Polish and Yiddish, not often spoken by the Western Europeans: French, German or English. The piece took the form of a fully functional piano bar where the visitor could sit down, read the newspaper, order a drink from the bartender (often the artist herself) and watch the six TV monitors present in the room. These latter displayed testimonies on the experiences of immigration, racism, societal exclusion and the loss of cultural identity. The testimonies given in English had been translated and dubbed into Polish and Yiddish, with discontinuous subtitles in English, German and French. Visitors not only experienced uncertainty about the nature of the artwork, wondering if it was in fact the museum's bar. They were also unsettled by the 'Babel' of languages surrounding them, against a background of piano music and the sound of moving trains. Being thus caught up in the situation of a stranger (other), the visitor is compelled to engage and sense for themselves one small aspect of the experiences of a global community of migrants.[25]

Dakić's art has evolved around the primary sites of languages such as tales and lullabies. Acquired in a mother tongue and at an early age, they cannot be fully retrieved in the new language. The artist's interest in these primary sites of language is present in her sound installation *Lullaby of the Earth* (Novy Most Bridge, Bratislava, 2000 and Sarajevo, Latinska Cuprija Bridge, 2002). Dakić recorded people singing lullabies, mostly during her stay in New York in 2001, and subsequently mounted speakers on the bridges of the two cities.

Dakić had already addressed the question of displacement in *Zid/Wall* (1998). Sixty-two close-ups of mouths speaking different languages were projected together on a screen, suggesting not only a brick wall but a speaking wall. For the purpose of *Zid*, Dakić had recorded people talking in their mother tongue about some personal experiences in her studio in Düsseldorf (Figure 2.6).

At first, the use of two stories in *Autoportrait* seems simply to evoke the tradition of tale-telling. Yet a closer examination of the two narratives shows that a different narrative dimension unfolds from what is first assumed. Indeed none of the narratives originate from the oral tradition of the assumed cultural backgrounds - Bosnia and Herzegovina or Germany. They are translations into Bosnian and German from two texts. The first one was originally written in English, and the second was transcribed from the oral language of the South-Western Australian Aboriginal ancestral group known as Nyoongar.

The narrative in Bosnian is a translation of 'The Isle of Voices' (first published in 1893), by the Scottish novelist and travel writer Robert Louis Stevenson (1850–94). It was included in *In the South Sea* (1896). The German narrative refers to an Australian Aboriginal story, *Weedah the Mocking Bird*. The artist provided me with the two versions of the texts she used in *Autoportrait*, explaining that they both came from collections of classic fairy tales.

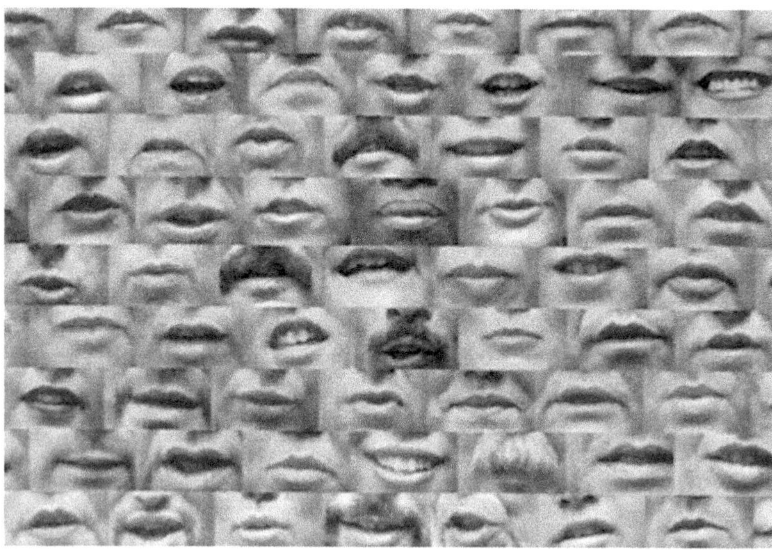

Figure 2.6 Danica Dakić, *Zid/Wall*, 1998. Video still. © VG Bild-Kunst Bonn.

Part of his fictions of the South Seas, Stevenson's 'The Isle of Voices' relates how Keola, abandoned on an island inhabited by invisible voices, marvels when he listens to them speaking all tongues on earth. The voices he hears act like a form of memorial, an unseen presence of other voices. He ignores the dreadful fate awaiting him of being eaten by a tribe of cannibals.

Weedah the Mocking Bird had been collected at the end of the nineteenth century by Katie Langloh Parker (1856–1940), a British citizen living in Australia. Parker published it in English in her now troublingly titled book *Australian Legendary Tales: Folk-lore of the Noongahburrahs as Told to the Piccaninnies* (1896). Parker's intervention was probably more of the nature of an anthropological gesture towards the announced death of a civilization – the Aboriginal one – than one made in the interests of literature. Even so, Parker was very cautious about finding an adequate translation methodology when transcribing the tales, as she describes in one of her letters:

> I am very careful to get them as truly as I can – first I get an old black to tell it in his own language – he probably has little English – I get a younger one to tell it back to him in his language, he corrects what is wrong – then I get the other one to tell it to me in English – I write it down, read it and tell it back again to the old fellow with the help of the medium, for though I have a fair grasp of their language I could not in a thing like this trust to my knowledge entirely.[26]

In an article on Langloh Parker, Judith Johnston points out that colonizers in Australia at the time were not only using material resources such as land, mines and so on for the purpose of their industries but turned Australian myths and legends into fairy tales to contribute to their own children's books industry.[27] Parker's honourable practices were not recognized as scientific work, and she described herself as 'an amateur', never acknowledging the anthropological value of her careful recording of oral culture.[28]

In *Weedah the Mocking Bird*, the Mocking Bird, left alone in a deserted village, goes from hut to hut, and as a gifted ventriloquist imitates the voices of the inhabitants in order to attract passing strangers before killing them. When the baffled strangers ask to whom these unseen voices do belong, the Mocking Bird gives this intriguing answer: 'I am alone here. Ask of your ears what trick they played you, perhaps your eyes fail, you know. Can you see any but me?'

In the postcolonial situation, anthropophagy appears as a cultural sign of consumerism. Keola is considered a consumable product, for the sake of the tribe and its survival. *The Mocking Bird* presents an inversion of 'The Isle of Voices', as the bird is haunting the village in a society which seems to have been either undone or destroyed – as the village has been deserted. Ingesting the culture of the other becomes a form of cannibalism close to the effect of collage.

In *Autoportrait*, both narratives bring to the artwork a dimension of geographical decontextualization, which makes one think about the instability of memory and the process of alienation. The power to create one's recollection through memory is at stake; memories are often connected to a loss, not only of the absence from a given home but also the loss of one's land(scape), the frame of one's home. In 'The Isle of Voices', Keola is lost on an unknown island, whereas in *Weedah the Mocking Bird*, the stranger, exploring new and foreign areas, seeks refuge in the village for the night.

Autoportrait takes on yet another dimension, relating to the phenomenon of globalization and the presence of geographically dispersed and expanding communities locatable only uneasily somewhere beyond territoriality. The analysis of the Self and the Other comes into play – to come back to Rimbaud's *I is an Other*. The native Bosnian and the adoptive German occur in *Autoportrait* as encounters between two different cultural identities contained by a single globalizing self. By proposing an interaction of something more than what is within or between two geographical spaces, this static body becomes a kind of non-place, embodying the experiment of global migration and exile that both eludes and retains specificity. The visual appearance of the subject in *Autoportrait* is devoid of any clothing or jewellery, and any indicators on the body of a possible cultural origin are absent. In this sense, to Reinhard Spieler it is 'a face detached from space and time'.[29] It refers to the perception of a global present and the dissolution of borders as well as ideas of how the notion of borders and boundaries has changed from a separating or a delimiting limit to what for Judith Butler has become a 'highly populated site' offering the possibility of encounter and which may confound identity.[30] The fictitious world of narratives finds its climax in the enchanted world of fairy tales, in which, according to Julia Kristeva, 'the generalized artifices spare us any possible comparison between sign, imagination and material reality'.[31]

Stevenson, a perpetual traveller in the attempt to restore his failing health, is known for being an author in voluntary exile. *Treasure Island* (1882) and *The Strange Case of Dr Jekyll and Mr Hyde* (1885) are among his most famous works. Stevenson left for the South Pacific for the first time on 28 June 1888. He eventually settled in 1890 on the island of Upolu, Samoa, where he remained for the last six years of his life, dying without seeing again his beloved Scottish shores.

If his voyaging in the south expanded his fictional vision, he stayed truthful to his former literary concepts. The island is the symbol par excellence of human isolation. However, Keola, the main character in 'The Isle of Voices', has to come across languages in order to survive on an uninhabited island nonetheless full of languages. Stevenson's *Scottish Islands* and *South Pacific Writings* are indeed full of islands inhabited by isolated characters. Literary critic Graham Tulloch makes the point that, unlike his Scottish fictions, for example, *Treasure Island* or *The Merry Men*, in which 'the islands are either linguistically silent when uninhabited or linguistically alien when inhabited',[32] Stevenson's *South Seas Fictions* show him to be aware of having found a place 'not of linguistic silence, but a place of talk'.[33]

Stevenson divided his time on Upolu between fictional and non-fictional writings; through his geographical wanderings, he became increasingly interested in anthropology and his long immersion in the area allowed him to start writing a history of Samoa. Being first of all a teller of tales, he found himself in his element while living in an oral culture. Accounts relate how he tried to narrate Scottish history and legends to the Pacific islanders, hoping to hear their local stories in return.[34]

He was sensitive to his status as the white foreigner/settler and the confrontation of his own with other cultural identities.[35] Scotland remained as the point of reference for him in order that he might understand his surroundings. At the same time, Stevenson produced damning analyses of the imperial powers in the Pacific. In 'The Isle of Voices', he openly accuses his fellow westerners of behaving uncivilly, observing that 'white men are like children and only believe their own stories'.[36]

While Western cultures tend to regard folk and traditional tales as fictional, reserved only for children, in the Australian Aboriginal view they are considered as part of a 'fundamentally narrative understanding of the universe'.[37]

In his extended research on myth, French social anthropologist Claude Lévi-Strauss noted how oral tradition relies more on sensory perceptions, compared to the increasing use of mental capacity privileged in modern Western societies:

> Today we use less and we use more of our mental capacity than we did in the past; and it is not exactly the same kind of mental capacity as it was either. For example, we use considerably less of our sensory perceptions.[38]

Lévi-Strauss was aware of the objection about his method of extracting the structure of American mythology, based on the fact that American myths were highly repetitive histories. He rejected the claim that myths of a given population can only be interpreted and understood in the framework of the culture of that given population.[39] There are several things I can say by way of answer to that objection.

I have argued that in *Autoportrait*, Dakić works on the recurrent theme of voices, which appear at different moments in different stories, thus evoking the Lévi-Straussian concept of myth. English speakers traditionally refer to the term 'The Dreaming' as the Aboriginal order of reality defined as 'an all-embracing system of signification, a complex of aspects of Aboriginal belief, including mythology, law and history'.[40] The use of *The Dreaming* as an English translation of the Australian Aboriginal concept *tjukurpa* has been criticized, as it could be denigrating or misleading, but there is as yet no preferable translation.[41] The modes of transmission of *The Dreaming* are contained in narrative forms and ritual dramatization, as emphasized by early twentieth-century Australian anthropologist William Stanner (and we have to tolerate but challenge the unreconstructed colonial terminology in quoting his text):

> The blackfellow has a mythology, a ritual, and an art which express an intuitive, visionary and poetic understanding of the same ultimates. In following out The Dreaming, the blackfellow 'lives' this philosophy. It is an implicit philosophy, but nevertheless a real one. Whereas we hold (and may live) a philosophy of abstract propositions, attained by someone standing professionally outside 'life' and treating it as an object of contemplation and inquiry, the blackfellow holds his philosophy in mythology, attained as the social product of an indefinitely ancient past, and proceeds to live it out 'in' life, in part through a ritual and an expressive art, and in part through non-sacred social customs.[42]

Dreamtime beliefs were passed down orally from generation to generation. The notion of custodians of the traditional stories is common to the Aboriginal view of the world. The world is here a symbolic universality taking its significance through myths and narratives, creating an order of reality implying every level of life.[43] As denoted in the English use of *The Dreaming*, a typical Aboriginal language possesses a certain degree of conciseness and detail, what is not easily reproducible in English, a language and a culture that does not inhabit either the imaginative or linguistic universe of the 40,000-year-old cultures of the Australian continent. Linguist Nicholas Evans reckons a linguistic diversity of ca. 250 languages in Aboriginal Australia. If dialects are included as distinctive languages this figure rises to 600.[44] I can, therefore, deduce that probably only the structure of *The Mocking Bird* is rendered into the German version in *Autoportrait*.[45]

Having the origins of the narratives chosen by Dakić to see what such investigation might bring to the reading of the work, I cannot escape from the fact that the collage of the two tales, two worlds, two positions in the world that she presents greatly differ from their original narrative content. In her use of mythical material, the artist has focused on paragraphs and sentences directly referring to *voices*. Their narratives, especially Stevenson's 'The Isle of Voices', take on, therefore, a new form. Through her use of voices, Dakić alludes to the ever-shifting functions of language, on which film-maker and postcolonial literary theorist Trinh T. Minh-ha has stated,

> Language is the site of return, the warm fabric of memory, and the insisting call from afar, back home. But here also, there, and everywhere, language is a site of change, an ever-shifting ground.[46]

Dakić chose fearful narratives. Yet by concentrating on the phenomena of the invisible voices, she avoids the dreadful destinies of the heroes of each tale – Keola will be eaten by a cannibal tribe, and the stranger dies, burnt in the fire prepared on purpose by the Mocking Bird. Both stories have been subjected to a double-procedure: first, the translation into their final versions and, then, through their shortening. The translation process itself bears its own opacity and disjuncture with that contained and purposed in the original text. In his famous essay on translation, Walter Benjamin comments on the translatability of the text and the 'vital connection' between the original and the translation:

> It is plausible that no translation, however good it may be, can have any significance as regards the original. Yet, by virtue of its translatability, the original is closely connected with the translation; in fact, this connection is all the closer since it is no longer of importance to the original. We may call this connection a natural one, or, more specifically, a vital connection.[47]

In a foreign language, thoughts wandering across the mind have to find a reasonable, translatable way of being articulated to the outer world while constantly impregnated by the perpetual return to the native language.

In *Autoportrait*, Dakić privileges the faculties of speaking and hearing, yet she signals in the narrative of *The Mocking Bird* how hearing can trigger a kind of blindness. The mocking bird states, 'You should ask your eyes instead, for they do not deceive you,' and this throws into doubt the piece's apparent privileging of language over visual representation. Art historian Horst Bredekamp comments on this particular aspect of *Autoportrait*, saying that although absent, the eyes are indeed expressed through the auditory aspect: 'Contrary to the audible comment to trust not language but our own eyes, the auditory aspect of the mouth does not efface but in fact expresses the *visus* of the eyes.'[48] *Autoportrait* conveys the sense of how the identity of persons, such as migrants, is constituted neither by their past selves alone nor solely by their adoptive language but by both. The artwork stands for an identity in perpetual transition.

Migratory trajectories

As I have suggested, *Autoportrait* needs to be approached from many angles and aspects: as a double or a split identity, as a human or social body, as the role of the foreigner within the self and as an inscribed body producing a kind of depth and meaning. To these should be added a post-communist dimension that to some extent refers to a postcolonial one. As Diane Amiel argues, 'artists from the Balkans have benefited from the postcolonial cultural critique developed in the West.'[49] *Autoportrait* becomes a site that enables the rearticulation of social and territorial conditions not only within Bosnia and Herzegovina and Germany but beyond. The questions of migration and identity have been the object of much scholarly discourse in other contexts. Due to the extended phenomenon of globalization and its subsequent virtually instantaneous worldwide activities and global migration, subjectivities tend to distance themselves from one, single and particular place. The diasporic self is considered an outdated model and has been replaced by what Swiss video artist Ursula Biemann calls 'Itinerary Identities'. Globalization has made migration shift from a historical to a geographic discourse. According to Biemann, who refers to 'Geographic Bodies',

> Geography as a discipline of geophysics is not what interests us here, but the postmodern understanding of geography as a distinct mode of producing and organizing knowledge regarding the way natural, social and cultural conditions relate to one another. The model operates as a theoretical platform from which to think about society in a networked, complex, and spatially expanded way that includes concepts of boundaries, connectivity and transgression.[50]

In this global and trans-cultural world in which geographies are possibly losing their importance, focusing on the specific geopolitics of the Balkans and more particularly of Bosnia and Herzegovina does not necessarily lead to an aporia. In the case of the reconfiguration of the former Yugoslavia, it is important to stress the central role of identity on social and political levels within a wider framework of the reworking of strategies, ideas and political values.

Irit Rogoff's writing on how geography inscribes itself as a practice includes changes occurring in the postcolonial, post-communist and post-migrational world. It implies the re-examination of its relationship with place and mobility:

> In this contemporary relationship, we no longer think of art as applying existing knowledge through other means, no longer illustrating or analyzing or translating. Rather, we think that it is both a research mode and a means of knowledge production in and of itself. Therefore art and visual culture are able to produce both new knowledge as well as new modes of knowing which have the potential to unframe some serious issues . . . away from the moralizing discourses that imprison it at a level that requires response.[51]

In a country led by what was termed Third Socialism, or subsumed into Iron Curtain Europe before 1989, Yugoslavians did not live as secluded as the citizens of other first-line communist countries. They enjoyed a controlled freedom to travel abroad. Getting a passport was an easy process and was even encouraged by the government, especially for Yugoslavian workers who could thus become temporarily employed in Germany as guest workers.[52] Moreover, culture was repressed less, and the state favoured a greater degree of freedom than was experienced in surrounding countries. Dissident East European writers and intellectuals were often first translated into Serbo-Croatian and published in Yugoslavia, a quite common transitional process before finding their way to the West.[53]

The Titoist regime's efforts to overcome regional nationalist identities by implanting a stable and common identity as citizens of one single state failed. These attempts proved insufficient to overcome economic downturns and the resurgence of nationalist forces, especially when these latter reached their climax in the 1980s. As mobility in post-communist countries increased in the early 1990s, in Southeastern Europe it was more a result of the threat of war.

In her work, Danica Dakić blinds and ruins the space of vision within the space of the body, opening to an allegorical interpretation: her face, endowed with multiple mouths and discordant voices is part of a collective memory. Thus, Dakić's *Autoportrait* expresses a double exile: on the one hand, the exile from the native land, on the other hand, from the mother tongue. Through the signification of the two narratives, the artist brings to the surface a political dimension and echoes the multi-ethnic portrait of Yugoslavia prior to its implosion.

Unfortunately, many Western scholars lacked this dimension when analysing the Balkan crisis. This latter was read more as a chain of sensational events and explained in terms of ancient ethnic enmities and blood-seeking ghosts. In her book on Balkanism, *Imagining the Balkans*, this aspect was heavily criticized by Maria Todorova:

> I would do much better if the Yugoslav, not Balkan, crisis, ceased to be explained in terms of Balkan ghosts, ancient Balkan enmities, primordial Balkan cultural patterns and proverbial Balkan turmoil, and instead was approached with the same rational criteria that the West reserves for itself: issues of self-determination versus inviolable status quo, citizenship and minority rights, problems of ethnic and religious autonomy, the prospects and limits of secession, the balance between big and small nations and states, the role of international institutions.[54]

With the collapse of communism, the opposition between democratic and totalitarian regimes and the old binary between West and East disappeared. Cultural identity has long since been theorized as a construct built through interaction between people, institutions and practices. British-Jamaican sociologist Stuart Hall explains,

> Cultural identity is a matter of 'becoming' as well as 'being'. It belongs to the future as much as to the past. It is not something which already exists, transcending place, time, history and culture. Cultural identities come from somewhere, have histories. But, like everything which is historical, fixed in some essentialised past, they are subject to the continuous 'play' of history, culture and power. Far from being grounded in a mere 'recovery' of the past, which is waiting to be found, and which, when found, will secure our sense of ourselves into eternity, identities are the names we give to the different ways we are positioned by, and position ourselves within, the narratives of the past.[55]

With the collapse of communism in the former Yugoslavia, the ideology of brotherhood and unity that used to prevail was replaced at the beginning of the 1990s by numerous identities defined by space. The reconfiguration of Eastern Europe was shaped along lines of ethnic, religious and regional identities. The multiplication of states within this geographical area destabilized the binary 'we', as a communist nationalist identification versus *the other(s)*, or the individuality of the 'I', on which democracy was partially grounded. The different *nationalities* contained in the Federation of Yugoslavia became more heterogeneous and consequently, an ethnic construct emerged immediately following the implosion of the country and led to a new sense of belonging.

The break-up of Yugoslavia raised issues of citizenship and residence status that afflicted hundreds of thousands of former citizens living abroad, particularly in Croatia. There had been a *before* and there would be an *after*, as Dubravka Ugrešić observes,

> A country disappeared, and it was replaced by a number of other countries – a whole fifty year period disappeared. Whether good or bad, right or wrong, it was the period in which we lived: these were the letters and words we had learned, the books we had read, the objects that were ours, the films we watched, the streets in which we walked. Suddenly everything had to change: address, books, the language and our names, our identity. [. . .] Everything changed with astonishing speed into old garbage, but nobody had found the opportunity to make a catalogue of it all, and put the right labels on.[56]

Dakić regards her own transplantation from one cultural context to another one in these words:

> My concept of home has utterly changed. In both cities I am a little at home, but also a little bit a stranger. My distance from both places has afforded me the position of a critical observer, a position that can be very fruitful for an artist. Learning to live with the difference and to speak from within the difference: that is the potential of incongruence.[57]

Voices, histories, languages represent different experiences that underlie a simultaneous absence or presence from one's location of origins. To grasp the sense and senses of a place is to understand how culture is a site of translation, of transformation. For Edward Said, migrancy involves 'a discontinuous state of being', and the knowledge that 'homes are always provisional'.[58] It presupposes the capacity of 'seeing the entire world as a foreign land'. Being aware of two homes, two cultures and realities 'gives rise to awareness of simultaneous dimensions'.[59] This potential of incongruity addressed by *Autoportrait* as a multiple positioning raises again not only the issue of diaspora. Intrinsic within the subjectivity of the expatriate is a shared and collective past in a homeland. According to Chambers, living in the new country involves the rearticulation of remembered past as *fragments*. Every stay in the return to homeland causes a reassessment of memories belonging to the past into the actual present.

In *Autoportrait*, the articulation of living between two places, two cultures and two languages questions the single point of view of one culture, one history and the sense of meaning we give to language. There is a dissemination of senses that challenges our imagination of ourselves as whole, unified and complete, and not as an open or fragmented subject. The significance of place in the artwork is furthered by the highlighting of the transitional nature of language. More than representing various geographical locations, the term 'migrancy' refers to cultural formations and the potential to develop new capacities. Among these, the capacity to listen becomes central in the process of acquiring new language and opens up the possibility of communicating in this language. Every linguistic, cultural and historical space functions in connection with a global *out there*, and the narratives in *Autoportrait* intend to demonstrate this through the epistemological value of the image. Dakić renounces the strict separation between these two worlds, bringing them into a simultaneous dialogue and represented in a single time. The whole is a negotiation of the gap keeping them apart and maintaining, at the same time, a certain balance.

By having attended to them as tales and language, I have been able to draw out the issues at stake in *Autoportrait*: How to express thoughts on absence, in a failed act of witnessing, without directly exposing one's personal experience? *Autoportrait* evokes space and displacement, hence exile, but through language. The artwork introduces an image of a speaking self but one alienated through its own sightlessness and multilinguality. The two narratives in *Autoportrait*, Stevenson's 'The Isle of Voices' and the Nyoongar story *Weedah the Mocking Bird*, serve here as examples of circulation not only of people – in terms of colonialism – but also of languages across continents. By being transposed into another language and another cultural context, these narratives become part of the phenomenon of globalization. Although the dangers present in both narratives become an underside of menace and allude to the violence of loss and strangeness, they are in no way less meaningful in this new contextualization. On the contrary, they retain all their original narrative strength across their travels in other languages.

3

Witnessing besides the forgotten

Maja Bajević's performances *Women at Work* (1999–2001)

In her trilogy of collaborative performances *Women at Work* (*Under Construction*, 1999; *The Observers*, 2000; *Washing Up*, 2001), Maja Bajević deals with memories of war and displacement. The artist asked women refugees in Sarajevo, who originally came from the area of Srebrenica, to perform this series of performances with her. Each performance took place in a different country, inside or outside a public building: *Under Construction* directly on the facade of the National Gallery in Sarajevo, *The Observers* in the garden of Château Voltaire in Ferney-Voltaire (France) and *Washing Up* at the Cemberlitas Hamam in Istanbul during the Biennial. The three performances took place over five consecutive days, at a rhythm of five hours a day, except *Washing Up*, which took place during two consecutive hours a day.

Under Construction was a contribution to the third annual exhibition organized by SCCA Sarajevo in 1999 and bearing the same name. The exhibition concept was to use the facade of the National Gallery in Sarajevo during its restoration works. During the whole summer of 1999, artists used the facade, week after week, for their sound and light installations and artistic performances. Bajević and five co-performers – Fazila Efendić, Zlatija Efendić, Amira Tihić, Hatidža Verlašević and Munira Mandžić – performed some embroidery works directly on the scaffolding security net, using it as framework. Unlike traditional stitching produced at home – during which women traditionally sing together – the task of embroidering on the facade was performed in silence. At the end of the performance, the embroidery works were left on the facade for four days, before being carefully cut off and later sold – the benefits of the sale going to the women performing with the artist. Men's work – the scaffolding and the rebuilding works – were integrated in the women's needlework, forming its basis. Moreover, a genuine juxtaposition of men's/women's work took place during the performance, as the builders were working on the facade during the day, carrying out their task of knocking down the plaster covering the external walls of the National Gallery while the women were embroidering (Figure 3.1).

The Observers took place one year later, during an artist-in-residence programme in the castle in Ferney-Voltaire (France). As *Under Construction* had been site- and time-specific, and could not be repeated, *The Observers*

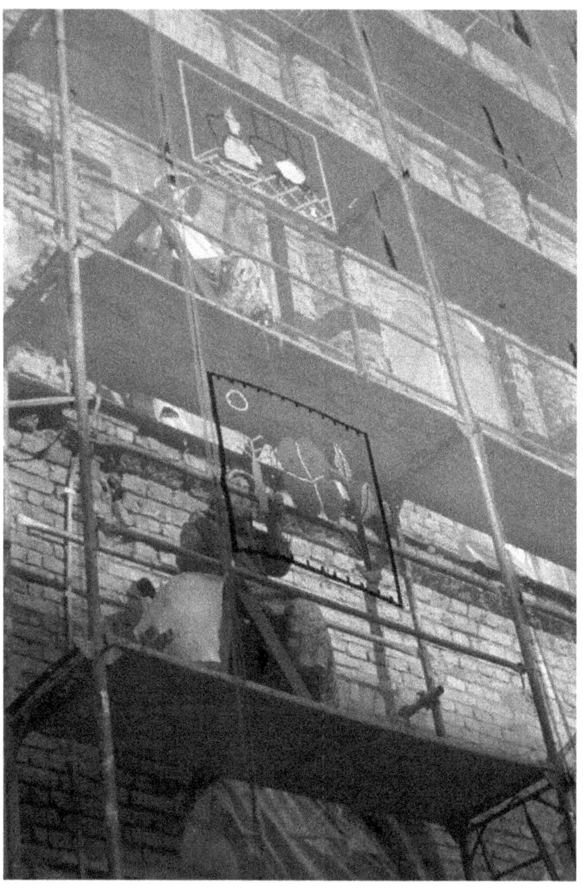

Figure 3.1 Maja Bajević, *Women at Work – Under Construction*, 1999, five-day performance / video installation (11'48") / photographs. *Under Construction*, SCCA Sarajevo, Bosnia and Herzegovina (Curator Dunja Blažević), 1999. Photo: Haris Memija, Dejan Vekić. Courtesy of the artist.

consisted of Bajević and four co-performers – Fazila Efendić, Zlatija Efendić, Hatidža Verlašević and Nirha Efendić – mostly sitting in the garden of the castle and embroidering in silence, dressed like the Regentesses in Frans Hals's painting *The Regentesses of the Old Men's Almshouse* (*c.* 1664, oil on canvas, 172.5 × 249.5 cm, Frans Hals Museum, Haarlem). The performance aimed to give the representation of the refugees experiencing a traditional castle life. The performance alludes at the same time to Voltaire's exile in Ferney in the seventeenth century, compared to the women of Srebrenica's refugee status in the twenty-first century, and, through the use of Hals's portrait transposed into both a photograph and a painting, to the Dutch involvement in the events of Srebrenica (Figure 3.2).

Washing Up was performed during the seventh Istanbul Biennial in 2001 in a traditional bathhouse, the Cemberlitas Hamam. *Washing Up* consisted of laundering pieces of white cloth, on which slogans from the time of Titoist socialism in former Yugoslavia had been embroidered, in three languages: English, Turkish and Serbo-Croatian. Following the rules of the hamam, the performance was restricted to a feminine audience, who had to first get undressed and undergo the usual cleansing ritual of bathing in the hamam before being allowed to the performance room, guided by recorded voices of adults reciting children's games in the three languages used for the slogans. In that room, the artists and her two co-performers – Fazila Efendić and Zlatija Efendić – fully dressed, were laundering the cloth. However, the fabric was never meant to become cleaned as the launderers were using dirty water. Through the constant washing process, the cloth and the slogans started to slowly disintegrate, becoming a parody of the slow disintegration of former Yugoslavia and the sudden acceleration of its breaking-up in the early 1990s (Figure 3.3).

The performances strategy, therefore, raised a twofold issue of displacement: first, the artist's, as an individual war refugee whose country has totally broken up, and the internal displacement of these women, as a group, a consequence of the events at Srebrenica in July 1995.[1]

Some of the women from Srebrenica, who had lost at the same time some family members and their homes, were relocated to Sarajevo. Deprived of widows' benefits as their relatives were still officially considered *missing* by the new Bosnian state, they were obliged to try to adapt to a new life, supported by local and international NGOs, waiting to know about the fate of their loved ones.

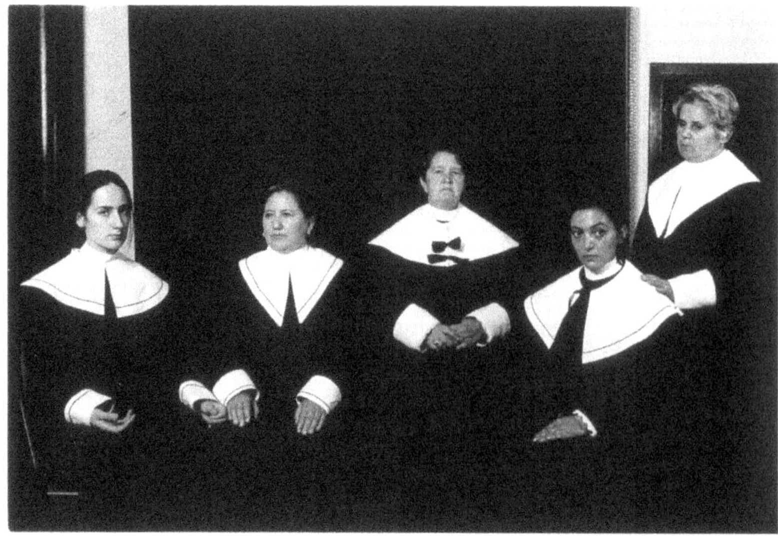

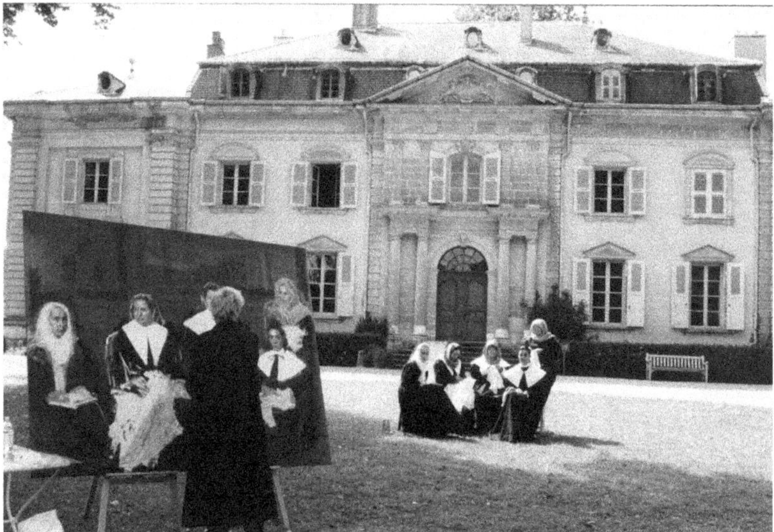

Figure 3.2 Maja Bajević, *Women at Work – The Observers*, five-day performance / video (8'20"), Château Voltaire, Ferney-Voltaire, France 2000. Courtesy of the artist.

This chapter explores the ways in which Bajević's gendered performances plunge the viewer into a public display of private/domestic tasks usually carried out in the realm of the home, while touching upon the complicated and delicate issue of the events in Srebrenica – often designated as the largest mass murder in Europe since the Second World War – and its consequent lengthy forensic identification process.

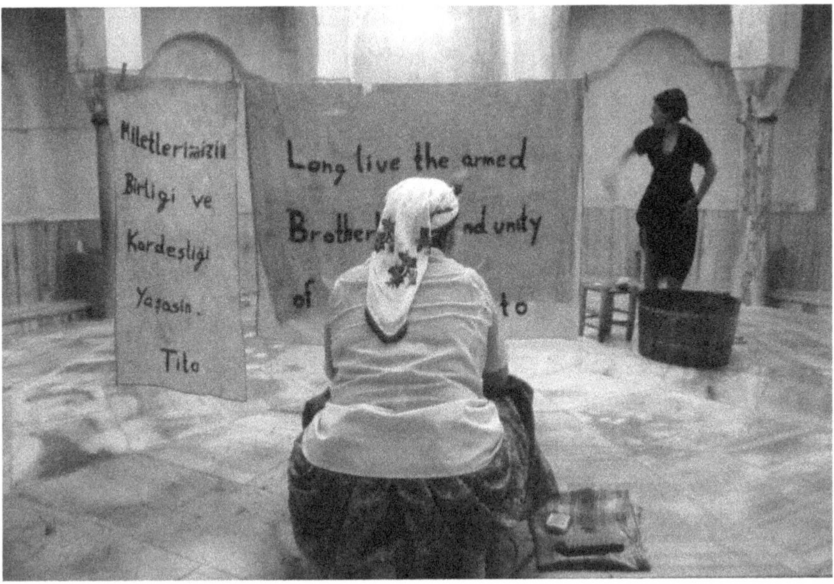

Figure 3.3 Maja Bajević, *Women at Work – Washing Up*, 2001, five-day performance / video (18'09") / photographs. Cemberlitas Bathhouse, seventh Istanbul Biennale, Istanbul, Turkey (Curator Yuko Hasegawa), 2001. Photo: Emmanuel Licha. Courtesy of the artist.

Srebrenica

Located in the mountains of Eastern Bosnia, off from the valley of the Drina river, Srebrenica was, before the Bosnian conflict, a small city inhabited by a mixed population: of the approximate 6,000 pre-war inhabitants, 75 per cent were Bosnian Muslims (Bosniak) and 23 per cent Bosnian Serbs.[2] It is estimated that after the beginning of the conflict in 1992, between 40,000 and 50,000 Bosniak people took refuge in Srebrenica, dramatically changing the demography of the city in an area of the country dominated by Bosnian Serbs. Declared a safe area by the UN in June 1993, Srebrenica had been protected by a small peacekeeping contingent of UN troops, first Canadian UNPROFOR (750 lightly armed soldiers), replaced on 3 March 1994 by a Dutch battalion of 570 soldiers, commonly called the Dutchbat.

Events of July 1995

Serb tanks, led by Ratko Mladić, overran the enclave on 6 July 1995. While women, children and elderly people were forced to get on buses and driven to the nearest Bosniak city, Tisca (from there, most of them were transported to Tuzla), 3,000 men of military age – according to witnesses, that meant from their early teens to almost their eighties – were separated from their families, forced onto separate buses and sent to nearby detention sites in order to be questioned. Five thousand other men and boys tried to escape, walking on the only road out of Srebrenica; others hid in the surrounding forests. Most of them were never seen again. During the next six days, it is known that ca. 8,000 men and boys were systematically executed, and their bodies disposed in mass graves.

Croatian writer Slavenka Drakulić gives us a detailed chronicle of the killings that took place at the Branjevo farm on 16 July 1995, based on the testimony of a Bosnian Serb soldier, Dražen Erdemović, in The Hague:

> A bus was coming towards them. [. . .] It stopped before the main building. [. . .] The commander assembled his unit and told them that buses would be brought in carrying civilians from Srebrenica. He meant captured Muslim men who had surrendered to the units of Republika Srpska. They are to be executed by our unit, the commander told them. [. . .] Never before had they been assigned such a task. But nobody said a word. [. . .] Dražen looked at the prisoners. They were standing with their backs to the soldiers. One man half turned his head towards them, as if he expected something. Was there something he wanted from them? Dražen felt a strong revulsion and he was afraid that he would vomit. [. . .]
>
> Dražen took his place at the end of the squad. His heart was still beating loudly when he aimed at an elderly man whose face, luckily enough, he had not seen before. [. . .] Once he started, Dražen kept shooting every few minutes without thinking much about what he was doing. The only thing he was aware of was trying to aim at elderly people rather than young ones – it seemed less of a waste. Soon the bus had been emptied.
>
> When Dražen looked at his watch, he was shocked: it had taken them only fifteen minutes to execute some sixty people! A second bus had already arrived.[3]

During the trial, Erdemović always expressed remorse for the acts he had committed, emphasizing how he was forced to do so by his commander, who would have shot him if he were to disobey his orders.[4]

In the months following the killings, Bosnian Serbs disinterred the bodies from the mass graves, scattering them in what would later be called secondary mass graves. The phenomenon of secondary mass graves rendered the identification process difficult, some remains of the same body being split between primary and secondary mass graves.[5] As the head of the International Commission on Missing

Persons (ICMP), which was founded during the G7 conference in 1996, Amor Mašović has underlined, it raised the issue about the exact number of victims as well:

> To this day we do not know where we stand with the recovery of the Srebrenica victims. If we take into account that there are somewhere around 8,500 missing from Srebrenica, today we have in the mortuary in Tuzla more than 7,000 bags, bags with mortal remains, but I wouldn't be able to say what number of bodies [that represents].[6]

Analyses of the events and of who bore the guilt for the atrocious acts committed in Srebrenica were not restricted to the trials in The Hague. Due to international involvement in the events and the lack of intervention of the international community in July 1995 – largely talked about due to an application for NATO intervention that was not filled in on the right form and faxed in due time – different official reports tried to assess the failure of the international community to act: a Report of the Secretary General to the General Assembly resolution 53/35 (1999), a report commissioned by the French Assembly (2001) and a report commissioned by the Dutch government to the Netherlands Institute for War Documentation (NIOD).[7]

Forensic identification process

Aerial photographs already revealed the existence of mass graves in August 1995, but the first exhumations only began in July 1996. Initially, the ICTY mobilized teams of forensic experts to conduct post-mortem identification for the purpose of the prosecution of war criminals. Soon, it became judicious to use the data collected for judicial purposes in order to provide the families of the missing with the available information on the fate of their relatives. In the months following the killings, most relatives of the victims were still hoping that their missing family members were still alive, hiding themselves in the forest, as was the case of a small group of men who lived in the forest for four months before reaching a UN base.

In that sense, successful forensic identification would bring an end to an unbearable state of uncertainty. In 2003, only 1,327 corpses had been identified and buried near the Potočari Memorial Centre.[8] DNA analysis became the primary tool of identification and the technologists created specific databases and computer software able to match blood samples from surviving family members and bone samples from the recovered remains. Although establishing the software and the databases was a long process, by June 2022, the number of successful DNA identifications reached the total of 6976 of the ca. 8,000 missing.[9]

In her book *To Know Where He Lies: DNA Technology and the Search for Srebrenica's Missing* (2008), Sarah Wagner relates the poignant encounter with families every time a DNA identification succeeds. Case managers working for the ICMP usually visit the family of the identified missing to bring the news. But, to most families, establishing the death of their relative through a complex process such as DNA identification is difficult to accept. To them, technology does not bring the tangible proof that a usual identification of a body and its belongings could.

The meeting generally ends with a discussion about their wish regarding the funerals. The families have the choice to establish the place of the gravesite: they decide either to bury their relatives at the Potočari Memorial Centre during the commemoration ceremony taking place every year on 11 July or to hold private funerals in the location of their choice. Most families actually choose the first option. By July 2020, up to 6,580 remains of individuals have been buried in that way in the Potočari Memorial Centre.[10]

Widows and refugees

Having been separated from the men, the women, children and elderly took refuge in different areas of the country or in Croatia. Some, supported by local NGOs, came to Sarajevo and lived as a community. Uncertain about the fate of their husbands and sons, most of them were without jobs, friends or family in Sarajevo. The violence of the 1995 massacre had shattered their family networks and made other social networks collapse, in times when intercommunal trust along ethnic lines had ceased to be the rule. It seems that Sarajevans were sometimes socially resentful towards the flood of refugees arriving in their city from the villages in the direct aftermath of the war, in such a way that establishing durable social connections turned out to be arduous.[11] Other women whom war had sadly widowed were normally granted the social status of widows by the state and allocated a meagre state allowance. In this case, however, as their relatives were officially missing and not accounted for as dead – due to the absence of corpses by which death is typically confirmed in normal circumstances – the widows of Srebrenica were extremely destitute. It was not until October 2004 that the Bosnian parliament eventually adopted a Missing Persons Law granting them this status of widow and securing them a minimal income.[12]

Women at Work

The collaborative performances *Women at Work* inscribe themselves in Bajević's will to work with invisible, often marginalized people. The end of the war and the artist's first return to her home city triggered her reflection on nomadism and diaspora, based on her constant commuting between Paris and Sarajevo since 1998. Since her return to Sarajevo after the war, Bajević had in mind to work on a project involving women refugees. In 1999, the artist was asked by Dunja Blažević, the director of SCCA Sarajevo, to take part in the centre's third annual exhibition. Through a humanitarian organization she met a group of ten to fifteen women refugees from the area of Srebrenica. After presenting and explaining to them her idea about the performance *Under Construction*, five women accepted the invitation to participate: Fazila Efendić, Zlatija Efendić, Amira Tihić, Hatidža Verlašević and Munira Mandžić. By collaborating with these women, Bajević sought at the same time to position herself and her co-performers in this post-war society; the artist was strongly determined to distance the women from the way they were usually perceived, that is, defined and stigmatized as victims of war. During the performances, the five women refugees appeared as active performers, encouraged to express and use their creativity in ways they themselves had chosen.

Bajević was not only the instigator of the group of performers; she was always part of it, and never left the women performing alone. As underlined by Dunja Blažević, 'The triad *Women at Work* most strikingly exemplifies those works that possess the characteristics of social and moral *detector and catalyst*, in which Maja is both *a participant and an observer*.'[13] This idea of belonging to a group is significant in the three performances. The performative dimension of the performance itself generated the feeling of having found a sense of belonging to a community that valued their competences.

Bajević always considers her collaborative way of working as a tribute to the people she includes in her performances or video works, as she pointed out in an interview with Italian curator Angela Vettese in 2008:

> I have always seen all my collective performances and videos that include other people as a homage to them. My theme and work is their life, and I am trying to treat it with as much respect as possible. In a way I am trying to put them on a pedestal through these works, give them a public space in which they will exist for the essence of what they stand for: refugees, immigrants, people from a psychiatric hospital, workers out of work. [. . .] Often I had the feeling that although I was approaching them, involving them in an artistic project, I was

> the one receiving and learning. There is a certain kind of wisdom that can only be learned through life experience.[14]

Her respect is shown by her habit, during press interviews, of always giving the full name – name and surname – of the people working with her for the purpose of an art piece. One striking example took place during the Istanbul performance, *Washing Up*, where Bajević insisted during press interviews on giving Fazila Efendić and Zlatija Efendić's full names. The press reaction was disappointing: the media commonly referred to them as *Bosnian women* or *Muslim refugees*, conferring on them once again the anonymity of the de-individualized and othered group. In spite of the artist's particular care about individual identity, none of the reviews regarding Bajević's performance at the Istanbul Biennale or Manifesta 3 revealed the names of the participants.

Common to all these performances is the use of fabric, which the artist utilizes in building the interaction between intimate/private and social/public realms. Using traditional craft in the production of contemporary art was, however, perceived as a kind of contradiction. Bajević draws attention to the hierarchical division between fine arts and craft: how an ancient, traditional art such as embroidery has become a minor art since the industrial revolution and its resulting mass production process. In Sarajevo, crafts were neither part of the permanent collection nor of the curatorial program of the National Gallery of Bosnia and Herzegovina.

In her book *The Subversive Stitch*, Rozsika Parker makes an interesting observation on this division between art and craft along gender lines in the canonical Western hierarchy of the arts:

> The art/craft hierarchy suggests that art made with thread and art made with paint are intrinsically unequal: that the former is artistically less significant. But the real differences between the two are in term of *where* they are made and *who* makes them. Embroidery, by the time the art/craft divide, was made in the domestic sphere, usually by women, for 'love'. Painting was produced predominantly, though not only, by men, in the public sphere, for money.[15]

Drawing on this insight, I would suggest that Bajević's work critically intervenes in this hierarchy, not only in terms of the craft being part or not of the collection of the National Gallery but in terms of both the value ascribed to and the visibility of work made with fabric by women. In placing women at work embroidering on a major building, the artist creates a gendered juxtaposition of women's embroidery work with men's building and painting work on the facade of the gallery. Hence, on the facade, crafts become more significant in terms of artistic expression than the men's act of painting it.

Dressed Up (Sarajevo, 1999)

In the spring of 1999, Bajević had held a performance in Sarajevo, named *Dressed Up*, during which the artist was raising awareness of the significance of political changes in the former Yugoslavia since the beginning of the 1990s. The seven-hour performance was based on the artist cutting and sewing a piece of cloth on which a coloured map of the former Yugoslavia had been printed (Figure 3.4).

In the city gallery of Sarajevo, Bajević measured, cut and sewed this fabric in order to make a dress for herself. The performance was punctuated by the noise of the sewing machine and the amplified sound of the artist's breathing. At the end of the performance, the artist put the dress on and walked out of the gallery. Considering this performance, Bajević reflects on its particular meaning, insisting on the symbolic loss of a home country and its impact at a personal level: 'Tragedies like war and the disintegration of a country are usually seen as political, general things. Actually, they are personal, very intimate events in our lives that we carry, pasted on, like a dress.'[16] Both Dunja Blažević and Bojana Pejić consider *Dressed Up* as the starting point of *Women at Work*. This first performance is thought to have triggered the theme unfolding in the three performances.

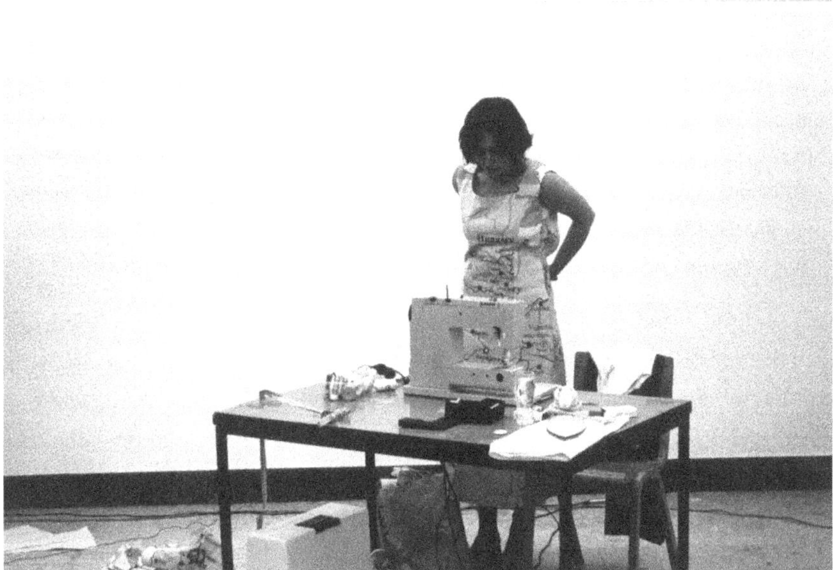

Figure 3.4 Maja Bajević, *Dressed Up*, 1999, seven-hour performance / video (60'55") / dress. *Minimum*, City Collegium Artisticum, Sarajevo, Bosnia and Herzegovina (Curator Dunja Blažević), 1999. Photo documentation: Danica Dakić. Courtesy of the artist.

Under Construction (Sarajevo, 1999)

From the existing documentation footage of the performance *Under Construction*, one can clearly distinguish how the performers are helped by the builders to get on the scaffolding, each taking position at different levels and places on the facade. Using wool threads, the women either start by delimiting the frame of their embroidery work from the security net or directly start with the motif, framing it later during the performance week. Day after day, the women at work were completing their task, during the night, thanks to lights displayed next to each of them, illuminating the facade in an interesting way. The last image on the documentation shows the holes in the security net, attracting the eye to spots where something had emerged but in the meantime had become invisible again.

By elaborating and displaying in public the traditional craft normally produced in the private realm of a home, the artist invited the audience – in this case passers-by – to reflect not only on this particular domestic craft related to the interior of the museum but also on their status as war refugees. She was, therefore, raising the question of their apparent anonymity and extending it to an allusion on the amnesia surrounding the Srebrenica case.

Maja Bajević has pointed out how *Under Construction* was an attempt to make a synthesis of these two aspects, providing the following statement on the complexity of meanings present in the performance:

> I wanted to make a synthesis of two histories: one that symbolises the interior of the National Gallery, and a new one – the reality of my country marked by war and refugees. Aside from this, I made a connection between needlework (outside) as part of the national folklore and the art collection (heritage) contained inside the National Gallery. An interesting shift occurred – the new history began to speak in a traditional tongue.[17]

This traditional tongue was very well perceived by a viewer starting a discussion with the woman filming the performance by saying, 'It is so interesting, and what is going to happen with the pieces? Are they going to take them off, or will they stay there?' When she gets the reply that the pieces will stay for four days and then should give way to a new piece by another artist, she is afraid the embroidery work might be destroyed or become fragmentary. 'That's too bad, they should take them off and exhibit them somewhere else, as a piece of art, as a piece for itself.' Moreover, the same passer-by considers that, even if the pieces are cut off they will just be part of the work of art, not the whole. And the woman insists, saying that 'It is not just embroidery, it is embroidery done on scaffoldings, which is different'.

The Observers (Ferney, Château Voltaire, 2000)

For the purpose of *The Observers*, Bajević brought to Ferney-Voltaire a photographic group portrait, taken prior to the artist-in-residence programme and representing all performers, the artist included, in an interior in Sarajevo. This group portrait was actually conceived as the contemporary transposition of Frans Hals's painting *The Regentesses of the Old Men's Almshouse*.

As suggested by the title of the performance, Bajević's first citation, through the use of Hals's portrait, goes to the Dutch involvement in the events of Srebrenica. The name *The Observers* unmasks the fact that members of the Dutch battalion were powerless observers in the summer of 1995. Its commandant, Lieutenant Colonel Thomas Karremans, clumsily tried to negotiate with General Mladić before retreating with his troops to the Dutchbat's headquarters. Château Voltaire is not a place normally dedicated to contemporary art, and Bajević's intention was threefold: to intermingle Voltaire, Hals and Srebrenica, all through the representation of the refugees experiencing a traditional castle life. In her modern reinterpretation of exile, Bajević wanted to transpose and reconsider this refugee aspect in the twenty-first century.

Bajević had invited Alma Suljević, another artist from Sarajevo, to be part of the performance. Suljević's role was to paint the portrait of the group of women on a large canvas while they were sitting in the garden and embroidering. The existing documentation of *The Observers* shows how Suljević, although painting outside in the garden, is indeed, as in the photograph, reproducing Hals's interior painting, replacing the faces of the women of that time with those of the participants in the performance. On the last day of the performance, the audience was allowed to approach the group of performers. Whereas most of the viewers spent time contemplating the portrait executed by Suljević, the group of performers was of little interest. They were considered models rather than active participants at the core of the performance.

With *The Observers*, Bajević raises the complex relationship between painting and photography, especially the truth-like quality of the photographic gaze. Which medium is the most accurate, the closest one to displaying reality? Is what we see always what we think we are seeing? Although the performance was recorded in a video called *The Observers*, the photographic portrait remained the most significant piece of the performance, the one around which the entire performance had unfolded. Produced prior to the performance, the photograph, faithful to Hals's portrait, was taken in an interior, while the performance in

Ferney took place mainly outside. In the photograph, none of the women wear their headscarves whereas all except the artist were wearing one during the performance at the castle – in the Balkans wearing a headscarf in rural areas is quite common regardless of the woman's religion. The most important aspect of this distorted gaze is that neither the photograph nor the painting display any kind of truth related to their real lives back in Sarajevo.

Through the question of the gaze, the performance alludes to issues related to the UN observers in Srebrenica. In order to paint, the painter has to be an observer. So were the UN troops stationed as observers in order to report to their higher authorities? This distorted question of observers is reinforced by the fact that Alma Suljević was not known as a painter, her art practice mostly involving performances about the sensitive question of minefields, especially in Bosnia and Herzegovina.

Bajević's choice to use Hals's portrait comes from the fact that the artist considers Hals (1580–666) and Voltaire (1694–778) to have lived almost at the same time. Having this in mind, she worked on the idea of refugees through Voltaire's perspective, who was himself living in exile in the castle of Ferney at the border of the kingdom of France. In 1753, François-Marie Arouet, better known as Voltaire, was forced into exile by the king of France Louis XV and his powerful mistress Madame de Pompadour. These latter were feeling threatened by this political dissident who was also a fervent defender of civil liberties and freedom of religion, a topic the philosopher was denouncing in his polemical pamphlets.

Hals's *The Regentesses of the Old Men's Almshouse* is often associated with a men's group portrait, *The Regents of the Old Men's Almshouse*, also painted in 1664. Hals, aged eighty-one, delivered, with the help of his apprentices, a rare and deep psychological observation of the group of women. The expression of the faces, the detailed joints of the hands of the portrayed first catch the eye of the spectator, while rich details of their dresses and a landscape in the background hung on the wall of the room reinforce this impact. Relying on his long experience of portraiture, Hals masters here the psychological portrait, displaying the women's individual personalities. All have different gestures: the first in the right as if begging for money for their charity, while the secretary with the book sits opposite to her. Art historian Pieter Biesboer interprets this particular gesture as receiving money with the right hand and giving it away to charity with the left one.[18]

Although paintings of charitable and humanitarian people were quite common in Amsterdam in sixteenth-century Holland, they did not appear in Haarlem before 1641.[19] Such a group portrait of women was, therefore, still rare at the time, and the identification of the women a complicated task for art historians. A wooden plate bears the name of four of the five women. If we know the names of the women portrayed, we do not know how to identify them with precision on the canvas. Still, the question who are Adriaentje Schouten, Marijtje Willems, Annavan Damme and Adriana Bredenhof in the painting, whether they sit or stand, remains without answer.[20]

There are two opposed interpretations of the *Regentesses*, on which Bajević relied for her performance. One considered them as the counterpart of the men's group portrait and, therefore, seen as patriarchal, in a Calvinist area. The women could appear totally introverted and a certain sadness could be read on their faces. The other interpretation is about representing self-conscious and independent women undertaking some charitable work and choosing to represent themselves in their charitable, organizational duty.

The Observers, therefore, plays with these two meanings, since patriarchy is still quite predominant in rural areas of Bosnia and Herzegovina, and with Srebrenica being one of them. Yet, the performers, expelled from their milieu, had to become independent women, standing up for themselves and their children.

Washing Up (Istanbul, 2001)

With *Washing Up*, Bajević had here chosen another domestic task, normally restricted to the realm of the private home, transposing it to the meaning of washing off the burden of a historical past: the heritage of the communist past or rather the consequences of Tito's regime in former Yugoslavia. Slogans such as 'Long live the armed brotherhood and unity of our nations', 'We live as if there will be peace for a hundred years, but we prepare ourselves as if there will be war tomorrow', 'A country that has youth like ours, should not worry for its future' were all authored by Josip Broz Tito.

The artist reflects on her view of how the performance, although taking place in the public realm, reveals how this latter can sometimes work as a better place than a more intimate, private one:

> Both of these performances [the second Bajević mentions being *En Attendant*] have been done in public spaces: one in a Turkish bath, the other in a backyard. But these are public spaces that are the temple of female intimacy, and as such function as even more private than a private space can be. Nevertheless, this time a typically female activity, like washing, is exposed through a performance.[21]

As Bojana Pejić commented on this performance comparing it to the two previous ones, stating the importance of its historical context,

> Contrary to the decorative motives embroidered on the façade's netting, and the needlework with geometrical patterns crafted during the residence in the castle, the cloths being washed in the bathhouse carry phrases with ideological meaning; these 'epic' messages are particularly familiar to those who lived in the now vanished country – 'Titoist' Yugoslavia.[22]

The way the slogans had been embroidered on the white fabric reminds me of the silent monthly protests that took place in the streets in Tuzla on the eleventh of every month, commemorating the events of Srebrenica and organized by the Women of Srebrenica. According to oral historian Selma Leydesdorff, these peaceful demonstrations have regularly taken place since October 1998. The women were inspired by similar demonstrations carried out by the Abuelas Plaza de Mayo in Buenos Aires (Grandmothers of the Plaza de Mayo).[23] Using embroidered pillowcases bearing the names of their missing relatives, friends and neighbours, women from the Srebrenica area tie the pillowcases together in a long line, holding them at waist level and momentarily blocking the traffic. Sarah Wagner, who had witnessed many of these silent demonstrations, states,

> In total the Women of Srebrenica have more than 4,000 such pillowcases, each bearing the name of a different victim. Stretched along the line of women – some fifty or sixty members who regularly attend the protests – they form a colourful banner of names, yet another collage of the missing that the women of Srebrenica hold up to the public as testimony to their relatives' unaccounted-for absence.[24]

Month after month this silent campaign drew attention to the absence of the missing, whereas the use of the slogans in *Washing Up* alludes to the disappearance of the homeland, which cannot be complete as traces and stigmas of it are still visible.

Body of pain, body of mourning

Interpretations of the performances *Women at Work* have focused on the aspect of the disintegration of Yugoslavia through the metaphoric use of fabric – particularly in *Washing Up*, which, by being obsessively washed actually disintegrates rather than being preserved through the repetitive action of laundering.

Following the Second World War, Tito and his Third Socialism had been holding together geographic areas dotted with exacerbated enmities between them. By giving them a sense and a rule of collectivism, resorting to different stratagems to encourage this brotherhood unity, the use of slogans being one of them, Tito provided all with the same standards of living and income. Yugoslavism was based on the myth of 'brotherhood and unity' and hold together by propaganda of communist ideology and the cult of personality surrounding its president until his death. Josip Broz Tito was expressing this unity and the importance of thinking in terms of a multi-ethnic country, with no dominant ethnic groups, a way to distance his political views from the interwar kingdom led by Alexander Karadjordjević. Yugoslav communists were building their definition of patriotism as including social and national justice. Tito firmly believed that the unity of the working class would assure the unity of Yugoslavia.[25] In his text 'No Compromise with Nationalism' (1969), Josip Broz Tito was stressing about the importance of this federal unity:

> The name Yugoslavia is somehow heard less lately while people write and talk mostly of the 'federation'. We must lay some stress on Yugoslavia. We are Slovenes, Croats, Serbs, Macedonians, but all of us together are also Yugoslavs, all of us are citizens of socialist Yugoslavia. In this sense, we must strengthen the sense of belonging to the Yugoslav socialist community of equal nations and nationalities. This is not Yugoslavhood in the unitarist sense that denies the nation or endeavours to diminish its role. [. . .] What I refer to is the need to deepen awareness of belonging to Yugoslavia, of the fact that the strengthening of our Yugoslav community is the concern of all our nations and nationalities and that only if strong can it guarantee them true prosperity.[26]

The system could have worked out and truly seemed to have deeply reunited communities bound together by a common language, Serbo-Croatian.[27] As economic crises struck following Tito's death – a consequence of his widespread politics of borrowing – animosities still present underneath the surface of national unity reappeared and quickly took over, having as consequence the conflicts taking place throughout the 1990s.

While the performances addressed in this chapter took place at the beginning of the 2000s, DNA identifications of the Srebrenica victims were still at an earlier stage. Most women of Srebrenica, wives and mothers, were living without the tangible proof of the death of their male relatives. They were, therefore, unable to bury and mourn them according to Muslim customs. Maja Bajević reflects on how the performances, and especially *Washing Up*, were not only a work of mourning over the lost country; they were also about how political, collective events affect individuals at a personal level. Instead of washing it away, the obsessive and repetitive washing process retriggers the grief, underlining it rather than diminishing it. As Bajević comments on this repetition,

> The repetition that will destroy fabric in the end, is also a way to pinpoint the most hurtful place, the place where once something was and is now missing. It is the desire to stay in mourning as if, since nothing else is left, only the mourning stays and is there, to be preserved in a typically female way.[28]

Hence, the act of mourning is here metaphoric, though double. On the one hand, it touches the level of a national mourning, those of the former nation, alluding to a unity obtained through a specific political system. On the other hand, the metaphoric act of mourning touches a personal level, when thinking about the victims of Srebrenica. These latter are mourned at a familiar, intimate level. According to Muslim burial rituals, women and children stay at home and, therefore, do not attend the burial ceremony at the mosque, which is, therefore, exclusively attended by men. Men also have the responsibility of taking away the coffin from the house of the deceased and carrying it to the mosque, later to the cemetery. While the ceremony is taking place at the mosque, the women recite the mourning ritual *Tevhid* in the house. *Tevhid* is a social ceremony of prayers for the dead attended by women and normally held in an ordinary house.[29] *Tevhid* comes from Arabic *tawhid*, meaning 'faith in one supreme God' or 'praise of God'. In Serbo-Croatian, there are two definitions for the term:

1. Commemoration of the dead, which consists of the collective recital of religious declarations and prayers;
2. Collective recital by dervishes of religious declarations, which is held while sitting in a circle.[30]

The *Tevhid* is held five times following the death of someone, the first time taking place the day the body is taken away from the home. These prayers are not deprived of social connotation, as underlined by Tone Bringa:

> The women's Tevhid is an occasion for individuals to strive to impress others and prove their capabilities both in religious matters, as by displaying religious knowledge and reciting well, and in secular activities as by cooking and organizing the event. A woman will also signal the socioeconomic status of her household and earn its prestige by the manner in which she dresses, the number of guests she entertains, the number of Islamic instructors called upon to recite, and the amount and quality of the food served.[31]

During the *Tevhid*, the Bula – woman religious instructor – generally sits at the centre of the group of women, leading the prayers that the other women around her recite. The oldest women with a high degree of piety sit close to her, while the other, younger women sit on the floor, facing her. Up to ten women recite at larger *Tevhid*.[32]

Anthropologist Veena Das has researched and analysed the work of mourning in different societies – particularly in India after partition, elaborating on the division of labour between men and women in the work of mourning. Das observes how 'it is the transactions between language and body, especially in the gendered division of labor, by which the antiphony of language and silence recreates the world in the face of tragic loss'.[33] Das observes how women are more likely than men assigned the work of mourning and how this pain is located in the body. As Das writes,

> In the genre of lamentation, women have control both through their bodies and through their language – grief is articulated through the body, for instance, by infliction of grievous hurt on oneself, 'objectifying' and making present the inner state, and is finally given a home in language.[34]

In the series *Women at Work*, the silence of the women dedicated to the assigned tasks (embroidering or washing) contrasts with the ritual of mourning laments of the women closely related to the dead person. Only their white veil betrays their state of widowhood. Usually, as stated by Das in her analysis of the concept of pain, the mourning process 'makes the voices of women "public"'.[35] The work of mourning in *Women at Work* is processed through the acts and bodies of the performers, as second shore of expressing grief, and experienced as a bodily pain in the woman's body.

Das's argument has led Jill Bennett to draw on how pain can be applied in the works of artists, in her analysis of Doris Salcedo's and Sandra Johnston's: both artists, in their artistic practice, reflect on violence in their respective countries or home cities, Columbia for Salcedo and Belfast for Johnston. Bennett writes,

> As 'insiders', both [artists] are concerned with the ways in which memories of the bad death are represented within communities. [. . .] Both take up a position aligned with the body of a grieving woman – in one case in the public domain of the funeral, in the other in the domestic sphere – to explore this antiphony, and in this respect they actively contribute to what Das has called a 'genre of lamentation' in which women are afforded control of their bodies and language. For these artists, there is a sense in which their own gender position promotes identification with bereaved women, but this does not mean that their work advances a simplistic notion of a common feminine empathy of that it disregards

> the variety of audience responses. The self-consciously adopted identificatory relationships that inform the production of their works lead both artists to think through strategies for aligning audiences with the subjective position of those who grieve. What is essentially an alienating and distancing experience – the memory of the trauma of loss – thus becomes one that is mediated through affective connections between bodies.[36]

Bajević unfolds a reflection on how different experiences of displacement and suffering could join each other, if a space where the two can meet can exist: belonging to a diaspora, forced against their will out of their households, sharing uncertain living conditions and destinies are some of the common features. Stronger is the marginalization of the state of exile, and making them participate in a performance was allowing them to get back a certain dignity. The way the artist does it could not only give them self-confidence but reawaken their trust in the state system.

Still, the strongest common denominator between the artist and the other performers is their femininity. It is displayed through a typically feminine craft, usually transmitted from mothers to their daughters: the art of embroidery. Rozsika Parker has beautifully observed and analysed the relationship women maintain with embroidery and its ambiguity in terms of power and at the same time powerlessness. Parker writes,

> The manner in which embroidery signifies both self-containment and submission is the key to understanding women's relation to the art. Embroidery has provided a source of pleasure and power for women, while being indissolubly linked to their powerlessness. The presence and practice of embroidery promotes particular states of mind and self experience. Because of its history and associations embroidery evokes and inculcates femininity in the embroiderer. But it can also lead women to an awareness of the extraordinary constraints of femininity, providing at times a means of negotiating them, and at other times provoking the desire to escape the constraints.[37]

The embroidering task carried out by the women is a cry and a testimony to the absence of a real home in their lives of refugees. Why, if you had the comfort and the warm environment of a home, climb on a scaffolding on the facade of a public building in order to produce these traditional embroidered patterns? As Parker has stated, 'Embroidery is invariably employed to evoke home.'[38] How awkward can this approach be perceived by an audience? Through this artistic modus operandi, Bajević succeeds in making visible, beyond the material loss of a home, the extensive state of grief lying underneath.

Feminist thought: West versus East

Bajević's attempt to break down the boundaries between the forms of expression inscribes itself in the consideration of the marginalization of women's work, particularly in post-communist societies. The debate about feminism in Eastern countries is a complicated one, a result of the rupture produced by the Iron Curtain. Eastern feminist thinkers and artists were said to be isolated from the development of feminist thought in the West from the 1960s. Western feminism was at the time subjected to a wide non-acceptance in the East, to criticism and misunderstanding: an extension of the hostility often displayed towards Western European and North American art and art criticism. In her study of Polish and Czech women artists, Iva Popovicova has observed this negativity towards feminism:

> The resistance of artists to identify with feminism has deep roots extending far back into the past, and in particular, to past ideologies and notions of politics. Politics under the former regime meant 'high' politics for women, that is, an empty exercise of male power. [. . .] As in the past, feminism is still viewed as a form of 'high' politics. Feminism is still charged with the stereotypes that characterized the cold war rhetoric, namely those, representative of the belief that Western feminism is a form of colonization of the East. Despite much improvement in the East/West feminist debates over the past nineteen years, which finally overcome the notion of complete incompatibility between the two worlds, feminism still does not blend well with the 'East'. The myopic views of the general public that feminism is just a ludicrous impact from 'vain' Americans, and is thus a concept completely unfit for the former Communist countries, often clouds the mind of feminist art critics, curators and historians as well.[39]

Efforts to restore an objective view of feminism were not sufficient, and Martina Pachmanová regrets how Eastern European feminist art theory bears a state of a 'gray zone', of a certain in-betweenness leading to a marginalization of feminist thought:

> It is situated in between, and similarly ambivalent is the position of feminist and art scholars. [. . .] As they simultaneously face mistrust and sometimes even hate and ostracism against feminism in their own countries, they are doubly marginalized.[40]

Pachmanová insists on the importance of reflecting on the specificity of each local experience in analysing the 'cultural, social and historical constructions of gender'.[41] In spite of the a *priori* universality of communist ideology – which has long been demonstrated as not existing – enormous differences existed between countries, resulting in different social positions for women, which in turn had a significant impact on women's movements in each country.[42] Despite the state of repression, a generation of feminist militant artists appeared. While most of them were camouflaging issues of gender and sexuality in their works, the younger generation of women artists active since the 1990s have been confronting these same issues more frontally, for example, through performances sometimes on the edge of brutality.

In former Yugoslavia

The situation in socialist Yugoslavia was more contrasted, due to the milder form of communism imposed by Tito. If, from the West, the East has been considered as a quite homogenous block, one cannot overestimate the sometimes great cultural and historical differences between the countries actually forming that East, in terms of politics, economy, freedom, openness to the West, modernization, living standards, degree of censorship and so on. Therefore, the development of post-communist feminism is far from being univocal. In the context of an imposed tradition of collectivism, the quest for a new identity has led to exacerbated nationalisms, as seen in Ex-Yugoslavia, and had a non-negligible impact on the role of women in society.

As recalled by Bojana Pejić, although having in common with the other countries of the Eastern Bloc a Communist Party and an official, state-imposed 'gender egalitarianism', Yugoslav citizens could, from the early 1960s, freely travel to the West, and abortion was acknowledged as a legal right more or less at the same time.[43] Women who grew up under socialism could no longer seek support of the now-discredited women's official organizations during communism. As sadly stated by Daša Duhaček, women saw their conditions regress in the aftermath of socialism. Whereas the Communist Party of Yugoslavia had advocated an egalitarian communist ideology, patriarchy was soon to become the norm again:

> The women in Yugoslavia did not learn the lesson in citizenship as a way of constructing political subjectivity. Instead, a thin layer of ideologically based egalitarianism was superimposed on a stable patriarchy. [. . .] History took another course. The imposed ideology started withdrawing; the egalitarian layer cracked and revealed an almost untouched patriarchy. What happened? Instead of upholding what they could make use of, what had nominally been guaranteed, women renounced ideology and egalitarianism, and in doing so renounced themselves and fell, with rare exceptions into the nationalist trap.[44]

Slavenka Drakulić goes even one step further in the analysis of Yugoslavia, when she writes that 'We have to take into account that because of cultural and historical differences, standards of life, natality, and employment, and, finally, war and national divisions, there is no single Yugoslavia, and there are no "Yugoslav Women"'.[45] If the first non-governmental international conference of women took place in Belgrade in 1978, signalling the first public articulation of feminism on Yugoslav territory, the feminist groups fell victims of their own nationalisms.

Drakulić sustains this argument by narrating the case of Serb women protesting in the Serb parliament on 2 July 1991. Hundreds of Serbian mothers interrupted the parliamentary session, claiming back their sons fighting for the Federal Army during the attack against Slovenia – which had just declared its independence from the Yugoslav Federation. Asking for the immediate return of their sons, the women started a mass protest, some travelling to Ljubljana the following day, and triggering similar upheavals in Zagreb. But the protesters were defeated, victims of their nationalism, acknowledging themselves either as Croatian, Serbian or Slovenian more than first of all as mothers; they never managed to get their sons out of the barracks. Similar actions by women were undertaken in August 1991 in Sarajevo and Zagreb, demanding immediate discharge of their sons from the army. Drakulić writes how the outcome of these protests could have been different and, therefore, had a deep impact on historical events in Ex-Yugoslavia in the 1990s: 'If the women had succeeded in organizing across ethnic/nationality lines by pulling their sons out, the federal army would have been destroyed.'[46] This uprising was doomed, and the women manipulated by their respective governments. Therefore, and against their will, their national interests had overcome their maternal instincts to protect their offspring. And Drakulić concludes on this incident: 'The women fell victim, not only to their nationalism, but to their spontaneity, and to their lack of organization and political vision, itself the product of their alienation from politics over the past forty years.'[47]

The perpetual state of violence and war dominating the 1990s in the geographic area covering Tito's Yugoslavia took on a gendered aspect through the systematic practice of rape of women. Estimations range between 30,000 and 50,000 victims of rape during the Bosnian conflict alone.[48] These violent assaults on women's bodies were considered as war strategy and adopted mainly by Serb soldiers in order to change the ethnic demography of other ethnic groups, particularly Muslim ones. This practice was later largely denied by the perpetrators while most of the victims, ashamed of what had happened to them and afraid of social repercussions, preferred to keep silent about it. Popovicova underlines how women's bodies were clearly targeted in their function of 'bearers of inscriptions':

> More than quarter million casualties of the Yugoslav civil war on the *body* (due to the predominance of rape crimes and knife attacks) silently testify that bodies are not only one tool of communist or capitalist production but also foci of destruction and targets of racial ethnic or gender-oriented hatred. As cultural documents, surfaces of symbolic representations, and bearers of social inscriptions, bodies – both present and absent – will always signify both the dangers and the persistence of symbolic borders in the becoming of the borderless Europe.[49]

If feminist artists, described and analysed by Popovicova, often resort to sadomasochistic practices towards the artists' bodies and the bodies of others, the 1990s mark a shift in this practice. 'In the absence of an official culture', writes Popovicova,

> Is there any consensus regarding what 'body art' as an art form stands for in the fascinating in-betweenness of post-Communist Europe? [The body art of the 1990s'] target is no longer bureaucratic manipulation; rather it is concerned with issues as social justice, women's rights, and the rise of commercialization and consumerism in the new Europe.[50]

Nonetheless, powerful feminist groups developed in Belgrade and Zagreb in the 1970s, closely followed by a similar movement, based on psychoanalysis, in the 1980s in Ljubljana. Marina Gržinić notes that the history of performance and feminism in this geographic space is closely linked to the practices of body art and conceptual art in the 1970s and 1980s, to be later followed by postconceptual art. 'It is clear that public space under socialism', writes Gržinić, 'belonged to the Communist Party and that it was necessary to find another space, precisely to develop and take back the space of contemporary art and culture.'[51]

Today's most widely known performance artist from Ex-Yugoslavia is Marina Abramović, whose practice transgressed the considerations of Yugoslavia on gender, social and cultural norms, claiming a new freedom of expression in the 1970s in Belgrade. Abramović was not the only pioneer in her country, as other women performance artists were active in the 1970s and 1980s, such as Sanja Iveković and Vlasta Delimar in Zagreb. All contributed to create discursive practices towards a public and political space dominated by patriarchy.

Unlike Abramović's practice in *Balkan Baroque* (1997), for example, Bajević's *Women at Work* does not take the act of cleaning to such a traumatic extent. Bajević reaches the metaphoric suffering through repetition of domestic tasks, and not through the exhibition of overwhelming pathos and a sense of theatrality. In terms of bodily transgression, Bajević's consideration reverses the roles of what is traditionally called body art by requesting nudity from her audience, installing a powerful psychological barrier between it and the performers, all dressed in spite of the humidity and the heat within the bathhouse.

Gržinić differentiates between conceptual art from the 1960s and 1970s and postconceptual art from the 1980s and 1990s. Gržinić notes how postconceptual art is embedded in the context of the social, economic and political:

> Instead of fragmentation and 'becomings', or dispersion into micro-politics, the postconceptual insists on emphasizing the social antagonism that is not just a formally performed debate that takes place between different characters, staged as a theater play with the chorus acting as the judge.[52]

According to this, Maja Bajević is an artist working on the social construction of gender after Titoism and the way gender is articulated in terms of public/private realms. Bajević plays with the boundaries of these two realms, making her audience aware of the porous membrane separating them and the hidden trauma contained in her pieces. In addition, this would suggest that her work is about the expression of individuals through the articulation of social, political positions. The symbolism of the lost country joins the mythical belief in the former unity of brotherhood proclaimed by Tito in socialist time. In her work, Bajević critically articulates the contradictions of patriarchal societies in which women are still considered through family and the household, despite the promulgation of gender equality by the former regime. Through her rearticulation of the economic, the social and the political, Bajević intends to display the feminine as a political act:

> Even after the '60s and the '70s when feminist practices started, I think that it is important today to revise the feminine role in society. Especially today – and in contrast to the '70s – when society is going through phases of repression in many ways. The female, the feminine work. . . . Is it really as respected as the male? I still often have the feeling that it is not. And the art world is not an exception. So I consider that showing the female and the feminine is still and maybe even more than ever a political act.[53]

Drawing on this insight, Bajević's performances catch the individuals' experience within a historical event as well as the framework of intimacy. *Women at Work* has to do with a private grief which is also historically formed on a grand, public and political scale. Her work is inflected by all these sociopolitical dimensions.

The artist works with and beside people who are in a way victims or invisible, hidden behind a kind of invisibility. By being named as individuals, the women themselves become visible through the performance, yet they still have to live with the invisible death of the unconfirmed dead. Gender discourse in Titoist times was inflected by the feminists' questions about the invisibility of the women's work. Hence, the performances become a collaboration with the living embodiment of the women's work. They disclose the conditions of in/visibility as well as refusing the total obstruction of visibility without disowning the constant risk of its disappearance.

Throughout the performances, Bajević raises the question whether there exists a space for these radically different, almost opposed experiences of displacement and estrangement from the home to meet. By retracing the forensic and memorial processes surrounding the events in Srebrenica, I intended to frame Bajević's performances in this highly specific context. Forensics uses a scientific jargon that most families of the victims could not come to terms with, whereas Bajević chose a borderless, almost universal language: domestic tasks, turned into crafts through the artistic performances. The notions of time and space are signalled here through the washing away, in a symbolic act, of a political ideology – with which generations who were brought up are still struggling to come to terms with – inherited from the past and confined to a precise geographical space: Ex-Yugoslavia. The post-traumatic is expressed here as the possibility to make the invisible visible, not as a belated trauma but as giving a space where a painful past belonging to the structure of the co-performers' existence can be collectively worked through. The performances symbolically open up to a new temporal space while confronting the past socialist system in the geographical space of Ex-Yugoslavia and its consequent devastating implosion.

4

Journeys in time

Traversing generational memories with the moving image in Lamia Joreige's *A Journey* (2006)

First, there is the detail of a black-and-white photograph, displaying the face of a young woman leaning towards the large basin of a fountain. Then, the viewer is able to see the whole photograph, a group of young people, men and women, posing on the other side of the basin from the photographer (Figure 4.1).

The title of the video appears, *A Journey*, before the screen turns into black screen. A voice-over, a young woman's voice says, in French, 'I decided to make a movie on the family.' And another voice, of an elderly woman, answers, half in French, half in Arabic: 'A movie for the family? What for? Why? Some will get angry, others won't, some will speak.' While she is talking the screen is displaying a photograph, from probably the same period as the previous one, of a group of women posing in the front of a house. Two elderly women are sitting, facing the camera, one with a young child on her lap, the other with another child standing on an empty chair next to her. Behind them, a young woman is standing, the same woman singled out from the group of young people in the previous photograph (Figure 4.2).

On the soundtrack, the comment of the elderly woman is interrupted by the younger woman: 'Not the extended family, the family, us!', before the screen turns black again.[1]

It is thus that Lebanese artist Lamia Joreige (*b.* 1972) opens her video piece *A Journey* (41 minutes, 2006), during which the artist takes her viewers on a journey: a physical one along the coast, towards the south of the country, and an emotional one through her family's history over almost a century. Departing from contemporary Beirut, a city still marked by a devastating, long-lasting war, Joreige drives her car along the coast in the direction of the south of her country, and beyond the border, to the city of Jaffa. But her journey terminates at the Lebanese–Israeli border in the south of Lebanon. Jaffa, therefore, remains

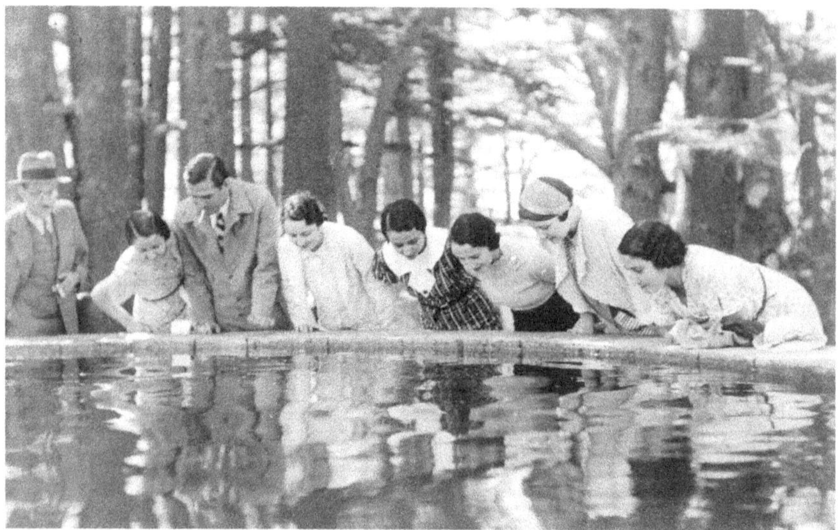

Figure 4.1 Lamia Joreige, Still from the video *A Journey*, 41 minutes, 2006. © lamiajoreige. Photograph from the Arab Image Foundation / Collection Rose Kettaneh © FAI.

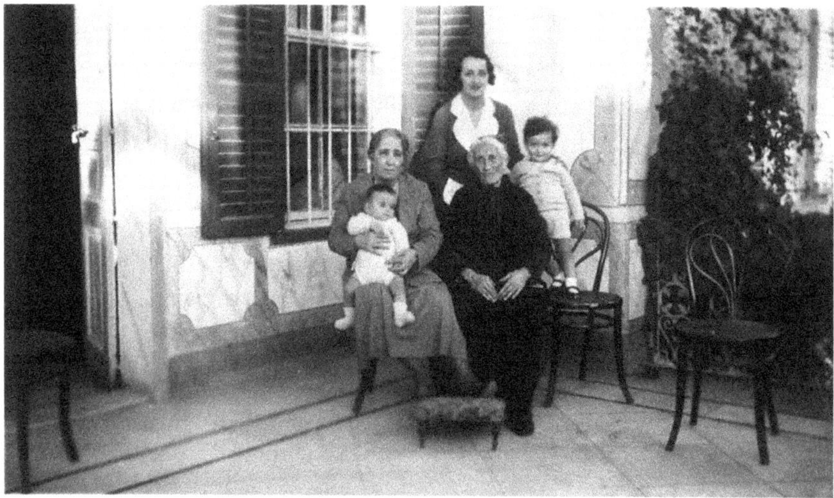

Figure 4.2 Lamia Joreige, Still from the video *A Journey*, 41 minutes, 2006. © lamiajoreige.

out of reach, replaced by the artist's phantasm of Palestine and its idealized past representation. Hence, the journey has a double dimension. On the one hand, there is the artist's perspective, which takes the form of an unfinished, symbolic journey. On the other hand, the video plots out a reverse journey of the grandmother and her family towards memory of the past.

The artist's approach to Jaffa is triggered by what her grandmother, Rose Kettaneh, remembers from her youth in this city. Born in Jerusalem in 1910, 'Teta Rose', as the artist calls her grandmother, grew up in Jaffa and moved to Beirut in 1930, the year she got married. Joreige helps her grandmother retracing her own journey from an intimate, personal perspective through the traumatic and disruptive changes that the Middle East as a geographic and political area has undergone since the 1940s: the consequences of the creation of the state of Israel in 1948 for her brothers and sisters – seeking refuge in Jordan and Lebanon, the Lebanese Civil War during which her son Alfred was kidnapped never to be found and the passing away of a generation who bore witness to the Middle East as a borderless area. Joreige's engagement is with both the moving and the still image, used as documentary modes or representation, in the process of taking the viewer between present and past, between the process of recording the present and remembering the past.

Lamia Joreige structures it by alternating present testimonies of her relatives with archival material, mostly family photographic and filmic archives. Images of the sea shot from her car recur throughout the whole video and divide its different sections, while the use of black screens is another structural means to separate them and give rhythm to the piece.

While being, most of the time, a voice from behind the camera, the artist expresses her own feelings and disappointments; Palestine becomes an unreachable zone of imagination and desire, in which Jaffa represents the roots of so many family memories, while her uncle Alfred Kettaneh's traumatic disappearance haunts the entire family. Family members still try to reconstruct the unfolding of his kidnapping on that day in August 1985 and never stopped their efforts to locate and liberate him in the years following his disappearance.

However, the encounter with Yaffa – the Arabic name of Jaffa used throughout the video – as an actual, physical place, where so many family memories are rooted, can never take place. Joreige's *A Journey* reveals the artist's missed encounter with this city. As a Lebanese citizen, she cannot travel beyond the Israeli border. There can, therefore, neither be a simple return to the family home nor an easy reconstitution of the identity of the former homeland after the breach inscribed by the formation of the state of Israel. Yet her uncle's abduction resists any narration and his fate and whereabouts remain to this day officially unknown.

This chapter will examine *A Journey* through a trans-generational discourse, the different (political) perceptions of the collective history of the Middle East of three generations of women: the grandmother, the mother and the granddaughter, the artist. These three subjects are positioned in time and history: they are witnesses of deeply lived and different stories throughout the twentieth century. Through the specific reconsideration of documentary art examining the archive and traumatic memory, as it has been developed in recent Lebanese artistic discourse in the 2000s, the artist's reflection can be linked, on the one hand, to the concept of nostalgia and, on the other hand, to Marianne Hirsch's work on postmemory.[2] Both concepts, nostalgia and postmemory, to which I will come back later in this chapter, catch the varying but mutually inflected positions of the grandmother, the mother and the artist. The grandmother is nostalgic about the place where she grew up, although she settled in Beirut a long time ago. Lamia Joreige takes over her grandmother's exile and tries in a way to experience it by this abortive journey that makes the viewers feel the border as a blockade against the movement that is possible in memory but no longer in the reality of contemporary political history. Postmemory, therefore, refers to the ways in which Rose Kettaneh's history becomes a memory for Lamia Joreige through the mediation of the photograph which holds before her eyes a space that is at once the past of her grandmother but also a space actually overwritten by modern politics, borders and the state that has taken Y/Jaffa into its own space, exiling both Joreige and her grandmother from what is promised or kept alive in the photograph. Hence, nostalgia would be a feeling of longing for what is past, whereas postmemory touches on the transmission of a rupture or a trauma, a severance from a lost past.

I suggest that the impact of geopolitics and postcolonial paradigm in the Middle East has, in effect, made its inhabitants become perpetual exiles in their own geographic area. For earlier inhabitants the same area formerly functioned as a space of open borders. As a result of colonialism and migration, French, Arabic and English are used as interchangeable languages throughout the video by the different family members.

Completion of the artwork

Although Joreige started working on *A Journey* in 1999, she only completed it in June 2006 and released it publicly for the first time in August 2006 – her grandmother and grandaunt, on whose testimonies *A Journey* is partially based, having passed away respectively in 2002 and 2003. Concerned that her work could be altered by the recent events of the war in Lebanon during the summer of 2006 – as she had been focusing on traversing Southern Lebanon by car, from which Israeli forces had withdrawn in 2000 – she added the following foreword to her video:

> *A Journey* was finished one month before the Israeli attack and shelling on Lebanon. This aggression against our territory and population, which began on July 12, 2006, has killed more than 1000 civilians, displaced more than 1,000,000 Lebanese to this day and destroyed the infrastructure of the country. I deliberately kept unchanged the content of this video, although this war already slightly altered its meaning and context. Beirut, August 25, 2006.[3]

In most interviews with her relatives, the artist rarely films herself, or only as a furtive shadow in a mirror. But her voice, her questions, clearly conduct the testimonies and make her become the other voice of the piece. *A Journey* ends with Joreige filming a friend at the fence at the border separating Lebanon from Israel, and the hills beyond it, repeating the same question: 'Do you see Israel?'

The grandmother

The first testimonial of Joreige's grandmother consists of her voice explaining, while the screen focuses on photographs from the 1920s: 'My name is Rose Kettaneh, I was born in Jerusalem, I was educated at the Dame de Sion. I got married in 1930 and since that year I live in Beirut, or I live in Lebanon.'[4]

A colour shot follows, showing an elegant lady standing at a table and going through photographs and documents disposed in boxes and brown paper in front of her. The camera switches back and forth between fanned photographs of her youth in Palestine under the British Mandate in the 1920s and the contemporary presence in front of the camera of an elegant elderly woman in post-war Beirut.[5] Her narration is sometimes interrupted by Joreige, who asks her for more details or corrects her on the exact date of specific events. Due to her slightly altered memory resulting from time and age, disruptions and alterations soon enter her testimony. When asked about the number of her siblings, the elderly lady hesitates and needs to count them on her fingers in order to give an accurate answer. Asked about the exact date of a Christmas party, she hesitates again, first giving 1958, to finally correcting it to the 1930s.

Joreige then shifts to Y/Jaffa and photographs of the 1948 events, explaining in voice-over the flight of her grandmother's siblings to Amman and then their exile in Beirut, where they eventually settled down. The recollection of these events is completed by Joreige's uncle Raymond (Kettaneh), her mother's elder brother. In voice-over, the artist's uncle retraces this family history while the camera slowly shifts from one photograph to another. His version is of interest, since he tells his niece that his mother did not talk so much about her youth and the 1948 events to her own children: 'My mother did not talk about it because she had become Lebanese and she wanted to become Lebanese.'[6] This aspect makes the artist realize that her grandmother's willingness to talk about the past represents more than reactivating an elusive past in the present, but it also instigates a feeling of nostalgia.

Nostalgia

The word 'nostalgia' has its historic roots in medical history, referring to a disease displaying physical symptoms of homesickness. In the framework of their workshop *History Workshop 20*, Malcolm Chase and Christopher Shaw observe that 'A perpetual staple of nostalgic yearning is the search for a simple and stable past as a refuge from the turbulent and chaotic present.'[7] Chase and Shaw stress the connectedness of the past to the present, often through kinship or another feeling of affiliation. They distinguish between three primary conditions triggering nostalgia at a collective level:

> These three conditions, a secular and linear sense of time, an apprehension of the failings of the present, and the availability of evidences of the past are by no means an exhaustive list of the prerequisites for a popular mood of nostalgia.[8]

Although these three conditions are present in Rose Kettaneh's account, evidences of the past are countered by the artist's own mother, as I will suggest while describing the mother's position. The grandmother presents to her granddaughter a past that seems continuous, whose history has become canonized. Each account throughout *A Journey* becomes indeed independent historical fragments composed of many people's experiences. The events Rose Kettaneh and her relatives experienced are those of disruptive violence, and, therefore, their own recollections represent a source of knowledge despite the permeability of the boundaries between official and private history. What seems like a unified past is indeed founded on the incoherence of the divided present between Beirut and Y/Jaffa.

The reconstructed past always seems more coherent than when the recollected events actually took place. The effect of *A Journey*, with its recourse to the framework of history and the archive, is to bring the viewer closer to a certain past, producing in him/her a kind of second-hand testimony and making him/

her the witness of the reconstructed events. The sense of melancholy prevails, facing the despair of having lost something that is now irrecoverable. The loss of reality is replaced by the acceptance of inauthentic historical versions because subjective, for which Joreige's mother Mona reproaches her daughter. Whereas history still has recourse to notions of objectivity, memory is tainted by the vagaries of both subjective history and amnesia. In her book *Screening the Past: Memory and Nostalgia in Cinema*, Pam Cook sees nostalgia as a way of coming to terms with the past, enabling individuals to exorcize it in order to move on. Cook associates nostalgia with a state of fantasy, regarded as 'even more inauthentic than memory'.[9] However, Cook's position towards unperfected memory shows more understanding towards the person endowed with this memory, because it is a result of subjectivity. Cook therefore distinguishes between history, nostalgia and memory, the latter building a bridge between the first two.[10]

The sense of loss in nostalgic encounters such as those contained in *A Journey* is a powerful acknowledgement that the past is gone forever, as the artist states,

> As history escapes us, only fragments remain, words and images; each fragment carries its own memory and its own history. These fragments are memory and oblivion at the same time, parts of an incomplete whole and assembled subsequently. Rearranged and re-interpreted, they border fiction. Similarly to the mechanism of memory, my work attempts to collect, record, erase, invent, forget, capture, miss and divert. I say attempts, because in all my work, I point at the impossibility of accessing a complete narrative, thus underlining the loss, the gaps of memory and history.[11]

Nostalgia intervenes in this desire to overcome the gaps between the representation of the past and the objectivity of the actual past events, to recover what was lost to the artist. Joreige reflects on the elusiveness of history in her voice-over narration.

The mother

Whereas Joreige filmed her grandmother within the confines of her house, she recorded her mother Mona's testimony at the Arab Image Foundation in Downtown Beirut. After her grandmother's passing away in 2003, Joreige donated the family archives to this foundation. Seeing Joreige's mother Mona wearing gloves to manipulate them contrasts with the grandmother's gesture of touching them with bare hands from a large box on her kitchen table. What used to be part of the grandmother's life has now the status of archives preserved for a given community.

The mother tries to pass on a message to her daughter: live in the present and do not try to interpret events you did not witness yourself. We are Lebanese and we live in Beirut. The artist's mother refuses this past heritage of Palestine, and when being reproached by her daughter – 'You never talked about Palestine and never told us that you were originally from Palestine' – she blankly asserts that 'I am not Palestinian, I am Lebanese. I was born in Lebanon, of a Lebanese born father, my mother was Palestinian, yes'.[12] And when Joreige pushes her on by saying, 'So you are half-Palestinian', her mother maintains her position, defending her country, Lebanon:

> You simplify because you know nothing about Lebanese history. [. . .] Lebanon is the only Arab country that paid such a price in the fight against Israel. In Syria, the Golan has been occupied for 40 years, and not a single shot was ever fired on the Golan, so I do not buy their stories. It is easy to make grand speeches but if you get back to history and you know history, you'll know the difference.[13]

At this stage, *A Journey* challenges the relationship of images with their constructed meaning and how these same images might contribute to an identity formation that goes beyond a family's structure, reaching national and political, historical levels. The camera, used as faithful recording witness and a tool of mediation, suddenly becomes a means of intrusion and unsettlement when the artist's mother firmly commands, 'Lamia, turn off you evil machine.'[14]

These different points of view of three women's consciousness on the same past events are embodied in a genealogical chronology and worked within the conditions, on the one hand, of loss and exile and, on the other hand, of hope. More than exploring her own identity through the past generations, Joreige poses the question of finding a general mode of receiving and transmitting testimony. The potential of the archival material she uses conveys this meaning by helping her to frame her quest through her own cultural space.

Postmemory

At this stage of the analysis, I would like to suggest that the artist's quest for what her grandmother remembers inscribes itself in Marianne Hirsch's postmemory process. Hirsch defines postmemory as 'the experience of those who grew up dominated by narratives that preceded their births, whose own stories are evacuated by the stories of previous generation shaped by traumatic experiences that can neither been understood nor recreated'.[15] Hirsch developed her concept in the initial context of Holocaust studies, and the children of Holocaust survivors, which seems extremely remote from my bringing it together with intergenerational transmission of a Palestinian Christian grandmother's memories from Y/Jaffa and the Lebanese Civil War. However, in a later contribution to the subject, Hirsch opens it up to other instances of trauma, acknowledging the predominance and relevance of postmemory in numerous other traumatic contexts. Hirsch, therefore, broadened the field of postmemory to 'describe other second-generation memories of cultural or collective traumatic events and experiences'.[16]

Postmemory is formed through family ties with those who have directly experienced these events. Hirsch also acknowledges that 'postmemory is distinguished from memory by generational distance and from history by deep personal connection'.[17] Although temporally and spatially removed from the events narrated by her grandmother, Joreige accesses the past through the photographs and through her attempt to return to its sites, interrogating the landscapes beyond the Israeli border. These photographs of Jaffa in 1948, of the rubble on the street of the destroyed houses, for example, represent traces of memory that become a way of exploring the two other subjects' positions, the mother's and the artist's. But the different levels of time and space forces her to acknowledge that the past itself cannot be located neither as a *there* nor as a *then*. Her efforts to give a personal, subjective transcription of the family past attach these events experienced from a private viewpoint to public, historical events. Joreige interrogates the status of the image's past and present, questioning its reliability as source of history.

In her essay 'Constructing the Image of Postmemory', Tina Wasserman reflects on postmemory in the work of two contemporary media artists, Daniel Eisenberg and Rea Tajiri. Like Joreige, both artists revisit their family histories: Eisenberg his parents' experience of the Holocaust and Tajiri his mother's interment in a Japanese American camp during the Second World War. Wasserman distinguishes between memory and history, although acknowledging the inextricability of their bond:

> History is the transcription of public events connected to the external world, and memory is an internal, subjective transcription of experience connected to the individual self.[18]

Wasserman's statement allows me to argue that to Joreige her grandmother's subjective memory becomes for the artist's generation within her family a kind of public history. To Wasserman the boundary between personal memory and public history is rather porous.[19] Such was the case for Joreige, who is aware of the historical versions of the same past recalled by her grandmother.

Middle East

Besides presenting the viewer with an historical mapping, Joreige uses geographic mapping, as recurrent motif in other pieces by the artist such as *Here and Perhaps Elsewhere* (2003), *Full Moon* (2007), *Beirut Autopsy of a City* (2010) and, more recently, in her film *And the Living is Easy* (2014). This geographical mapping takes the form of the filmed journey in the present of filmmaking along the Lebanese coast, but also around the city of Beirut and, to some extent, of Y/Jaffa. The reappropriation of space seems to matter to the artist. She told journalist and art critic Kaelen Wilson-Goldie in an interview that as a child growing up during the war, she used to know the streets as a site of violence.[20] I want to argue that by this mapping of the locations to which her family is historically linked, Joreige is in a way creating a Palestine for herself. Such is Sarah Rogers's argument in her dissertation, *Postwar Art and the Historical Roots of Beirut's Cosmopolitanism* (2008):

> The geographical mapping combined with the complex interweaving of documentary sources allows the artist to consider her own concept of Palestine as the locus of an identity and political position.[21]

Joreige also acknowledges how the Middle East once seemed to be a borderless area, when Joreige's mother recalls how her father and uncle used to leave for months. They would travel to Jordan, to Iraq, by car or on camel back, and Mona tells her daughter about her father's excitement and the dangers of such adventurous practices at the time. While the screen displays photographs and other documents such as a letter of her grandfather's expeditions, Joreige adds in voice-over her feelings about these transformations of borders between these regions. By displaying his travelling, she is in comparison disclosing her inability to follow his path, because the area has changed so dramatically:

> They travelled far away, for months, to Egypt, to Iraq, Iran, not worrying about borders. It was all one territory to them. [. . .] Did they dream of contributing to modernity? Of those days she evoked through the occupation of Palestine and the exile of its population unto the Lebanese war, what am I left with? An unattainable elsewhere? A fragmentary territory where past promises made way for an unbearable and irreversible reality.[22]

Joreige refers here to nation-state formations in the Middle East and the decolonization process. After the First World War, political emancipation of national aspirations was already put in action, following the political reorganization of the international system at Versailles. As I will expand in the chapter on Paola Yacoub's photographic practice, it was during the mandates of Britain over Palestine and of France over Lebanon that an agreement was reached in March 1923 over the border between Syria, Lebanon and at the time Palestine. According to historian Dietrich Jung, the facts Joreige deplores were in fact inescapable:

> On the one hand, the Middle East provided European powers with a convenient arena in which to fight out their rivalries with little risk, while on the other hand, regional and local forces were able to instrumentalize great-power politics to their own ends. This entire confusion of international, regional, and local levels is then expressed in the systemic characteristic that no outside state has been able to dominate and organize the Middle East, just as no state from within has been able to do so.[23]

Jung raised the issue whether colonialism did negatively impact on the actual political and national situations of these countries, underlying how the Middle East was at the time a *practical* area where European powers could host their own struggle. Joreige expresses here her concern as an individual who has no control, neither over the political past nor over the present of her geographic area. In colonialist theory, this debate is about foreign powers allowing themselves to take decisions for and in the name of entire populations. In this sense, Lamia Joreige's film is a work that contests colonization and its legacies by translating them into lived experiences and transmitted memories of other orders, such as being in that space as an inhabitant.

Y/Jaffa

Whereas the photographs of Y/Jaffa sustain the grandmother in remembering the place she lived in, the artist holds in her hand a photograph of a world to which she cannot go back. In Joreige's work, the trope of the journey mentally leads her to an imaginary site, the Yaffa of the 1930s (Figure 4.3).

She knows that she will never be able to reach this contemporary place called Jaffa. The city remains an inaccessible world to her, locked in the time of the photograph and barred by the events that have happened since it was taken.

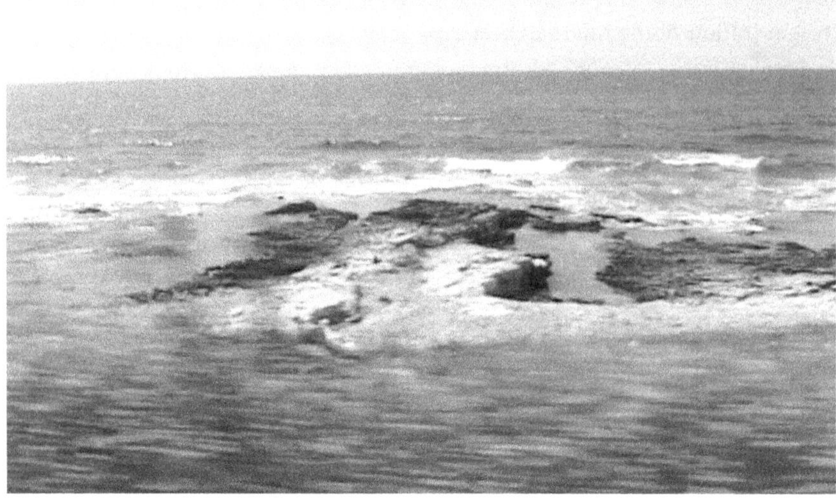

Figure 4.3 Lamia Joreige, Still from the video *A Journey*, 41 minutes, 2006. © lamiajoreige.

Thus, the barbed wire fence at the border between Lebanon and Israel not only represents the border that she cannot cross but also signifies the confrontation between memories of a past world and present reality.

The first long photographic sequence of the piece becomes an experience of connection between the viewer and the subjects of representation. Soon, the name Y/Jaffa enters the conversation between the grandmother and her granddaughter, reinforced by the old lady's laconic statement regarding her father's grave. Looking at a photograph of his grave, Teta Rose wonders, 'Who knows what it has become? We cannot even go and see it.' This sentence in the video triggers Joreige's real journey and explains why she does need to go on *A Journey*.

According to historian Mark LeVine, Jaffa is, together with Jericho, one of the oldest cities in the world and inhabited settlement in Israel/Palestine. The city has been constantly changing hands and has been destroyed partially or completely more than thirty times.[24] Before 1948, Yaffa used to be described as the country's most important commercial and cultural Arab centre in the time of Mandatory Palestine. Yaffa was a symbol of the modern urban landscape to many Palestinians. On 29 November 1947, the UN Resolution 181, to which Joreige refers, partitioned Palestine between two states: a Jewish one and a Palestinian

Arab one; Jerusalem and Bethlehem were meant to constitute an international zone. Although being surrounded by Tel Aviv and other Jewish towns, the city of Yaffa, due to its majority of Palestinian population and its status as economic and cultural capital of Arab Palestine, was meant to remain an Arab enclave. However, fighting for the city started in December 1947 and 13 May 1948 marks the surrender of Yaffa to Jewish forces of the Haganah, Irgun and Lehi. Of its pre-war Arab population of 70,000 inhabitants, only 3,500 remained. Yaffa was officially united with the city of Tel Aviv (founded in 1908) on 24 April 1950, of which it became a minor appendage.[25]

Those remaining in the community of Jaffa were among the poorest Arabs living in surrounding villages. In the early 1950s Jewish emigrants, mostly from the Balkans, settled down in Jaffa and were relocated to Palestinian properties. Arab representation in the municipal council of Tel Aviv did not occur before 1993. Today, the Arab population of Jaffa only represents about 2 per cent of the population of the Jaffa Tel Aviv metropolis.[26]

Two radically opposed representations of the city are still in circulation today. On the one hand, the city is visualized as poor and crime-infested since the 1960s. It has been often used for shooting crime movies and television shows as André Masawi stated in an article on 'Film Production and Jaffa's Predicament': 'It resembles Beirut after the bombardments – dilapidated streets, fallen houses, dirty and neglected streets, smashed cars.'[27]

On the other hand, extensive efforts to depict Jaffa as ancient, romantic and exotic have been deployed by touristic institutions to attract and promote touristic consumption. Jaffa represents in this case the archaeological and historic site of the city of Tel Aviv, a city devoid of ancient history. According to Levine, many of the Jaffa diaspora have accepted the erasure of the city. Those returning to visit it had envisioned it as 'a fragment of imagination' and replaced their nostalgia with a touch of cynicism.[28]

The post-1948 history such as recounted by Mark LeVine and Sharon Rotbard is that the exponential growth of Tel Aviv happened at the expense of Jaffa.

In his controversial book *White City, Black City*, Israeli architect Sharon Rotbard implies racism from the White City (Tel Aviv) towards some of its areas. In exploring the shadows of the White City, Rotbard not only raised the issue of Jaffa but raised the issue of all unprivileged south areas of Tel Aviv.[29]

Having explained some of the changes Jaffa has undergone since 1948, I am now wondering myself about this question: Had Joreige been able to get to Jaffa, how her encounter with the city would have been? Therefore, I became interested in the testimony of some returnees. Most of those who came back were looking for the family house and their roots. Salim Tamari's testimony illustrates the feelings most of them have, which are mainly of disappointment. Tamari says about the best way to deal with this confrontation with reality:

> After being slapped by the gentrified and de-Arabized city and treated to a laundered version of their history, they treat themselves to a sumptuous meal by the sea in order to forget.[30]

It is never easy to confront one's quest for an iconic city of loss and their dreams about it with today's reality of an everyday lived space. This testimony illustrates a reaction quite common to returnees. One of the personal experiences Lamia Joreige displays in *A Journey* is her attempt to remember a world, not only a place. Her real engagement with the place is a double encounter with absence and loss. She struggles with this temporal and geographical distance, together with cultural/generational difference. That prohibits her from experiencing a total sense of identification with the people in the photographs. Which elements does she have to support memory of this past, apart from some fanned photographs and her grandmother's fragile sense of memory? More than this, how do you actually give a visual representation of memory, of its maintenance and communication?

On Alfred Kettaneh's kidnapping

In August 1985, Alfred Kettaneh Jr., Joreige's uncle, disappeared while he was driving a Red Cross ambulance. The practice of kidnapping was common during the Civil War, the kidnapped being usually used for the purpose of exchange. A law issued after 1995 stipulates that after four years, the family of the kidnapped people could have the missing person declared deceased, a difficult decision to take for many families; 17,000 people disappeared during the war and were never found.[31]

This disappearance seems to be articulated according to the individual relationship everyone had with this person. The grandmother connects it to the war and the loss of her home, shelled the week of the kidnapping. To her the war took away part of her life that all her attempts to recover through finding her son remained in vain. Mona, the mother, remembers Alfred as being her closest sibling during her childhood. To her, the sense of being unable to locate him and reconstruct what happened to him even on the day of the kidnapping is traumatic. Mona was also the person who, for a long time, kept Alfred's belongings ready in case they could send him something before his release. She tells her husband, niece and daughter, how, a few years before this interview, she finally gave up, giving his belongings away. This gesture acknowledges that for her, her brother will never come back. The artist's viewpoint on this tragedy is to try to precisely reconstruct the events of August 1985 through seeking different testimonies among her family members.

Joreige not only makes her grandmother speak about this loss. She also records a conversation between her parents and Alfred's daughter, Gillian, who all try to make sense of the scattered elements; they have to reconstitute a chronology of the events and attempts to liberate him. Therefore, *A Journey* offers to the viewer the ways in which the different generations experienced this traumatic disappearance.

As recalled by Teta Rose

Building on this insight, the most remarkable sequence of the video is the grandmother's profoundly moving testimony about her son's disappearance, after many years of silence about it. The viewer watches Teta Rose, motionless, seated in an armchair in her living room. In the background, one can precisely hear her voice giving the account of the day her house was burnt down and she had to move to the mountains, and how, in the narrative, this is linked to Alfred Kettaneh's disappearance. Hence, this sequence is disorientating for the viewer because the artist actually filmed her grandmother while she was watching on television an earlier interview with her. This latter was recorded for the purpose of Joreige's series *Objects of War* (1999), a video piece for which the artist asked acquaintances to speak about an object on which their memories of war had crystallized. Joreige chose this indirect way of including this testimony into *A Journey*. This sequence is about listening to the testimony, for the people present in the room – grandmother and granddaughter, and for the viewer. The narrative explains in a calm and composed manner how Rose Kettaneh lost at the same time a son, whom she calls *Junior*, and a home, the one kidnapped, the second burnt within the same week:

> One hour after I had left when I arrived at Mona's, I got a phone call and was told 'your house is burning', they said. 'It's not possible,' I said. 'Nothing is impossible, if there's a will. You don't want to come with me, I'll go by myself.' And this is how I left with my son, with my two sons . . . because I had a son, Junior, who got kidnapped unfortunately during the war and who's no longer alive. And . . .

> my brother-in-law insisted that I join them, I told them: 'If I don't go to see my house, I won't come with you, I want to see my house.' I went, I saw my house in the state I described earlier to you and I understood that truly I had lost my home. The entrance doors were broken on all sides, the house literally robbed, burnt. So this is how I went up to the mountains.
>
> I cannot say I'm resentful . . . I'm resentful, certainly I am resentful! But I wouldn't go and harm them, no, because it is not in my nature. But if I knew who caught him, I would want to see that person die before me! That, that . . . I don't know, maybe I myself would kill him![32]

Suddenly, on her face, a tear appears, and the elderly woman loses her composure for a brief instant. This seems to me the most evocative and mediated image in the video. It provokes a greater respect for the other's repressed suffering, which is displayed for the first time as such. Joreige told me in an interview that this has been one of the rare moments of emotion she witnessed in her grandmother (Figure 4.4).

As recalled by Joreige's parents to Alfred's daughter, Gillian

The second articulation of Joreige's investigations is the recording of the discussion between her own parents and her cousin Gillian, Alfred's daughter. Joreige shows here how fragile memory can be, as the three of them first cannot agree on the exact date of the kidnapping. Did it take place on 17, 18 or 19 of August 1985? Were there any witnesses to the kidnapping who could help retrace

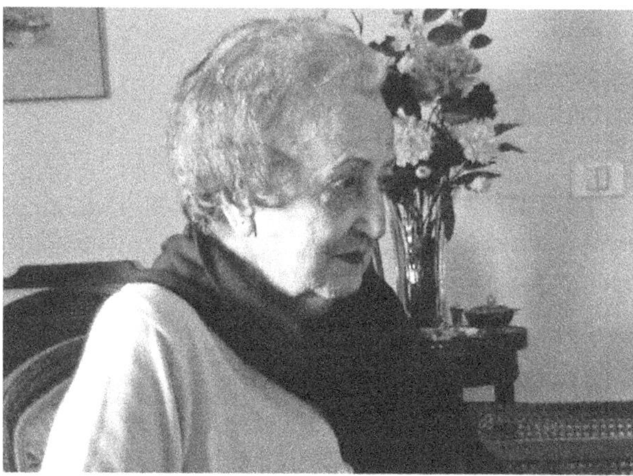

Figure 4.4 Lamia Joreige, Still from the video *A Journey*, 41 minutes, 2006. © lamiajoreige.

the chain of events? By whom was Alfred detained and where was he kept? Again, Joreige returns here to family albums and the different testimonies of family members as she retraces how everyone experienced this disappearance.

As worked out by Khalil Joreige and Joana Hadjithomas

Lamia Joreige is not the only artist in her family haunted by her uncle Alfred Kettaneh Jr.'s disappearance in 1985. Her brother, Khalil Joreige, and his wife, Joana Hadjithomas, worked on *Latent Images*, 8mm films retrieved from their uncle's belongings. As Khalil Joreige explains, 'My uncle was never found, and never returned. He is still reported as missing: and, the circumstances of his disappearance remain a mystery. There is very little evidence to explain what really happened.'[33]

Khalil Joreige by chance found the last film his uncle used. Realizing it might contain the last pictures Alfred took fifteen years earlier, when he eventually sent the film to be developed, the result was disappointing, since the film was opaque and irreparable. It only showed white images, with sometimes a few shadowy images appearing. Both artists knew that the result of this latent film and its images might be the cause of a disappointment if the images could not be properly developed. Since, Joreige and Hadjithomas had, among others, been working on the concept of latency. More than ever, they remained haunted, because, according to them, remaining haunted resists the enveloping Lebanese amnesia: 'by remaining haunted, we do not succumb to cynicism in the acceptance of images and of realities in a continuous present. Being haunted is refusing the mechanical state, the machine; it is time that refuses to efface itself. It is something that resists. Being here, today, is accepting to live with our ghosts, to long for them, to feed them. It is reminiscent of an image, of a knowledge that inhabits us, a knowledge difficult to pin down.'[34]

In *Here and Perhaps Elsewhere* (2003)

Lamia Joreige had previously worked on this kidnapping. In *Here and Perhaps Elsewhere* (2003), a 54-minute video directly alluding to Jean-Luc Godard's *Ici et Ailleurs* (1976), the artist probed the memory of abduction during the war. Showing a set of black-and-white photographs depicting the checkpoints that existed along the Green Line – the Ring Checkpoint, Harbor Checkpoint and the Museum-Badaro crossing point – Joreige asks the same question to inhabitants, passers-by and shopkeepers she encounters on her quest: 'Do you know of anyone

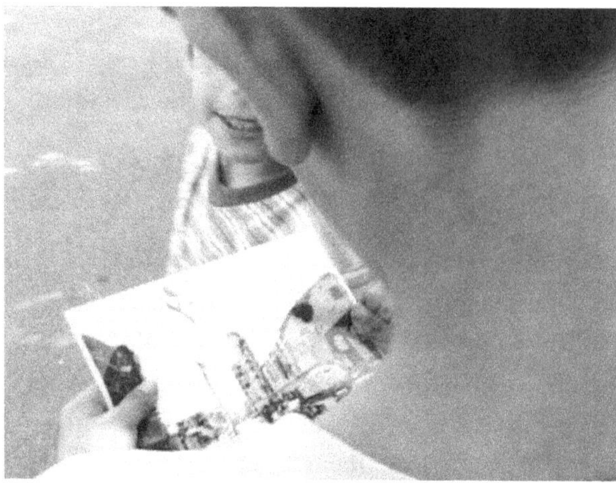

Figure 4.5 Lamia Joreige, Still from the video *Houna Wa Roubbama Hounak* (*Here and Perhaps Elsewhere*), 54 minutes, 2003. © lamiajoreige.

who was kidnapped here during the war?' Some people, showing distrust and fear, refuse to speak; others lose themselves in the incoherence of their accounts. While recording and moving along the former conflict line, Joreige draws at the same time a map of the city, the map of the city centre today compared to its map during the conflict. Joreige uses the juxtaposition of archival, still photographs with moving, colourful captions, recording her own moving in the city. Although the artist tries to recover recollection of past events, she gets only an interpretation of their memories (Figure 4.5).

Nonetheless, Joreige keeps a rigorous methodology, repeating the exact same set of questions at each location. As Kaelen Wilson-Goldie remarks,

> There is a repeated failure to match one view with the other, as if these images of the past and present refuse to conform to a singular notion of place, let alone a coherent, collectively understood historical narrative linking one with the other.[35]

This insistence makes it clear by the end of the piece that she is looking for one particular story: the account of her uncle's disappearance. The title Joreige chose is a direction allusion to Jean-Luc Godard's film *Ici et ailleurs* (1976), a peculiar film on the Palestinian uprising. Part of the Dziga Vertov Group's films, *Ici et ailleurs* was originally planned to bear the title *Till Victory*, and to be the result of Godard and Jean-Pierre Gorin's 1970 visit to Israel.[36] On the PLO's request, Godard and Morin filmed these Palestinian guerrillas during the so-called Al Fatah liberation struggle. When the duo returned to France, however, the project fell apart due to the change of political situation and Hussein's routing the Palestinian guerrillas in spring 1971. In *Ici et ailleurs*, Godard was willing to turn it into a critical analysis on how to film history in the making.

The film results in a commentary on its own state of unfinishness as in the Palestinian/Israeli conflict. It alternates between the footage from Israel and sequences of a family in France, mostly watching television. In this way, Godard created the digression between *Here* (France) and *Elsewhere* (Israel). In voice-over, Godard reminds the viewer from *Here* that most people seen on the *Elsewhere* images died five years earlier. Hence, Godard engages the *Here* not only with a geographical delocalization but also with a temporal one. Thus, the French film-maker succeeds in showing how images are disconnected from the reality they represent.[37]

Godard's reflexive cinematic Modernism, his ideologically self-conscious handling of image and text, were worked out by Joreige. Her practice in *Here and Perhaps Elsewhere* and in *A Journey* aims at revealing the structure within the close family in the context of a geographically discursive Middle East. Interested in memory and nostalgia in a broader context than themselves, Joreige asks if these aspects can become collectively discussed issues.

Documentary art

Joreige's *Journey* is emblematic of Lebanese art practices developed in Beirut throughout the post-war period. Without special filmic effects, the artist immerses us in the core of her family, transmitting to the viewer her own gaze on her relatives. The viewer is to take an active part in her investigation of past and her relatives' feelings – expressed as such or guessed. This apparent lack of effect through the elliptical montage, rather oblivious of aesthetics, provokes an immediate experience, which becomes a dynamic between the artwork and the audience. Sarah Rogers qualifies Joreige's technique of elliptical montage as 'a mediation of the failure of memories and photographs to meet seamlessly'.[38] Rogers states that

> In Joreige's film, the photographs presented to her interviewees not only initiate an attempt to remember but also visualize the frustrating inability to locate the past in the present landscape.[39]

The term documentary originates from the noun document. Its Latin root, *documantum*, means 'lesson of proof'. This definition leads to a notion of equivocal truth of the determined here and now, a debate already raised and largely discussed in the field of photography and its theory. Documentary, therefore, bears an antinomy to art in its aesthetic expression. On the one hand, technological revolution gave access to immediate filming, while the simplicity of its format, its apparent neutrality and transparency seek authenticity.

In order to understand the origin and acceptance of the documentary as an artistic form, I have to go back to 1978, at a time when video was at an early stage of development and struggling to become acknowledged as a form of artistic expression, to an influential essay by Allan Sekula, 'Dismantling Modernism, Reinventing Documentary (Notes on the Politics of Representation)'. Sekula made an intervention at the point of Modernism, making a case for a form that was excluded from the art world. He outlines the myth of the camera, which is simply a machine recording images, that there exists a rhetoric of these images and insists on the status of documentary which has nothing to do with realism, but with the artist's expression:

> The rhetorical strength of documentary is imagined to reside in the unequivocal character of the camera's evidence, in an essential realism. The theory of photographic realism emerges historically as both product and handmaiden of positivism. Vision, itself unimplicated in the world it encounters, is subjected to a mechanical idealization. Paradoxically, the camera serves to ideologically *naturalize* the eye of the observer. [. . .] The same picture can convey a variety of messages under differing presentational circumstances. [. . .] Documentary is thought to be art when it transcends its reference to the world, when the work can be regarded, first and foremost, as an act of self-expression on the part of the artist.[40]

Sekula's engagement with documentary art seems remote today, particularly since Documenta 11 (2002), which sealed a change in legitimating documentary film and photography. Its curator, Okwui Enwezor, wanted to raise awareness about artists' engagement with politics and history, and how these media became a dominant artistic language as ways of making artistic statements and their relations with social life. As Linda Nochlin noted later that year in the September issue of *Artforum International*, many works exhibited functioned at a level of interaction between images and social reality:

> The most striking aspect of Documenta 11 is the predominance of the documentary mode, for want of a better world. [. . .] Many of these works function in the documentary mode but transform and expand it, making it into a kind of hybrid that appeals not merely to curiosity, a quest for specific information about some topic, but to imagination, political consciousness, and unconscious fears and desires.[41]

Enwezor's intention was to bring visibility to a postcolonial order taking into account geographical and cultural areas different from the Western one. Enwezor stresses that documentary does not possess any absolute fixed messages attached to its designation. The ideas and works can vary depending on the locational and social context of its production, as well as the relationship between artists and their audiences.[42]

Enwezor answered to the critics of the exhibition by admitting that he could not wholly dismiss that many works in display could be confused with the documentary mode. In 2004, in his contribution to the exhibition catalogue *Experiments with Truth* (Fabric Workshop and Museum, Philadelphia), Enwezor reflects back on the Documenta, introducing the concept of *vérité* and differentiating it with truth and reality, drawing a distinction between the tension between the aesthetic intention and the ethical position vis-à-vis the subject of the documentary.[43] Enwezor was drawing on the 1960s French cinema known as *cinéma vérité*, and the mode of documentary.

Documentary art in Lebanon

In the face of dramatic instability, documentary art in Lebanon became a privileged site of avant-garde experimentation in regard to a city affected by violence, rapid growth and an intense urban transformation and reconstruction. Vit Havránek has pointed to these specific issues of documentary emerging out of dramatic, unique, political and historical circumstances in his definition of documentarism:

> Documentarism, in film and photography, could be described as a genre in which the director/artist carries out a transfer of his own or other people's knowledge, stances, and experiences through his own articulation of the media and technology. The decision to devote oneself to documentary is an acceptance of the condition to define one's creativity in direct connection with the complexes of social-historical issues, which the artist documents; what permits us to call a work documentary is the relation between the documenting and the documented. Thus, the decision to work in a documentary manner primarily situates the Not-I, other people, creators, works, social phenomena and so on, at the center of the thinking and acting of the creative subject.[44]

Personal archives used by artists – and I have in mind here not only the work of Lamia Joreige but also the work of Akram Zaatari, of Khalil Joreige and Joana Hadjithomas, of Walid Raad and the Atlas Group – break the monolithic historical narrative into subjective testimonials and highly personalized narratives. In a so-called post-war period, documentary, in its fictitious/sceptical or realist forms, mediates subjective experiences, offering different methods of envisioning through the camera. It results in an interplay between authors and their audience, between so-called memory and amnesia, the imaginary narrative versus its available materiality. Perpetual coexistence with conflict extends beyond these personal collections and self-reflexive acts; they truly convey what Mark Ryan Westmoreland has named 'a crisis of representation'.[45] In his research on experimental documentary in post-war Lebanon, Mark Ryan Westmoreland states as his main argument that the exactitude of the representation is not the key aspect of this crisis of representation that seems to have seized Lebanese art practices. Westmoreland argues that the most important aspect of these practices is indeed their signalling of the gaps or the holes left by amnesia:

> Rather these documentary endeavours are efforts to make manifest the imaginaries that haunt a landscape of forgetfulness, amnesia, and impossible representations. Documentary artefacts are thus not records of the real, but casings, hollow shells, empty remnants of remembering. [. . .] By re-enchanting these mimetic artefacts, Lebanese documentary experimentalists break through the blockages of amnesia, to see around representational eclipses, and to rupture ossified narratives that reify violence.[46]

In conflict zones, the quest for stable notions of truth, subjectivity and cultural identity are irremediably doomed by a sense of urgency. Joreige's *Journey* inscribes itself in the resulting imperfection of any attempt to make sense of the war by juxtaposing personal narratives with collective traumatic memory and experience of euphemistic historical events. Documentary art in Lebanon disrupts the official historiography of the country and the official refusal to bear memory to the chain of conflicted events. Art is an attempt to address the legacy of a past veiled by threat of censorship and political arrest. The lack of official and public equivalent to a 'Truth and Reconciliation Process' presumes that the Lebanese were not enabled to start a process of collective healing, a conscious act of putting the war behind them. The use of the term 'post-war' itself might not be the most appropriate in framing a time stretching between 1991 and today, as violence still structures life of the different communities and their respective war narratives. The recurring return to the war in documentary art suggests the difficulty of transcending these traumatic events. These attempts convey a deeply buried desire to make sense of this past. In Lebanon, official amnesia is felt as a public secret whose limits of permissibility are tightly controlled by the government. A general state of depression and social malaise emerged from this permanent state of instability.

It is nothing else than this state of instability, together with the possibility of a historical narrative, that artist Akram Zaatari and assistant professor in art history Hannah Feldman pointed out in a joint application to the Fulbright Visiting Specialist Program submitted in 2006:

> The implied 'versus' that traditionally separates ('fact' and 'fiction') has generated much of the scholarly focus on art produced in Beirut since the civil war. Indeed, critics from Lebanon and beyond have consistently noted, if not perhaps prescribed, that one of the most prevalent features of contemporary Lebanese artistic production is its preoccupation with the reassessment of the role and place of documentary evidence in constructions of historical truth [. . .] a number of Lebanese artists have spent the last fifteen years producing work that attempts to register the irresolution of the civil war's legacy.[47]

At stake in the work of these Lebanese archivists I mentioned above, archives and photographic collections not only (re)present a referent of the past but are also objects of the present, blurring the boundaries of time and generations. Walid Raad does not imply that his practice is sceptical or fictional but that the memories and fantasies present in the Atlas Group's work are a manifestation of a truth and reality of a subject's state of mind.[48] T. J. Demos remarks about Raad's project *We Can Make Rain but One Came to Ask* (2008) that 'Raad's account significantly redefines the status of "fiction" as a mode of inventive construction by taking seriously the psychoanalytic symptology that is its basis'.[49] Drawing on this insight, Jalal Toufic came up with the concept of the 'undead', while working on the representation of vampires in a cinematic culture. Vampires are on the threshold between living and dead. For Toufic, the undead serve the purpose of mediation in a post-conflict society tainted by amnesia. Toufic uses the undead as an allegory for subjectivity in the aftermath of the Lebanese Civil War.[50]

Lamia Joreige's documentary practices

In a way Joreige's work draws on its audience a certain artlessness, a concept I am writing down while having in mind Claude Lanzmann's monumental work on his film *Shoah* (1985). Lanzmann's documentary approach to keep powerful testimonies – of survivors from the camps, Polish peasants and German perpetrators alike – as intact as possible succeeds in transmitting to its audience the state of horror and degradation innocent civilians had to live through. Lanzmann's monumental film became a benchmark of the representation/non-representation of the Holocaust. At the same time, in the history of cinema and documentary, it represents a point of reference for anyone using the documentary form post-1985, as Stuart Liebman puts it, 'Twenty years after its premiere, we can say with confidence that this work of surpassing ambition [. . .] marked a caesura in the representation of a vastly complicated episode.'[51]

Yet, Lanzmann consciously renounced making historical documents prominent in his film and *Shoah*'s particularity lays in the absence of archival photographic or filmic footage of the camps. Although it looks like a documentary, Lanzmann calls it a work of art, since it functions at the level of the image, the way images are put together, particularly the powerful image of the journey. *Shoah*'s apparent artlessness results from its director's intention not to over-inscribe it with his own subjectivity. By contrast, if Joreige uses testimonies without altering them, in Lanzmann's cinematographic way, she does include many historical documents tracing back to her family past. Hence, in spite of its apparent artlessness, Joreige's aesthetic elements in *A Journey* are numerous: from the selection of appropriated footages and archives, the building of sequences and their narrative throughout these sequences, their continuous or discontinuous fragmenting, the choice of recurrent patterns, the title and subtitles, all the interventions are the consequence of a conscious and thoughtful choice by its author.

Unlike Walid Raad's practices, Joreige does not link historical investigation with fictitious narratives; she does not perform a mimicry of the archive. Both artists, however, denounce the way individuals remember and fabricate history. Joreige does not claim any historical truth, but her quest of reconstruction of the past, even in the framework of a single family, produces disruptions and imprecise narratives of the same events. It raises the question of subjective impressions and personal experience denounced by Raad. This aspect explains why the latter critiques the circulation of facts and their understanding. Joreige gives a sense of intimacy through her use of documents and testimonials. Yet at the same time she reaches the limits of her possibilities to write her own history and inscribe it in a collective context. Joreige gives to her audience a sense of observational subjectivity, and not a truth telling, creating a kind of officiality and objectivity. Joreige herself, describing her own work, brings the argument that this never-determined and endless state of war cannot allow her to imagine a future; she feels trapped in an everlasting present, although aware of the time going by:

> In voice-over I describe the 'just liberated and still-unknown South', finally asking: *What has been left to me of this war that is fading day by day – images of boat departures, the impressive sound of repeated shelling, fear of checkpoints, my grandmother praying day and night . . . ?* Watching *A Journey* today, I can't help but

> talk back at my own voice. The south is no longer liberated; it has been destroyed. The similarity between the present situation and events decades ago – and the sense of war beginning without the previous one ending – shakes my understanding of history, as well as my relationship to it. The war continues, the images and sounds have returned. But my grandmothers are dead, and there is no one to pray.[52]

A Journey appears typical of documentary testimony, with one exception: if the survivor, in this case mainly Joreige's grandmother, is recounting memories accompanied by archives, the actual historical site triggering these memories stays out of reach. Joreige uses the gaps within the subjective accounts to let the impossibility of narration become obvious. Reflecting on the exhibition *Out of Beirut* (Modern Art Oxford, 2006), T. J. Demos writes that 'for her, the documentary mode remains one viable tool to contest forgetting and the challenge to hysterical and psychosomatic effect of suppressing memory when trauma goes unacknowledged'.[53]

This may seem like Joreige's elliptical montage focuses on rendering a larger picture as a productive principle rendering the juxtaposition of a combination of multiple events and facts closely intertwined. Throughout *A Journey*, the montage comes to signify more than a common expressive tool. It actually accentuates the gaps and the dissonance of a particular historical discourse.

The slow motion from photograph to photograph in some sequences opens up a new dimension of the documentary genre which belongs to the specific context of post-war Lebanon: a physical evidence of an age of innocence, ignorant of the surrounding turmoil at the time of the British Mandate and today's post-1948 and post–Civil War Lebanon. The medium of the moving image allows the movement of time to be shown. Joreige does not presuppose that there is or was one history that it has always been and acknowledged as such. Instead she attempts to think history with and through its representations and gaps as a certain history in the making. Time becomes an interval in time. It is no longer a continuous flow. The gap between the images and the reaction achieved through them has an effect of suspension in time, of rupture. There is no way of telling when and where objective description begins to become something different or even opposed to it. By performing attempts of giving a historical account, Joreige wonders if her family members have a history and whether *this is history*. The video unfolds an inscription of the law of the gap, a spacing I shall call 'in-betweenness'. This in-betweenness is positioned at the threshold between memory and history, between subjectivity and objectivity.

By presenting the present as her own journey along the sea and her presence at the fence separating Lebanon from Israel, Joreige creates her own space in time. This space in time is requesting the audience to decide which landscape the camera discloses. Does the end of Joreige's message lie in her question 'Do you see Israel?' Is this her way of letting the viewer know how aware she is about the actual borders of the Middle East? Joreige cannot represent this actual space but she can still designate it: 'Your shadow is in Israel.' By naming Israel, she acknowledges her own position anchored in a contemporaneity in *A Journey*'s trans-generational discourse.

In this chapter, I have been focusing on the relation between a form of postmemory practice, initiated by narratives of memory supported by photographs, and the use of the documentary essay in video. This produces a particular configuration of the double axis of space and time. The postmemory dimension allows Joreige to travel in time through her grandmother's memories while she undertakes with the documentary aid of video an actual journey to a border. Hence, the border stands not merely within the city but between a moment of the past and the present as well as Israel and Lebanon are woven together. The artist's undertaking traces back events that put her family in the forefront of some historical happenings and tries to make sense of a war she endured as a child and a teenager. Joreige knows her *A Journey* will not have the outcome outlined by the beginning of the video: this double reunion with a place, and, by means of the place, with the past. Nonetheless, her undertaking, through her collection of remembrance, the juxtaposition or in some cases, confrontation of some personal narratives with collective traumatic memory, lifts up some of the accumulated burden of amnesia. The particular use Joreige makes of documentary art disrupts the historiographic notion of the continuum, signalling that imperfected memories are often replaced by a kind of amnesia when it comes to war. Thus, the documentary essay allows the artist to display a crisis of representation and memory proper to Lebanon and to find a way of transcending these traumatic events.

5

Wounded places

Architecture and landscape in the photographic work of Paola Yacoub

The photograph depicts the entrance of a building. Through the raw concrete literally framing the image, the damaged floor and the lack of decoration, the building looks either unfinished or in ruins. Only a few posters appear on the wall as sole decoration in the mass of concrete constituting it. The room photographed looks imposing; its monumental perspective runs through an oblique line formed by four massive pillars. In the centre a circular motif carved in the ceiling indicates the planned location for some lighting system. Instead, this one is simply crossed by an improvised electricity cable. The only furniture consists of three white, cheap plastic chairs, scattered around the room, and the wooden board onto which the posters have been applied. The colour is a dominant tone of greenish grey, while white graffiti and traces of white paint debate this shade on the pillars and the ceiling. Moreover, to an attentive gaze, the pillars clearly reveal impacts of shelling, forming regular, circular holes in their materiality. The photographer chose with exactitude to position the viewer at the threshold of the room, pushing him/her inside the inhospitability of the place with no possible escape into the street. On the posters, the knowledgeable viewer can recognize Hafez Al-Hassad and his son Bachar, the former and the actual heads of the state of Syria. From this image of threatening desolation emanates a sensation of unease, an underlying feeling that the scene does represent something the viewer is not supposed to see, something that has been hastily registered by the camera and displayed as such. Yet, at the same time, this meaning is somehow escaping him/her (Figure 5.1).

A second photograph displays a green, rural landscape, the vista of a small valley with its cultivated fields and hills closing it in the background and earthy paths running through it. As in the first photograph, the sense of symmetry,

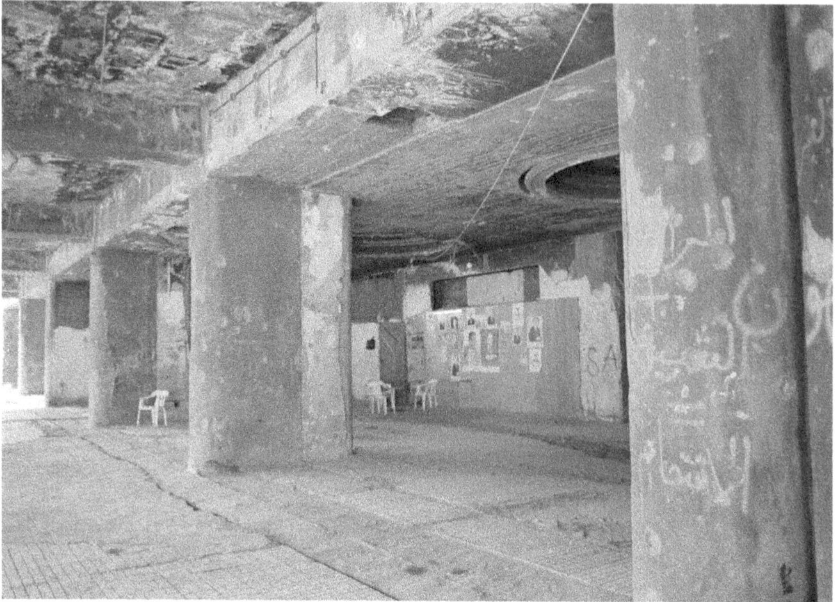

Figure 5.1 Paola Yacoub, *Hall of the Holiday Inn*. Beirut, 2001. Chromogenic hand print, Aluminium, 40 × 60 cm. Courtesy of the artist.

articulated here through the line of cypresses demarcating the cultivated from the uncultivated fields and a small road running almost like a straight line from the bottom to the top of the picture, is striking. The picture appears still, peaceful, out of time as no human subjects are to be seen in it. It can even remind of some landscapes found in Italy, for example, in Tuscany, with its cypresses and their idyllic appearance. Yet, in a reverse strategy, the camera holds back the viewer at the threshold of the image. Whereas the previous photograph was pushing the viewer into the picture, here, although the landscape unfolds in front of us, we cannot enter the picture: the camera holds us back through the blurred appearance of the left and right sides of the image (Figure 5.2).

Through their lack of conventional visual appeal, both pictures unsettle the viewer, raising some questions in his/her mind. What is the artist's project about? What are the effects of the photographer's choices and processes? What is the purpose of these photographs, of what first appears as a sense of emptiness in these different locations?

In his book *The Fate of Place* (1997), Edward Casey observes how far space is from being a universal concept, inherent in Western culture. Casey provides different reasons for considering place as a crucial concept. One is that place can become momentous as a result of major events:

> Still more saliently, certain devastating phenomena of this century bring with them, by aftershock as it were, a revitalized sensitivity to place. Precisely in its capacity to eliminate all perceptible places from a given region, the prospect of nuclear annihilation heightens awareness of the unreplaceability of these places, their singular configuration and unrepeatable history. Much the same is true for any disruptive event that disturbs the placidity of cities and neighborhoods.[1]

It is in the framework of the sensitivity of place about which Casey is talking, that I would place these two photographs depicting two radically different locations, city and countryside.

The author of these pictures is Paola Yacoub (*b.* 1966), a Lebanese artist. The first photograph is entitled *Hall of the Holiday Inn*, and was therefore taken in the lobby of the hotel Holiday Inn in Downtown Beirut, which was, at the time of Syrian occupation, said to accommodate the Syrian Secret Services, the *Moukhabarat*. The second photograph is part of a series of three photographs, entitled *Elegiac Landscapes*. These were taken in the region of Marjayoun in Southern Lebanon in May 2001.

Both photographs mark two very different but specific sites of the Lebanese Civil War and its aftermath. The Holiday Inn is situated in Beirut Central District (BCD), which used to be a no-man's land during the war. Almost no civilian had access to it between 1975 and 1991, since the area was held by militias. The region of Marjayoun had been a battlefield during the war, strategically positioned not far from the border with Israel. Southern Lebanon was occupied by Israeli troops until May 2000. Apart from its inhabitants very few people had access to this area until then. Both photographs, therefore, represent sites synonymous

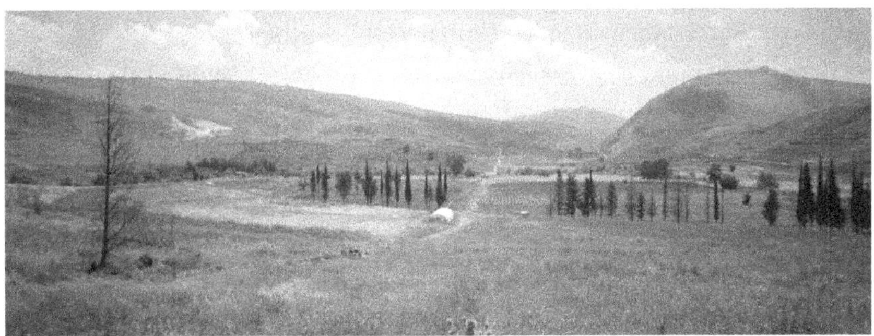

Figure 5.2 Paola Yacoub, *Elegiac Landscape 1. Region of Marjayoun.* Southern Lebanon, 2001. Chromogenic hand print, Aluminium, 35 × 94 cm. Courtesy of the artist.

with restricted access, sites in which spatiality has rarely been experienced by a common Lebanese citizen throughout recent events.

Paola Yacoub grew up during the war, during which she learned, by following a war photographer, to *take pictures*. Her photographs discussed in this chapter represent architectural structures, such as streets and hotels in Beirut or landscapes in Southern Lebanon. They embody the artist's analysis – together with her French collaborator Michel Lasserre – of the Lebanese space, where pain and memory still persist. They are therefore twofold. On the one hand, her photographs convey the experience of the fabric of the city of Beirut. Painful is the rediscovery of post-war Beirut compared to its past and remembered state. There, demolition and reconstruction processes of its city centre overlap, witnessed through the camera.

On the other hand, Yacoub's photographs are part of a rediscovery process by the Lebanese population of the space of Southern Lebanon at the beginning of the 2000s. Through the analysis of the variations of aspects or what Yacoub and Lasserre name 'circulation of territory', they reflect on the perceptions of these landscapes, particularly in conflict zones. This work is anchored in how elements of the territory – to which architectural elements belong – move and circulate in the present day, against the background of a history haunted by traumatic events.

The artist touches further upon the phenomenon of the border, especially the one, called by Israeli historian David Eshel the 'border enigma', separating Lebanon and Israel.[2] A further series of photographs picks up on the topic of a security zone put in place by Israel back in 1948: there, Yacoub's gaze rests on remaining physical traces of the line agreed upon by French and British Mandate authorities in colonial times – during their respective mandates in Lebanon and Palestine set up in May 1916 by the Sykes-Picot Agreement. This unaligned continuum of concrete blocks resonates with the line of blockhouses erected on the Atlantic coastline by Nazi Germany in the early 1940s, and extensively discussed by urban theorist and historian Paul Virilio.[3]

My reflection on Paola Yacoub's practice is articulated around the fact that her photographs do contain something uncanny. Somehow their description, for an audience looking at them, leaves us with the sense that describing them does not cohere with what they might really tell us. In a way Yacoub's photographic practice contains gaps and holes. Moreover, they seem to display an absence, or an absence of words. 'This is the location of a story I cannot talk about' seems to be the message embedded in many of her photographs.

In some way, Yacoub's photographs of the streets of Beirut remind of Eugène Atget's *empty* photographs of the streets of Paris. These same photographs seduced members of the Surrealist movement, Man Ray in particular. In 1926,

Man Ray approached Atget, seeking permission to publish his photograph *L'Eclipse – Avril 1912* on the cover of *La Révolution Surréaliste*. Atget granted permission but asked Man Ray not to put his name on it, remarking that his photographs 'are simply documents I make'. In her monograph on Atget, Berenice Abbott, who bought the content of his workshop after his death in 1927, promoted the Parisian photographer as a styleless photographer. In 1930, Walter Benjamin wrote a review of the book and commented on Atget's style:

> They [the photographs] are not lonely but voiceless; the city in these pictures is swept clean like a house which has not yet found its new tenant. These are the sort of effects with which Surrealist photography established a healthy alienation between environment and man, opening the field for politically educated sight, in the face of which all intimacies fall in favor of the illumination of details.

And Benjamin added later in that same essay this well-known comparison: 'Not for the nothing were pictures of Atget compared with those of the scene of a crime.'[4] If Atget's photographs appear to come from a frozen time, this finds an explanation in the exposure time needed to take a photograph at the time: passers-by would have blurred the shot because of their movement. Yacoub herself made reference to Atget's practice during our conversations. She considers Atget both as a precursor of modern photography and as an isolated character in Paris in the late nineteenth and the beginning of the twentieth century, who put a different gaze on the subjects he photographed.

Through the nature of photography confronting an absence, this raises the question of the gaze, and therefore, in a certain sense, the nature of a palimpsest. Andreas Huyssen uses the terminology of 'palimpsests of real and diverse experiences and memories'.[5] Artists working in post-war situations are themselves part of the reconstruction process or part of memory, since part of their work inscribed itself in these notions. Yet, if Yacoub acknowledges that some traumatic events, such as war, do exist, she underlines how every individual has his/her own experience of these events. To her it is, therefore, quite inappropriate to talk about it, as one might fail to find the appropriate, descriptive language. Hence, Yacoub undertook to register the fabric of the urban in the city of Beirut with her camera rather than using a narrative by speaking about it or describing it. In his essay 'World Cultures, World Cities', Andreas Huyssen explains what he means by urban imaginary, and that this singularization of events, the same worked out by Yacoub, stays out of reach:

> Beyond its fictional premise, however, the title [World Cultures, World Cities] suggests that no real city can ever be grasped in its present or past totally by one

> single person. That is why urban imaginaries differ depending on a multitude of perspectives and subject positions. All cities are *palimpsests of real and diverse experiences and memories*. [. . .] An urban imaginary marks first and foremost the way city dwellers imagine their own city as the place of everyday life, the site of inspiring traditions and continuities as well as the scene of histories of destruction, crime, and conflict of all kinds.[6]

Paola Yacoub's photographs of Beirut and Southern Lebanon discussed in this chapter tacitly engage with these debates, not only of Huyssen's 'palimpsest' but also of Ulrich Baer's 'spectral evidence'.[7] Moreover, the origins of Ludwig Wittgenstein's *Tractatus Logico-Philologicus* and Stanley Cavell's scepticism provide me with a framework in which to analyse Yacoub's artistic practice – an ongoing reflection on Wittgenstein and Cavell being part of her collaboration with Lasserre.[8]

I am looking at Yacoub's artistic practice from the perspective of crossing points, hotels being important crossing points in the fabric of the city and borders representing the crossing point between neighbouring states. The specificity of Yacoub's practice of the urban fabric in the lingering context of the war is echoed in Paul Virilio's emphasis in an interview with Sylvère Lotringer. In this interview, Virilio declared that his interest in war is inseparable from his interest in the city and its urban planning.[9] Though not formally trained as an architect, Virilio became one, and his work revolves around questions of architecture and urban spaces. Yacoub, therefore, as a trained architect, shares some points of interest with Virilio.

The city

Note on hotels

In her essay 'The Holiday Inn Cycle' (2010), Yacoub writes about the urban context of the specific geographic area of Downtown Beirut, an area she has been photographing and remapping throughout her career. Moreover, it is precisely in this area that she has been working after her graduation from the Architectural Association in London. With the archaeologists in Martyrs' Square, Yacoub witnessed, on a regular basis, the destruction of archaeological remains of ancient architectural structures. The team of archaeologists applied in vain to the UNESCO in order to have some parts of BCD classified as world heritage sites. In 1999, after completion of the excavations, the archaeologists were dismissed.

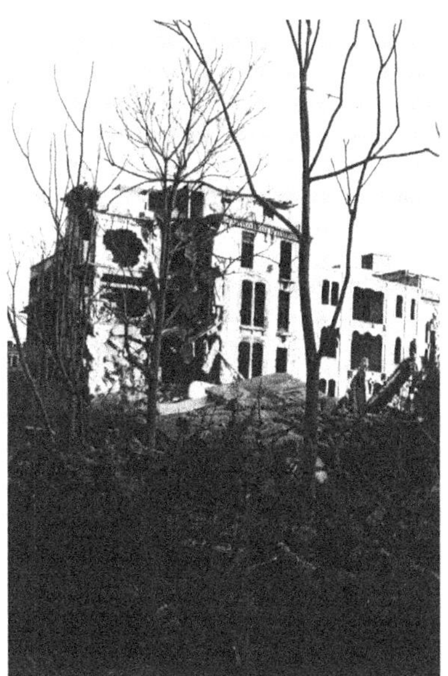
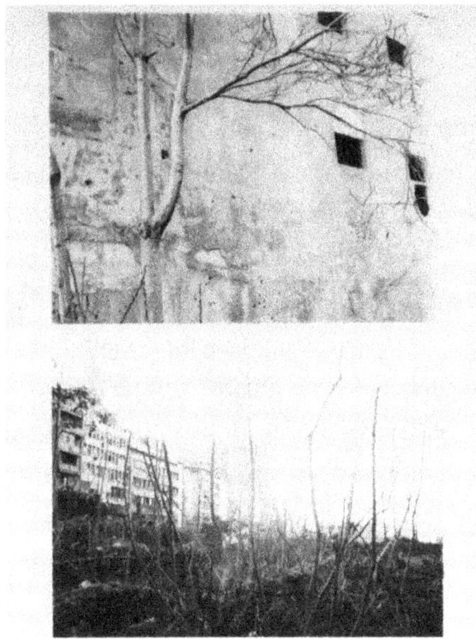

Figure 5.3 Paola Yacoub, *Untitled (Summer 88)*, Beirut, 1988. Black and white hand print, 12 × 15 cm each. Courtesy of the artist.

Yacoub's bond to the city centre is expressed in one of her first series of photographs, *Untitled (Summer 88)*. The series was taken during the war, in the then inaccessible city centre of Beirut. It resulted in pictures taken hastily under the threat of possible targeting by snipers or militias. *Untitled (Summer 88)* displays, from various black-and-white angles, parts of buildings full of bullet holes, vegetation growing over rubble of former houses, the impact of shelling on the floor and the sky overhanging the buildings (Figure 5.3).

The origins of Yacoub's practice rests on the symbolism she attached to the Holiday Inn, an emblem throughout her childhood and adult life. In an essay on the Holiday Inn, she expresses how, as a child, she wanted to work in a hotel later. But the war did not give her this opportunity. Instead, she became an architect, and an artist:

> The Lebanese civil war began in Beirut in 1975. The battles started in the high-rise hotel district, but no one knew it would last for more than fifteen years. In that year, I was nine years old. [. . .] Since then, I am still highly sensitive to events taking place in hotels all over the world. Stories of battles moved from one hotel to another. Elements reached me here and there in the rhetorical form of diegesis. [. . .] I wanted to work in hotels. But clearly my studies as a hotel manager were not going to be possible. Since the battle of the hotels, hotels and architecture haunt me. This is why I wanted to become an architect – because of the war, because of hotels and their modern architecture.[10]

Genesis of the shot

In 2001, the artist went back to the former no-man's land, photographing, among others, the Holiday Inn. First, from outside, her photograph reveals the threatening facade of the hotel building because of its height and its overlapping aspects of both ruins and unfinished building (Figure 5.4).

Then, Yacoub enters the building, photographing the lobby. *The Entry Hall of the Holiday Inn. Beirut, September 2001* looks away from human interaction and rests on the architectural elements of the hall, the pillars and the ceiling. It was taken for the purpose of the Ayloul Festival. Yacoub intended to exhibit it in the entry hall of the Holiday Inn. This hotel is an important symbol for an entire generation of Beiruti, who grew up with the image of the hotel, during and after the war; because of a struggle between heirs it has been the only building left standing untouched since the end of the conflict. When the artist started to take

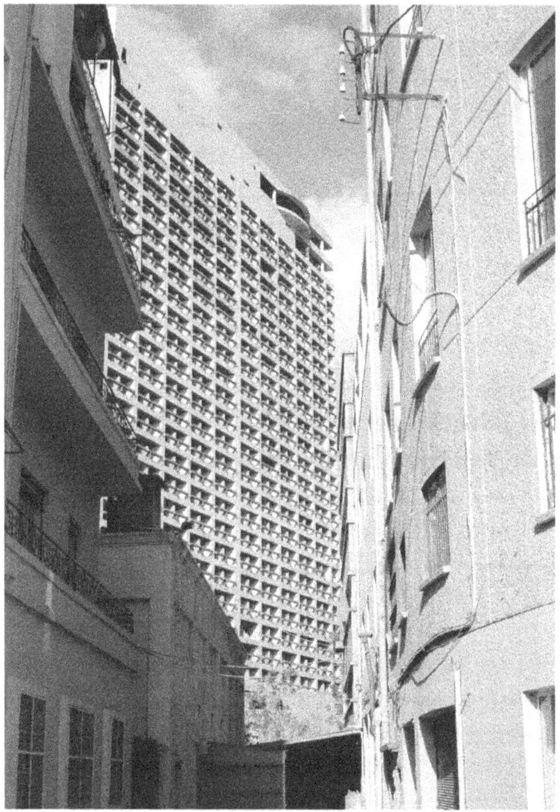

Figure 5.4 Paola Yacoub, *Holiday Inn*, Beirut, 2001. Chromogenic hand print, Aluminium, 45 × 35 cm. Courtesy of the artist.

pictures of the hall, an angry Syrian guard snatched her camera from her, took out the negatives and destroyed them in front of her. In the remains of the film the artist recovered, one single negative was developable, precisely this shot. It goes without saying that Pascale Feghali, the curator of the Ayloul Festival, and the artist were never granted permission to exhibit in the lobby of the Holiday Inn. Instead, they found their exhibition venue in a building located across the street. This picture takes also another meaning: to indicate that, particularly during the Syrian occupation, artists were subjected to arbitrary censorship.

On the significance of hotel buildings

This focus on hotel buildings not only raises the issue of their function in war. It also refers to their primary function in times of peace. Hotels represent central elements of modern cities as they signify both circulation and movement. They act as a substitute home for their clients. In normal times, hotels employ people, putting them in a continuous exchange with guests coming from the outside. Yet, in times of conflict, the significance of hotels shift, sometimes taking dramatic new meanings. In war and conflicts hotels become headquarters: for the different conflicting factions, for the mediators and peace negotiators, for the press. In Beirut, while the Carlton was the place where negotiations on the release of hostages took place, the St Georges was where secret services from all over the world used to meet.

Yacoub's photograph proposes a different encounter with reality, a reality that cannot be spoken of but could be *shared* through common perceptions mediated by the camera. In the conclusion of an essay published in the catalogue of the Venice Biennale in 2003, Yacoub and Lasserre phrase their approach in the form of three questions:

> The question of Beirut could be formulated thus: how and where do territories circulate through the activities of alternative spaces? How productive is our gaze on the city, here or elsewhere? And what is the role of artistic actions in this circulation?[11]

Another Lebanese artist and writer, Walid Sadek, addressed the criticism towards the commitment of Lebanese artists to the visual:

> What we try to do when we write is slow images down. We try to give them weight. We experience, we who live in the third world, that to be in an image, to be photographed, is almost like a death warrant. But we are equally uneasy about standing behind the lens. We work and live somewhere between the lens and the photograph.[12]

Although considering the image as suspect, Sadek nonetheless concedes that artists in Lebanon, whether writing or photographing, confront this uneasiness of expression or gaze. In the introduction to his book *Negative Horizon*, Paul Virilio remarks how our visual and cultural conventions make us see the perspective of a picture from one collective viewpoint. In his commenting on painting, Virilio articulates his reflection on vision and seeing. Virilio wonders whether we could allow other perspectives, not only visual, but also historical or political, to appear within an image:

> The phenomena that obscure our perception of the world deprive us of sources of energy, our relative blindness masks from us inestimable sources of information. In order to survive, we must change our view [*vue*], just as we must change our lives [*vie*] to subsist. It no longer suffices to speak negatively of 'zero growth', it is necessary to endeavor positively to reinvent our vision of the world.[13]

While Virilio's position is articulated as a change of *vue*, Yacoub and Lasserre speak in terms of 'variations of aspects'. I would rather suggest that both Virilio and Yacoub and Lasserre are close to Stanley Cavell's argument expressed in *The Claim of Reason*. Concluding his chapter 'Natural and Conventional', Cavell wrote,

> In philosophizing, I have to bring my own language and life into imagination. What I require is a convening of my culture's criteria, in order to confront them with my words and life as I pursue them and as I may imagine them; and at the same time to confront my words and my life as I pursue them with the life my culture's words may imagine for me: to confront the culture with itself along the lines in which it meets in me.[14]

There is, indeed, a genuine interest in Cavell's scepticism demonstrated by Yacoub when she writes about the uncertainty of the result of her photographic experimental act. Drawing on Stanley Cavell's thoughts about photography, Yacoub acknowledges how much her own protocols are inscribed in the field of scepticism. To her, to acknowledge that she cannot know in advance what she does with her camera is being sceptical. As Stanley Cavell puts it, 'You cannot know what you have done to the camera, what has been revealed to it, as long as the results have not appeared.'[15] Drawing on this insight, Yacoub reflects on her own practice and powerlessness towards the photographic medium, even in times when digital cameras are privileged over analogic ones:

> It is basic, but essential. When I draw a line with a ruler, I expect the result I will see. The surprise, if there is any, will be tiny. In the drawing of the stroke,

> a causal chain perfectly links the gesture to the result. When I take an analogic photograph, I am impatiently waiting for the print. That is the charm of the dark room. Today, I just have a quick look on the control screen. [Still] I do not know what I will obtain, whatever my mastery.[16]

The landscapes

Southern Lebanon

Having now discussed the urban aspects of Yacoub's artistic practice, I would like to address the specificity of her landscape photographs in Southern Lebanon. Yacoub and Lasserre's common project in Southern Lebanon dates back to 2000, that is to the moment shortly after the withdrawal of Israeli troops from Southern Lebanon. Yacoub and Lasserre's first visual encounter with Southern Lebanon took place on 25 September 2000, exactly four months after the Israeli withdrawal on 25 May 2000, in compliance with UN Resolution 425 (1978). At this time, the Lebanese army had not reached the region yet, leaving Hezbollah's militia in charge of the protection of the border with Israel and its general security. Yacoub and Lasserre's project, texts and photographs, conveys the long silencing of the architectural state and the landscapes in the region at that time.

During the Israeli occupation, houses and sometimes entire villages had been destroyed. Some populations, therefore, left their villages and relocated further north. Moreover, the area generates a sense of abandonment that Yacoub and Lasserre describe in one of their essays accompanying the photographs:

> It is only on the basis of the current struggles between populations that certain aspects of southern Lebanon can be perceived, like the sharp feeling of this region as an anomaly. This aspect is clearly perceived by the inhabitants of this region. These inhabitants suffer the arbitrary will of the Israelis, the abandonment of the Lebanese state, the consequences of the occupation, and the effects of the new world division of labor in the rural sector. And in their isolation, they try to resist these multiple forms of oppression. By all possible means, the inhabitants reject the stigmatization of southern Lebanon as a disaster region.[17]

Southern Lebanon is a particular site. Cut off from the rest of the country, this region was in a way separated from, while still being within, Lebanese territory. In Yacoub's photographs, it is disfigured by demolition; houses opened to the wind are still awaiting inhabitants long gone, while idyllic fields covered with grass and orchards are hiding minefields or former battlegrounds.

Elegiac Landscapes

The series of three photographs entitled *Elegiac Landscapes* were taken in the region of Marjayoun in Southern Lebanon in May 2001. The landform in this geographic area consists of successions of hills and plateaux, whose altitudes vary between 200 and 800 metres above sea level. Small towns and villages are scattered among the fields, generally along the peaks. The area is known for being an agricultural one, where tobacco, cereals, olives, citrus and bananas are grown (Figures 5.5, 5.6).

The three photographs are indeed three different views of the same landscape, a small, cultivated valley closed by two chains of hills, taken from different angles. As if, observed together, they illustrate the photographer's will to register a 360-degree view of this small valley, experimenting with the photographic medium by using a disposable camera modified with a plexiglas lens. They all reveal how cultivated and uncultivated fields alternate with small bushes and cypresses. Paths and stretches of roads are visible, running through the slope of the hills.

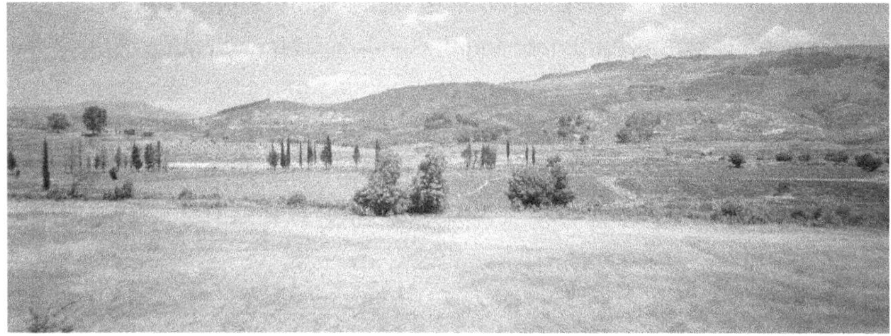

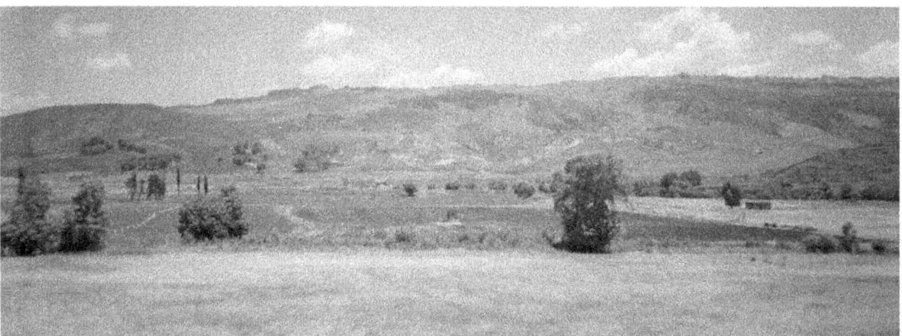

Figures 5.5 and 5.6 Paola Yacoub, *Elegiac Landscape*, Southern Lebanon, 2001. Chromogenic hand print, Aluminium, 35 × 94 cm each. Courtesy of the artist.

From the series, I would like especially to examine the second photograph, the one I described in the opening sequence of this chapter, in the light of landscape theory and of the concept of spectral evidence proposed by Ulrich Baer.[18] Its frame is closed by the hills in the background and opened by fallow land in the foreground. A second visual articulation in this landscape is initiated by an alignment of cypresses and pines delimitating the cultivated fields beyond them. Finally, a strong sense of symmetry is given to the picture by a path running exactly down the middle of the photograph, forming almost a straight line separating right and left sides. This image appears peaceful, yet its eerie stillness catches our attention and stimulates our critical response. This image poses the issue of the disarticulation in the legibility of this landscape. The viewer feels the need to connect with some specific extra-pictorial information, be it historical or cultural. Landscape is reckoned as a major genre in the history of art on which art historians, as Nicholas Green reveals, have taken on new approaches:

> On the one hand we have the apprehension of spatial/perceptual relations in terms of a well-established and self-assured repertoire: the debate about mimesis, the division of space into foreground, middle-ground, and horizon, and the naming of different modes of perspective, aerial as well as linear. On the other hand, we have the commitment to historical specificity. The question is: how far do these techniques and strategies add up to a schema of general analytical value, whether for art history itself or for disciplines, such as anthropology or geography, also intimately concerned with the perception and interpretation of space?[19]

Writing of the new developments in landscape painting in nineteenth-century France, Nicholas Green is arguing that art historians need to develop new strategies to integrate the formal and socio-historical axes. Green juxtaposes the formal and conventional critical language in which landscape as an aesthetic form is typically appraised with the recognition that these forms can and do encode historical and ideological specificities. In a similar vein, W. J. T. Mitchell links landscape and power, insisting on this interrelation between the representation of space, place and its historical narrative and actions.[20] Mitchell considers landscape as an instrument of cultural force that creates and sustains national and social identities. He remarks how a landscape embodies these narratives, whether readable or not: 'Landscape could be seen as the first cognitive encounter with a place, and an apprehension of its spatial vectors (thus, an appreciation of landscape may well include a reading – or an inability to read – its narrative tracks or symbolic features).'[21]

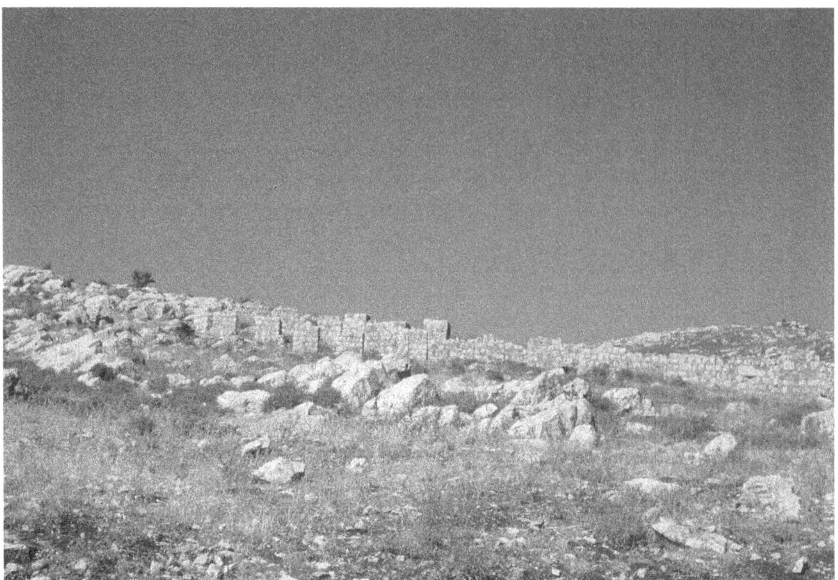

Figure 5.7 Paola Yacoub, *Cease fire line*. Southern Lebanon, 2001. Courtesy of the artist.

In order to understand Yacoub's aesthetic framing in her landscapes of Southern Lebanon, I want temporarily to leave this particular photograph and read as an excursus Yacoub and Lasserre's description of another landscape photograph taken in Southern Lebanon, in the area of Meadow in June 2002. Yacoub and Lasserre start by stating that 'Neither the subject nor the structure of the photo is special. It documents nothing. It is an anonymous image' (Figure 5.7).[22]

Systematically, Yacoub and Lasserre slowly distil few but significant elements of the historical background of the photograph, sometimes even withdrawing some of these same elements:

> It was taken in Southern Lebanon, at a border area between Lebanon and Israel. Today the region is more or less under the control of the Hezbollah. In our photo we are near the border, but we will not tell you here what a border is. Still, this photo documents nothing. It could have been taken anywhere. It is intransitive.[23]

And only after these preliminary remarks do Yacoub and Lasserre acknowledge the presence of some architectural elements and a stretch of road within the picture. Only then do they point these elements out, which indeed form the ground of their reflection.

> Let's suppose now that we learn that somebody has just been murdered here. The road finds itself suddenly accentuated. Its aspect changes completely. A whole new territorial equilibrium is set in motion. The road finds a singular expression in the event. The aspect is the event merged with the architecture. A free, subjectless expressiveness unfolds in front of our eyes.[24]

Hence, the two artists unfold their artistic protocol, explaining their thoughts about it and the elements – formal and historical – contained within a single photograph. The same process can apply to the photograph from *Elegiac Landscapes*. Yacoub and Lasserre give to this particular landscape the duality of either being considered as elegiac, an allusion to its stillness and reminding of some Italian landscapes, or as battlefield, what it has been in a past not so remote, as underlined by the pair:

> Certain landscapes of Southern Lebanon recall Italian genre paintings. One can also see them as territories for military operations, invaded twice since 1978, without counting the intensive bombing of 1976. One can also see them as fields exposed to the bombardments, or simply as fallow lands, after the collapse of the agricultural structures. The Litany valley takes on the aspect of both an elegiac setting and one of the most hotly contested battlefields of the recent wars. To see the latter aspect one need it merely locate [*sic*] the destroyed Israeli positions on the heights, the Hezbollah posts under the cover of the woods, the abandonment of many houses in the villages.[25]

This landscape actually shifts from one to the other representation, elegiac and battlefield. Shall we, therefore, reproach Yacoub for her aestheticizing of such a place referring to battlefields and conflicts over territoriality? Or is her practice a way of approaching facts too traumatic to be deliberately displayed with full assertion of past memory?

Ulrich Baer's discussion of photographs evoking trauma in terms of landscape art gives us a further insight into Yacoub's photographs. In a chapter of his book *Spectral Evidence* entitled 'To Give Memory a Place', Baer writes on Holocaust photography, and on how the sites of suffering, witness to atrocities, and the landscapes can become the support of a collective memory in the face of the failure of full recognition and memorialization. As both Holocaust landscapes and the Lebanese war landscapes photographed by Yacoub have specific burdens of memory, there can be forms of analogy. Baer's analysis, therefore, provides me with an important insight in the way I am looking at Yacoub's photographs of war landscapes. Baer offers a reading of an image taken by Dirk Reinartz of a clearing bordered with pines, on the location of the former extermination camp of Sobibor, and Mikael Levin's photograph of Nordlager Ohrdruf. Both Reinartz's (1995) and Levin's (1997) photographs do not show any physical evidence of past events connected to these two places and associated with their names. Reinartz depicts a clearing with pines, formatted in a large panorama leaving little importance to the sky. Baer notes how 'the exactitude devoted to portraying this place' sharply contrasts with 'the site's lack of conventional visual appeal and absence of identifiable markers'.[26] Also depicting a landscape, Levin's photograph displays this time not the closure but the vastness of a meadow. As Baer points out,

> They [the two photographs] contain no evidence of the sites' historical uses, and they rely explicitly on the aesthetic tradition of landscape art and [as I will explain] on the 'auratic experience of place' to commemorate the destruction of experience and memory.[27]

Baer acknowledges how these two images call for a historicizing or contextualizing of the image in terms of narratives.[28] Baer asserts that this necessity to get some extra-pictorial information comes from a Eurocentric and aesthetic approach to landscape mechanical reproductions. What Baer calls an 'auratic experience' requires, therefore, a new way of being looked at. Ulrich Baer's analysis of Mikael Levin's image of Ohrdruf concludes that the image does not narrate a story, although it does contain that same story:

> Although they are bereft of documentary information, however, these images nonetheless tell the truth. They challenge the notion of what constitutes knowledge by calling on our deep-seated trust in photography's reality effect and, thus showing us that really nothing is pictured there or, put differently, that nothing in this picture is real.[29]

Hence, Baer's examination of photographs that touch the mown event of the Holocaust belatedly is about the parallel between the way the traces of historical events are perceived by the camera – as a mechanically frozen moment – and the way that memory works psychologically either for those who experience it or for those who came before the landscape with historical knowledge. The dissociation takes place between representation and remembrance registered in a photographic image. A viewer not familiar with the specific political situation of Southern Lebanon can fail to observe the solicitation in Yacoub's photograph to contemplate the fact that beautiful, fertile fields' pictures can index political instability. Although the picture's aesthetic strategy might fail in the way that the viewer does not become aware of its significance, its apparent *emptiness* is striking. But, in the artists' common reflection, the shift between elegiac and battlefield leads to a further statement. Instead of looking in the picture for the representation of a landscape of war, Yacoub and Lasserre affirm that this latter historical truth cannot be found as such in what we see before our eyes. The viewer has to live with the idea that the change operates not at the level of the picture but at the level of the gaze. Yacoub and Lasserre build their reflection on these two notions, elegiac landscape versus battlefield:

> [But] these two aspects are not symmetrical. The first [elegiac] implies the total isolation of the landscape; the second [battlefield], the disparity of architectural and territorial elements in transit, like a military position on the top of a hill, a tumulus, the folds of a valley. All one now finds are elements. They alone can traverse the events of recent history, passing from one to the next. To the contrary, one does not find landscapes of war.[30]

Interestingly, both artists consider Beirut as no exception to the state of absence of landscapes of war. These landscapes are, therefore, never graspable as sites of war, and only an attentive eye can catch these elements and make sense of them. Yet, Yacoub and Lasserre imply that attempts to reconstruct them are doomed:

> The elements can no longer even associate to form a place, they are swept up into the events, separately from each other, in so many different perspectives, which they enter and leave according to the chance circumstances of life.[31]

Hence, for Yacoub and Lasserre, landscape is not inert. It has the connotation of combining not only space and place but also time and society, changing through historical events such as the creation of a new state or violent strife. It changes structure through human activities, too, as noted by Alan Baker: 'The plurality of cultures is reflected in the landscape, giving it its distinctive identities.'[32]

Beyond its history, this landscape has foremost a present, and an important social function. It represents indeed the means of survival of a mainly rural population. In Southern Lebanon, modernization and economic growth stagnated during the 1950s and the 1960s, a situation that went on throughout the Israeli occupation (1978–2000). Jala Makhzoumi gives to the landscape two aspects, an investigative one and an expansive one: 'As an open-ended, investigative framework, landscape frames rural culture, unfolds local perception and decodes traditional valuation of place. As an expansive, spatial framework, landscape becomes a medium for configuring multifaceted, humanized recovery narratives.'[33]

Thinking about battlefields, my first statement is that most non-urban sites of battles are remembered as such through the presence of memorials, or cemeteries for some. It is their respective monuments which, to me, make them appear as battlefields, which makes me see beyond the grass, beyond the trees and beyond what nature reclaimed from this site of human murderous activities. But, what if I were to be confronted with a landscape devoid of any physical markers of memory? How would I react? Would I get a sense or imagine the events that took place there?

By reflecting on their common practice, Yacoub and Lasserre make certain sensibilities emerge from the architectural and natural landscapes and how the elements of the territory circulate in Lebanon today:

> We present aesthetic practices, regimes of the gaze that are not played out in the artistic field. This work effects an intrusion. The intrusion of the architectural and territorial elements. It is a matter of introducing shifts which do not conform. [. . .] The idea is to allow this gaze, by the impact of the facts and the work of publication. [. . .] The subjects being treated are not without effects: they teach people to discriminate among the architectural and territorial elements. The interest of this field is to give rise to other architectural circulations.[34]

In terms of circulation of elements, to Yacoub architecture represents a structure, which, rather than being fixed, evolves through elements and events crossing it. To her, elements of architecture are turned to ruins when an event too strong overcomes them. Yacoub observes not only the violent changes – that she and Lasserre name 'city trauma' – but also the more subtle one, like renovation work of entire areas or expropriation. On the one hand, the act of destruction, the one that took place long before the taking of the shots, indicates a suffering of the urban fabric – implying a suffering of the social fabric, too – that cannot be shown at the moment of impact. Hence, Yacoub seeks symptoms or traces of this suffering. During our conversations, the artist quoted many times Wittgenstein's *Philosophical Remark* on pain, commenting on the notion of the hair: 'Can I imagine pains in the tips of my nails, or in my hair? Isn't that just as possible or impossible as it is to imagine a pain in any part of the body whatever in which I have none at the moment and cannot remember having had any?'[35] This idea, which became a long-term reflection throughout her artistic practice, makes us wonder how could the gap between certain traumatic historical events and traces left years after be linked? Yacoub tries to find a way of approaching places charged with traumatic memory, when events are too painful to be recounted. The blank objectivity performed by Yacoub's camera is real, while, in her *Elegiac*

Landscapes, violence is nowhere to be seen. It is, although, somewhere, embedded in the stillness of a landscape. To the viewer, the most disturbing aspect is indeed keeping up with the chain of events contained outside the picture.

A brief note on the notion of border

Before calling in the specificity of the border in Southern Lebanon, I would like to draw here a parallel between the circulation of territory Yacoub and Lasserre are negotiating in their project and an exhibition held in Paddington, Australia, in 2008. Called *The Resilient Landscape*, obviously drawing on Boris Cyrulnik's concept of resilience, curators Phillip George, David McNeill and Khaled Sabsabi decided to apply it to an exhibition bringing together artists who are both Lebanese and Australian.[36] The purpose of the exhibition was to reflect on how two events taking place in these two areas, so remote from each other – the so-called Cronulla race riots in December 2005 and the war in Lebanon in the summer of 2006 – do indeed not affect some similarity they might share.[37] The exhibition curators raised the issue of the artificiality of borders while explaining their exhibition concept:

> To state the obvious, borders are an artifice designed to both include and exclude. [. . .] The instability and porosity of borders, and hence the complex interdependency of seemingly bounded entities, is explored through an artistic survey of two distant border incidents whose geographical remoteness is belied by their political and cultural proximity.[38]

The events the exhibition *The Resilient Landscape* address, are, therefore, twofold. Not only does it convey a sense of violent events, but it also confronts the notion of borders and their artificiality. Whereas borders are often considered sites of strict separation, sometimes leading to zones devoid of movement, Yacoub sees these boundaries as sites of action. Yacoub's photographic series, therefore, is about crossings, intersections and their interaction: of countries, of conflicts, of populations of different origins. Far from being static territorial zones, frontiers are sites of action, often delimitating parts between states, sometimes creating lines of conflict. Hence, borders are considered symbolic territories of state control in a world becoming always more fluid through the globalization process.

Malcolm Anderson acknowledges how borders are predominant markers in the construction of national identity, what is generally considered as constitutive to the political identity of a modern state.[39] In Lebanon, this border and the occupation of the area around it during so many years led to a situation of fracture. This fracture does not only happen on a state level, between Lebanon and its neighbouring countries Israel and Syria, but also between the populations of Northern and Southern Lebanon. The poverty and marginalization of Southern Lebanon date back to the 1930s, to the demarcation of the border by French and British mandates.[40]

It is these issues that Yacoub and Lasserre raise in their project on Southern Lebanon. There exists a photograph by Yacoub displaying the crossing of three border areas: the Golan Heights, Southern Lebanon and Northern Israel. Both artists comment on it in terms of artificiality of the border, since there is nothing else to be seen than a continuous landscape:

> But these three regions embraced in the same gaze do not form so much a landscape as a synoptic picture, or table. A landscape forms a whole and is grasped all at once, whereas the elements of a table come and go, according to events, and do not necessarily add up to the whole. This photograph offers a synoptic table, dated September 2000. Nothing more.[41]

The Lebanon–Israeli boundary, today called *The Blue Line*, was designated by the UN in 1948 and follows almost the same trace as the border agreed between French and British mandates in 1923. It has been set in 2000 under UN Resolution 1701 as a withdrawal line, although it is usually designated as the effective border between Lebanon, Israel and Syria, guarded by UN soldiers.

In 1923, this final agreement on the border issue between French and British partly ignored topographical natural obstacles, or worked to secure vital resources. Even though a joint Anglo-French commission was mandated to properly demarcate the border, the line agreed upon never materialized on the ground.[42]

During the Second World War, the area became a site of conflict when the British, afraid of repercussion the French collaboration with the Nazi regime during the Vichy government could have in the Middle East, decided to invade Lebanon and Syria. In 1943, Lebanon gained its independence from the French Mandate. Hence, 2000 is important since it marked an accessibility to the border: not the frontier itself, which still remains closed, but the area close to it, which used to form the security zone. As underlined by David Eshel, the disagreement over the border is far from being solved, as 'according to international experts, some sixty percent of the 120 km borderline is not delineated in any formal agreement between Israel and Lebanon'.[43]

As I have pointed out many times already, the issue of territory is not an innocent one. Territorial boundaries generally address two considerations: a geographic one and a demographic one. The demographic one implies, as argued by Allen Buchanan and Margaret Moore, a political authority: 'Questions of political and legal authority are inextricably bound up with the issue of territory because of the close, interconnected relationship between territory and governance.'[44]

The Great Wall

Taken in June 2001, a further series of photographs by Yacoub revolves on the fortifications erected by the British in 1940 at the border between Palestine and Lebanon. During a journey with curator Catherine David around Southern Lebanon, Paola Yacoub saw for the first time these lines of scattered concrete blocks in the landscape. Both wondered what these lines were or represented, and Yacoub took many shots of them that day. It was only after their return in Beirut that they found out that this fortification line, looking more like a ceasefire line, dates back to the Mandate.

Afraid of how the Second World War would spread in the Middle East, the British used these fortifications to protect Palestine from the French stationed in Lebanon. France was at that time under Vichy government and could potentially become an enemy because of its collaboration with the Axis powers. Yacoub's series displays what can barely be seen as a fortification today: in a state of abandon, victims of natural elements, these alignments of disordered blocks do not look like a threatening wall, but more as remnants of a certain past in the area. In their writing about it, Yacoub and Lasserre stress that, sixty years after being put in place, the Lebanese can finally see them for the first time.

These fortification lines trigger a reflection on the trace, as argued by the artists: 'Why are they seen at present? It is not simply a question of reading the traces that the colonial power left on the territory, but of showing the rise of a new aspect today.'[45] This line, which looks so awkward nowadays, nonetheless illustrates how a colonial power does mobilize forces in a given landscape by durably leaving its imprint on it.

Yacoub's gaze rests on the architectural details of the fortification lines. With Lasserre she remarks how their shape does not raise any particular interest: 'Stone blocks aligned in staggered rows', looking 'like residues of some abandoned worksite'.[46] Like *Elegiac Landscapes, Now The Great Wall of China in Southern*

Lebanon – the name Yacoub and Lasserre gave to this series – stimulates interest when its narrative comes into play:

> They aroused no interest, not the slightest curiosity. Why indeed should they? [. . .] As though we were supposed to be concerned about all the unfinished or abandoned constructions that dot southern Lebanon. [. . .] But these blocks now appear as former colonial military fortifications. And only since the moment of Israeli withdrawal. Perhaps because southern Lebanon, which in theory has been liberated, still remains beneath the control of others – namely Syria, via the Lebanese state. Perhaps because the colonial past surfaces in the repeated formatting of this region as a battlefield. Thus, these fortifications run through the political space of southern Lebanon, into which the borders also plunge.[47]

There is an important parallel here to be drawn between this defensive line in Southern Lebanon and the erection, in the early 1940s, of concrete blockhouses on the Atlantic coast by Nazi Germany. Paul Virilio's *Bunker Archeology* extensively examines these blockhouses and their meaning in the generic context of war. Virilio notes the role played by fortifications in the case of a violent conflict:

> The fortification answers to the accidental, the duel between arms and armour leaves its mark on the organization of territory by progress in its means and methods, by the potentialities of its inventions – war is thus present in peacetime. A history unravels itself parallel to the history of civilian production; powers and energies develop ceaselessly in the constantly renewed perspective of conflict, but this production, secret and surprising, is ignored.[48]

By encountering these physical remains, Paola Yacoub uncovers a hidden aspect of the past. War is therefore always present in peacetime, in the landscape, and it is this relationship between war and peace that I would like to underline here. Between war and peace there is considerable permeability and the presence of these fortifications reminds us of their overlap. There is an attempt to master or control the landscape, which has deep political and ideological implications. Their function is narrowly tied to a specific terrain's spatiality, which contradicts their inertia in their appearance of useless, unordered collections of poured concrete blocks (Figure 5.8).

Walls always have great significance in historical discourse, but also in the verbal and visual ones, as remarked by art historian Michael Moore: 'It is my thesis that, in addition to their versatile physical functions, walls possess an immense measure of signification and that these two realms – the concrete and the symbolic – interact with each other.'[49] Walls are by definition impenetrable, and assure a defensive function, but in the case of the 1940 British fortifications

Figure 5.8 Paola Yacoub and Michel Lasserre, *Now the Great Wall of China in Southern Lebanon*, Lebanon, 2000. C-print, 50 × 75 cm. Courtesy of the artists.

in Southern Lebanon, these latter raise another question: those of the indeterminacy of the wall. Both artists touch upon this issue while describing these walls. They even conclude that, although they are part of the landscape, it might be better to decide not to see them, to ignore their existence and, moreover, their significance:

> The architecture of the wall gives no indication of its orientation. Composed of regular blocks set in staggered rows, it is not oriented like bastions, observation posts or loopholes, which point in the direction from which the attack is expected. The wall turns as you wish, its orientation belongs to its aspects, and not to its form. We can see the wall as a prefiguration of the border between Lebanon and Israel. We can also decide not to see it.[50]

Playing on the signification of the wall, Yacoub and Lasserre refer to the Kafkaesque considerations on the Great Wall of China. Yacoub and Lasserre quote, for example, this passage from Kafka's essay, which calls for a comparison to their case study of Southern Lebanon:

> But how can a wall protect if it is not a continuous structure? Not only can such a wall not protect, but what there is of it is in perpetual danger. These blocks of wall left standing in deserted regions could be easily pulled down again and again by the nomads, especially as these tribes, rendered apprehensive by the

> building operations, kept changing their encampments with incredible rapidity, like locusts, and so perhaps had a better general view of the progress of the wall than we, the 'builders'.[51]

Written in March 1917, only six years after the end of the Ch'ing dynasty, Kafka's fragmentary essay 'Constructing the Great Wall of China' emerged despite the fact that the novelist had never set foot in China. Kafka's text attempts to give an objective account of the construction of the Great Wall. Yet, at the same time, it reflects on the functioning of imperial institutions, critically pointing out its failures.[52]

The narrator in Kafka's essay mentions how the 2,400-kilometre-long Great Wall was originally planned to protect the Chinese against the so-called Barbarian people of the north. Interestingly, Kafka's essay avoids direct references to the new China and its post-revolutionary malaise. Rolf Goebel gives the following interpretation of Kafka's silence on the new Chinese regime: 'Kafka's refusal to offer unequivocal statements on China resembles this attempt to delineate an ambiguous space for China beyond definitive statements and interpretive closure.'[53]

Kafka's silence on the new Chinese regime reminds me of the official silencing of the war in Lebanon. Hence, Yacoub's photographs of the Great Wall try to denounce this silencing of the political issue of Southern Lebanon. Goebel points out how Kafka's silence on Chinese politics is expressed by his writing style throughout his essay: 'Kafka breaks off his stream of writing, approaching silence and nondiscourse, a decision that can be seen as an effective counterstrategy to the interpretive closure, impositions of definitive meanings, and exercises of political hegemony typical of many traditional orientalists.'[54]

In my view, Kafka's approach of breaking off his stream of writing draws a further parallel with Yacoub's series. The artist experiments with the photographic medium, by letting silenced elements linger like fragments on the surface of her photographs.

Now that I have described three series of photographs by Paola Yacoub, one on the Holiday Inn in Beirut, the others on Elegiac Landscape and the Great Wall, both in Southern Lebanon, I would like to discuss the artist's practice. As noted earlier, Yacoub's practice focuses on architectural fabric, rarely portraying human beings. Her work nonetheless displays landscape carved out by human intervention and architectural features. Allusion to the deep affects of political imbroglio on human beings is always implied, through the narrative of a landscape, for example. Yet, it never reveals their cognitive contents and perceptual properties as such. Even so, this visual ambiguity provides a highly political framework with which the viewer is confronted, sometimes unwillingly. Yacoub returns the aesthetic to a silenced compatibility with the historical. Traces of the historical are present, scattered elements in her representations inviting the viewer to find them and make sense of them.

The artist's practice goes against the Lebanese political will either to forget or to restore the past of the country. Whereas her photographs give to architectural elements a value, a sense of being preserved for generations, architectural wounds of war are being effaced by some large-scale reconstruction projects. Reconstruction, in that case, does imply destruction of the remains, even from ancient civilizations, a situation Yacoub witnessed on a daily basis while working with archaeologists in Downtown Beirut. Yacoub's experimental practice, which can already be found in her series *Summer 88*, profited from her diploma project at the Architectural Association. Yacoub's main reflection was to experiment with different objects put in water and observe the resulting effects. 'Put things into water | See what happens'. This experimental way of approaching architecture was first not appreciated by her examiners, who referred her. She could later prove that she was using architectural theory calculations in her work, and passed. The artist underlines how the 'put things into water' is still today the performative part of her practice, as, for example, experimenting with new cameras or framing her pictures in an unexpected way. The 'see what happens' represents the discursive, interpretative part of her practice, the part with which she has been struggling the most. For a long time, she was unable to find the appropriate language to describe it. She was stumbling over language, especially since she was trying to transpose the 'see what happens' to the fabric of Beirut and, more generally, to the generic framework of Lebanon. It is through the reading of Wittgenstein's *Tractatus Logico-Philosophicus* (1922), on which was partly based her common practice with Michel Lasserre, that she could begin to articulate the interpretative part of her work. Wittgenstein's quest for an ideal language in philosophy was driven by the fact that ordinary language might misrepresent reality.[55] Wittgenstein commented to a number of people that the origin of the *Tractatus* came from his reading of a court trial in Paris in the newspapers in 1914. The courtroom case was about a traffic accident, and the reconstitution of the facts was carried out through the use of scale models – dolls, model automobiles and buses – during the trial. Soon, it became impossible to accurately reconstruct and describe this particular event in detail. While entering into details, Wittgenstein noticed that there would have been a plurality of possible descriptions for one unique, single reality. In his book *Wittgenstein*, François Schmitz reflects on this infinity of possible reconstitutions of the accident in the courtroom. Schmitz points out that the small objects or *modèle réduit* used can only show 'what *could have been* the case'.[56] But in no way can this state reproduce the state of reality as it took place. And Schmitz concludes that 'something simple cannot be described, one can only *name* it'.[57] Yacoub and Lasserre's approach relies on their decision to apply this failure of description to the fabric of Beirut and Lebanon.

Through the taking of still photographs, Paola Yacoub's work operates within the space or place and memory on the one hand, and with the absence of the markers of time on the other hand. Although the artist does travel around the country to specific locations, her photographs do not convey this sense of movement; they remain fixed within their specific space. Some of these places have personal memories; others are sites of forgetfulness. The empty streets and the idyllic landscapes, therefore, become the field rather than the borders of divisions of space. The visual ambiguity of her work, this apparent stillness, displays the artist's unwillingness to directly represent post-war specific elements and her own powerlessness in face of the war and the confrontation to its memories. There is a sense that her photographs convey to the audience a perception of the state of amnesia ruling over these places. Remembering – in time – becomes an act of connecting one's memories of war to the places or objects chosen by the artist.

Concluding words

Since I first began to think about post-traumatic art in the cities of Sarajevo and Beirut, ways of thinking about the relations between art and place have gone in new directions. I have focused on the concept of *wounded* places. These have proliferated in these last years in cities across Syria, Lebanon's neighbouring country, while former ones try to recover from profound disruption. Even after the 'stitches' of recovery have been removed, both places and their inhabitants are still left with indelible scars. Sarajevo and Beirut have been shaped by conflicts and the different interpretations of their histories. Hence, in addition to the notion of the post-traumatic, this book has outlined two specific major lines of reflection. Besides being clearly sites of trauma, in the sense of extreme events endured over a prolonged period involving violent assaults, death, disappearance and reduction of life to the barest, this book has used the double axis of space and time to examine both the situation in the two cities involved and the four artistic practices I selected. This introduces a new dimension into the field of trauma studies, which has tended to deal with arrested timelessness and buried space. The spatial axis arises from the fact that the artworks I have analysed can be read as coming from or dealing with the situation of exile and expatriation. At the same time, the artworks involve a sense of temporality through their preoccupations with history, memory, remembrance, invisibility and the unsayable.

There is in addition the spatiality involved by the geographical separation of the two cities through their own lines of conflict. Sarajevo was encircled and separated from the territory around the city and the rest of the country so that the military stranglehold also functioned as a newly imposed border, enclosing, separating and redefining the city as a novel entity isolated from what had hitherto been passages and exchanges locally and even internationally. Beirut's spatiality was otherwise redefined because the city was clearly cut in two halves with different areas of the city becoming inaccessible to each other. Each city, therefore, bears a different imprint of separation through systemic violence.

Another axis has been memory and remembrance. A central question for this book has been how war, understood not as military action but as civilian experience of prolonged traumatizing violation of the conditions of life, remembered (or not) is aesthetically mediated.

The development of memory studies, distinct from traditional historical understandings of the past, only indicates how complex 'memory' is as a term. A classic definition of memory such as Samuel Hynes's as 'the mental faculty by which we preserve or recover our pasts, and also the events recovered'[1] completely underestimates that complexity by seeing it only as a mental faculty rather than one mediated by many personal, hence psychological, and cultural factors. Scholars have moved beyond the individual psychology of memory to address its socialized forms, collective or cultural memory.

But even there, memory seems unstable and unreliable. In his seven-volume collection of essays, *Les lieux de mémoire* (Realms of Memory), French historian Pierre Nora outlines a thesis on the end of a tradition of collective memory through the increasing confusion between history and memory in times when history is often considered an explanation of the past.[2] Whereas Nora concentrates on *lieux de mémoire* associated with specific moments of French history, his perception nevertheless gives a general insight into the way modern society is trying to make sense of the complicated and disrupted relation between past and present. Nora dwells upon a collective memory which, shattered by modernity, was turned by historians into dead traces, devoid of ritual, and how, in this loss, we are trying to recreate memory through sites of memory. Nora's thinking is articulated, on the one hand, by memory as part of a lost tradition such as peasant culture and, on the other hand, by official historical narratives. This disruption between the two provokes, postmodernly, a crisis leading to a kind of memory fever. It is, however, the interaction between history and memory that creates sites of memory. Although Nora's definition of *lieux de mémoire* is broad, taking into consideration physical places as well as objects within which a crystallization of memory can take place, there are two particular aspects of his concept in which I am interested here. First, Nora considers that, in order to have a site of memory, 'a will to remember must be present initially'.[3] A commemoration, therefore, can become a *lieu de mémoire* by briefly interrupting the continuous flow of history – Nora specifies the commemorative minute of silence as example. Second, besides underlining the topographical aspect of some sites of memory, Nora emphasizes their functional dimension. Speaking of some veterans' organizations, Nora remarks that these '*lieux de mémoire* are clearly intended to preserve an incommunicable experience and are doomed to vanish with those who shared that experience'.[4] Using these two notions, I would argue that, due to the siege, Sarajevo, while being part of the Bosnian collective memory as a site of trauma, can also be turned into a site of memory through official commemoration. Moreover, the artists who create artworks have elaborated something different alongside commemoration; these artworks become *memory works*. Nora's *lieux de mémoire* allows me to view Dakić, Bajević, Joreige and Yacoub as working between trauma and cultural memory, generating artistic forms to address both the shock and its amnesia, while stressing the necessity for its passage into a public form as something other than dead history, as something that might survive those who lived through it, able to transmit some sense of it to further generations.

The event of 6 April 2012 in Sarajevo is such an example of a collective act of historical remembrance interwoven with a specific artistic memory work. That day was marked by the commemoration of the start of the war in Bosnia and Herzegovina twenty years earlier; 11,541 red plastic chairs were aligned on Titova Street, between the Presidency and the Mosque Ali Pasha, forming an installation called *Sarajevo Red Line*. Each chair symbolized one victim of the siege, forming a red river on which inhabitants of Sarajevo could mourn or remember a lost one, having the opportunity to leave flowers or gifts. Most poignant were the 643 little chairs, suggesting the slain children who were victims of the siege. The main initiator of this artistic commemoration was the film and theatre director Haris Pašović. Red, the colour of blood, spread too many times in these years, is still recalled by the presence of the Sarajevo Roses: the shelling impacts in the shape of flowers on the pavement on many streets across the city. Attempting to cover them with a kind of red asphalt highlighted them instead. Moreover, red is evocative of the colour no one should have worn during the siege while walking on the street, since it would have attracted the snipers' attention. Press agencies widely reported the comment of Asja Rasavać, an inhabitant from Sarajevo in tears at the sight of the chairs: 'It's as if the whole tragedy materialised, became visible. One cannot even describe the feeling. It's not hatred. It's not anger. It's just endless sadness.'[5]

Through the motif of the chairs and the act of commemoration, *Sarajevo Red Line* engages in a way with Doris Salcedo's installation *Noviembre 6 y 7* (2002), the artwork on which Mieke Bal grounds her theory of the traumatogenic event in her book *Of What One Cannot Speak*. Salcedo used the façade of a gallery – Alexander and Bonin in New York – for her 53-hour performance, where 280 chairs, all different, appeared, commemorating, hour after hour, the mass killing that took place 17 years earlier in Colombia. As Bal remarks on the significance attached to the motif of the chairs, 'These chairs are not exactly traces. But they do bear witness; they propose evidence of something, a violence that happened in the past. They do this by embodying a statement of absence.'[6] Following Bal's attempt to make trauma less psychological and pathological and belong more to the realm of politics, *Sarajevo Red Line*, through bearing witness to the absence of people killed in the siege, reconnects a traumatic past with the political conditions of its occurrence and the politics of remembering certain people, places and situations in an acutely social way. *Sarajevo Red Line* does not only temporally establish a designated space to remember, it creates the possibility of having such a space, a site of memory, where the act of remembrance can take place.

Using various media such as video, performance and photography, the four artists whose work I have considered are addressing a wide range of issues: public history versus personal experience, heritage of war and memory, without forgetting the landscape of their surroundings, shaping environment through the perspectives of local and global power relationships. I have been collecting site-specific stories that the artworks convey. I tried to give the sense of how much the geography and the history of these places are closely entwined with people's lives. The inscription, mediation and transformation of memory took place over time and generation. In Lebanon there is a sense that the history has fallen prey to generational amnesia. While reading Craig Larkin's recent analysis of second-generational narratives in Lebanon, and particularly of 'war residual memory', I have the sense of a presence, in these artworks, not of narratives preceding their birth but of particular narratives or images connected to the artists' childhood and their memories of it.[7]

It seems that the presence of childhood memories becomes an element embedded in works that are about more immediate political events. A precise image either affected them or had a long-lasting impact on their deep personal memories. The articulation within an artwork, of the wounded place, passes through an image of the artists' childhood. These images thus bridge the moment of the lived experience and the moment of its remembering.

Dakić went back to her favourite book of tales she remembered reading as a child, and could not rest until she got hold of a copy of it, integrating these narratives into her *Autoportrait*. Through the narratives that marked her as a child, Dakić challenges the dissemination of the senses and highlights the transitional nature of language. Bajević went back to the stitching/embroidery activities she may have witnessed many times as a child in former Yugoslavia: a group of women gathering at someone's home in the afternoon and chatting together while concentrating on their embroidery work. Joreige goes back to family stories she either heard about or indirectly witnessed as a child, reflecting on her own grandmother's youth. Finally, Yacoub had her mind impregnated by the Holiday Inn as a child, which today not only symbolizes her decision to study architecture but still shapes her artistic practice. These images are integrated in their grown-up reflection on the events they lived through or stood by. They invoke a deeper past in works about more recent events. They suggest a kind of layering of various pasts and the deeper one seems to emerge to provide a story of an association for the artist to contain the newer more violent, or even traumatic memory.

Another aspect I would like to underline is the invisibility that takes place at different levels in these artworks and its connection to memory: the invisibility of the subject's gaze in *Autoportrait*, the invisibility of refugees, even IDPs in Bosnia and Herzegovina, and the invisibility of something that was once a home and was transformed into a different space, Jaffa, the contemporary place remains invisible throughout Joreige's *A Journey* towards the past. Yacoub retains traces of war as invisible in order to negotiate the experience of war. Hence, out of the artists' attention of the otherwise invisible they create memory: memories of people, events or places that did exist or take place in the past, but are, in the contemporary present, kept alive through the artworks.

Memory has become a central issue in the transition taking place in a contemporary landscape, which undergoes perpetual changes, sometimes violent ones. As Andreas Huyssen has emphasized, memory can be a transitional link between a violent past and a better, more peaceful future. He writes, 'As particular nations struggle to create democratic politics in the wake of history or mass exterminations, apartheids, military dictatorships and totalitarianism, they are faced, as Germany has been and still is since World War II, with the unprecedented task of securing the legitimacy and future of their emergent polity by finding ways to commemorate and adjudicate past wrongs.'[8] Thus, Huyssen takes memory into a third space beyond its relation to history, its relation to even deeper personal memories. Huyssen makes memory a political issue in which the nature of the commemoration will shape the future. This includes being able not merely to remember but to adjudicate. The artists I have studied are not directly engaged in judgements as such. But a sense of adjudication might emerge precisely from the fact that they refuse to allow absence to remain, invisibility to persist and oblivion to continue.

More than inscribing itself alongside the vast issues of trauma, memory, history and art, this book has provided a study of an art that came into being through the experience of violence and suffering in the everyday. These embodied, aesthetic practices catch individual experiences that do not particularly rely on the scheme of historicism and the inherent belatedness of trauma. This book aims to reconnect the traumatogenic events with their political and social conditions of occurrences. The artworks do not produce a vicarious trauma in their viewers. They call for another kind of reading, materializing an absence or oblivion into a kind of perception close to memory. These works preserve a certain intimacy with the symptoms of war or with particular remembered events, conveying some disparate and fragmented elements of a specific lived experience – the journey, the landscape, the alienated subject and the performance. Thus, they add to the notion of time and space present in the artworks the artists' connection to particular places, not only topographical ones – Beirut and Sarajevo – but also places that are themselves the sites of memory and continuing memory work.

Notes

Introduction

1 Founded in 1299, the Ottoman Empire once ruled over most of South-Western Europe, Western Asia, the Caucasus, North Africa and the Horn of Africa. Its capital was Constantinople, modern-day Istanbul, and thus was the hinge between East and West for many centuries. In the sixteenth century, its forces were at the gates of Vienna, although they were defeated there. Declining during the nineteenth century, the Ottoman Empire allied itself with Germany during the First World War and after the defeat, its territories were partitioned by the Treaty of Sèvres in 1918. The Turkish War of Independence followed (1919–22) that led to the establishment of a modern democratic state of Turkey, and the Sultanate and the Caliphate were abolished in 1922 and 1924 respectively.

2 According to this treaty, Croatia, Slovenia, Bosnia and Herzegovina and the region of Vojvodina were to become part of the Austro-Hungarian Empire, whereas Serbia, Montenegro and Macedonia stayed in the Ottoman Empire. It was only in 1918, after the First World War, that all these federations were combined to create the 'First Yugoslavia', with a rigid centralist system established in Belgrade. 'Second Yugoslavia' was reunited after the Second World War, under the communist leadership of Marshal Josip Broz Tito.

3 The French Mandate for Syria and Lebanon (1923–43/46) was established by the League of Nations when the Ottoman Empire was partitioned between the Great Powers. Against the background of uprisings and conflicts, French authority was eventually established. The French divided the areas into six states: Damascus, Aleppo, Alawites, Jabal Druze, Sanjak of Alexandretta and the State of Greater Lebanon. In 1943 two states were formed when the French Mandate was ended: Syria and Lebanon.

4 Bosnia and Herzegovina was formerly a region of the country of Yugoslavia. It had been formed in the aftermath of the First World War as the Kingdom of Serbs, Croats and Slovenes and then renamed the Kingdom of Yugoslavia (union of Slavic peoples) in 1929. It was invaded in 1941 by Axis powers (Nazi Germany, Italy and their allies). The resistance movement eventually declared a Federal Republic in 1943 which was recognized as Federal People's Republic of Yugoslavia in 1946 with a communist government under partisan leader General Tito. Renamed the Socialist Federal Republic of Yugoslavia it contained six republics: Bosnia and

Herzegovina, Croatia, Macedonia, Montenegro, Slovenia and Serbia. In the 1980s, Yugoslavia began to break up along these borderlines leading to the Yugoslav Wars with conflicts well into the twenty-first century. Independence for each of the countries, finally including Kosovo as separate from Serbia, was completed only in 2008.

5 Florian Bieber, 'Bosnia-Herzegovina and Lebanon: Historical Lessons of Two Multireligious States', *Third World Quarterly* 21 (2000), p. 270.

6 Gijs van Hensbergen, *Guernica: The Biography of a Twentieth-Century Icon* (London: Bloomsbury, 2004), p. 3. Emphasis mine.

7 Jean Baudrillard, *The Gulf War Did Not Take Place*, trans. Paul Patton (Bloomington: Indiana University Press, 1995), p. 85.

8 See Carl von Clausewitz, *On War*, ed. and trans. Michael Howard and Peter Paret (London: Campbell, 1993).

9 Michel Foucault, '7 January 1976', in *Society Must Be Defended: Lectures at the Collège de France, 1975–1976*, ed. Mauro Bertani and Alessandro Fontana, trans. David Macey (London: Penguin Books, 2004), pp. 15–16.

10 Ingo W. Schröder and Bettina E. Schmidt, 'Violent Imaginaries and Violent Practices', in *Anthropology of Violence and Conflict*, ed. Bettina E. Schmidt and Ingo W. Schröder (London: Routledge, 2001), p. 4.

11 This figure is contested, as Phalangist militants are believed to have killed twenty-eight people and wounded nineteen others. Samir Khalaf, *Civil and Uncivil Violence in Lebanon: A History of the Internalization of Human Contact* (New York: Columbia University Press, 2002), p. 229.

12 Lina Kathib, *Lebanese Cinema: Imagining the Civil War and Beyond* (London: I.B. Tauris, 2008), p. xx.

13 Sarah Rogers, 'Forging History, Performing Memory: Walid Raad's The Atlas Project', *Parachute* 108 (2002), p. 68.

14 In spite of the signing of the Dayton Agreement in Paris on 14 December 1995, the siege was not lifted until 26 February 1996, when the northwest passage to the city was reopened and the Vagosca and Ilyas districts were liberated. Suada Kapić, *The Siege of Sarajevo 1992–1996* (Sarajevo: FAMA, 2000), p. 143.

15 See Chapter 1, *Setting the (Art) Scenes*, pp. 21–49.

16 These artists' practices include more traditional patterns than video practice, such as embroidery, painting on canvas and photography. They are Mladen Miljanović, Nenad Malešević, Radenko Milak, Zvjedzdana Veselinović, Ana Banja, Boris Glacomin, Miodrag Manojlović, Sandra Dukić.

17 Walter Benjamin, *One-Way Street*, trans. Edmund Jephcott and Kingsley Shorter (London: New Left Books, 1979), p. 45.

18 Ibid., pp. 351–2. Emphasis in original.

19 Walter Benjamin, *Illuminations*, trans. Harry Zorn (New York: Schocken, 1969), p. 261.

20 Jean Said Makdisi, *Beirut Fragments: A War Memoir* (New York: Persea Books, 1990), p. 19.

21 Ibid., p. 22.

22 Ibid., p. 28.

23 The term 'trauma' itself derives from the eponymous Greek word, and means 'wound'. Trauma originally refers to a physical wound, an injury or physical harm. In the seventeenth-century medical vocabulary, it used to designate a 'bodily injury caused by an external agent'. The idiom "trauma" has since shifted to the mental realm, understood in psychiatric literature as a wound of the mind and became an increasingly debated term, both in its understanding and its application process, particularly in the field of literary and cinema studies.

24 *The Diagnostic and Statistical Manual for Mental Disorders* lists possible traumatic experiences, particularly contemplating: 'Traumatic events that are experienced directly include, but are not limited to, military combat, violent personal assault (sexual assault, physical attack, robbery, mugging), being kidnapped, being taken hostage, terrorist attack, torture, incarceration as a prisoner of war or in a concentration camp, natural or manmade disasters, severe automobile accidents, or being diagnosed with a life-threatening illness. For children, sexually traumatic events may include developmentally inappropriate sexual experiences without threatened or actual violence or injury.' American Psychiatric Association, *Diagnostic and Statistical Manual of Mental Disorders*, fourth edition (Washington, DC: American Psychiatric Association, 1994), p. 424.

25 The name shell shock refers to the splintering shell and its consequent shock on the brain of soldiers. Shell shock is connected to the mechanization of artillery and its impact on the soldier's behaviour and level of stress following the battles. Its symptoms and signs as a traumatic neurosis have been largely observed and analysed on soldiers involved in trench warfare during the First World War. For an analysis of shell shock, see Peter Leese, *Shell Shock: Traumatic Neurosis and the British Soldiers of the First World War* (Basingstoke: Palgrave Macmillan, 2002).

26 American Psychiatric Association, *Diagnostic and Statistical Manual of Mental Disorder*, p. 424.

27 Mary Kaldor, *New and Old Wars: Organized Violence in a Global Era* (Stanford: Stanford University Press, 2007), p. 9.

28 João Biehl and Peter Locke, 'Deleuze and the Anthropology of Becoming', *Current Anthropology* 51, no. 3 (June 2010), p. 332.

29 Charlotte Eager, 'The War Is Over but Sarajevans Cannot Find the Peace They Seek', *Daily Telegraph*, 6 September 2003.

30 Hirsch goes on with his argument: 'Its significance for the purpose of this argument transcends the literal referencing of any particular experience of trauma or vicarious trauma – of surviving atrocity, witnessing it, or seeing images of it – and

lies, rather, in the staking out, in the language of various media, of a discursive space pertinent to all these experiences. One may be traumatized by an encounter with the Holocaust, one may be unable to assimilate a memory or an image of atrocity, but the discourse of trauma – as one encounters it in conversation, in reading, in film – gives one a language with which to begin to represent the failure of representation that one has experienced.' Joshua Hirsch, *Afterimage: Film, Trauma and the Holocaust* (Philadelphia: Temple University Press, 2004), p. 18.

31 Hirsch, *Afterimage*, p. 19.

32 In her book *Unclaimed Experience*, Cathy Caruth writes on the belatedness and delayed re-enactment of the past: 'Trauma seems to be much more than a pathology, or the simple illness of a wounded psyche: it is always the story of a wound that cries out, that addresses us in the attempt to tell us of a reality that is not otherwise available. This truth, in its delayed appearance and its belated address, cannot be linked only to what is known, but also what remains unknown to our actions and our language.' Cathy Caruth, *Unclaimed Experience: Trauma, Narrative, History* (Baltimore and London: The Johns Hopkins University Press, 1996), p. 11.

33 Ernst van Alphen, *Caught by History: Holocaust Effects in Contemporary Art, Literature and Theory* (Stanford: Stanford University Press, 1997).

34 Van Alphen, *Caught by History*, p. 10.

35 Griselda Pollock, *After-affects | After-images: Trauma and the Aesthetic Transformation in the Virtual Feminist Museum* (Manchester: Manchester University Press, 2013), p. 20.

36 Veena Das, *Life and Words: Violence and the Descent into the Ordinary* (Berkeley: University of California Press, 2007), p. 103.

37 Ibid., p. 102.

38 Jill Bennett, *Empathic Vision: Affect, Trauma and Contemporary Art* (Stanford: Stanford University Press, 2005), pp. 3 and 4.

39 Ibid., p. 21. Emphasis in original.

40 Mieke Bal, *Of What One Cannot Speak: Doris Salcedo's Political Art* (Chicago: University of Chicago Press, 2010).

41 Ibid., pp. 211–12. Emphasis in original.

42 Kristine Stiles, *Concerning Consequences: Studies in Art, Destruction and Trauma* (Chicago: Chicago University Press, 2016), p. 23.

Chapter 1

1 Lewis Mumford, 'What Is a City?', in *The City Reader*, ed. Richard T. LeGates and Frederic Stout (London: Routledge, 2000), pp. 93–4 (American spelling of the original retained).

2 Ida Susser and Jane Schneider, 'Wounded Cities', in *Wounded Cities: Destruction and Reconstruction in a Globalized World* (Oxford: Berg, 2003), p. 16.
3 In cities overwhelmed by displaced persons the acceleration of the process of ownership restitution positioned returnees claiming their rights to property against displaced people. Both groups were competing over scarce resources: the displaced for the right to settle in the new place of residence and the returnees for the recognition of their ownership. See Christophe Solioz and Svebor Dizdanevic, *Ownership Process in Bosnia and Herzegovina* (Zug: Karl Popper Foundation, 2001).
4 Peter Andreas, *Blue Helmets and Black Markets: The Business of Survival in the Siege of Sarajevo* (Ithaca and London: Cornell University Press, 2008), p. 32.
5 Ibid., pp. 58–64.
6 Martin Coward, 'Urbicide in Bosnia', in *Cities, War and Terrorism: Towards an Urban Geopolitics*, ed. Stephen Graham (Oxford: Blackwell, 2004), p. 158.
7 Ivana Maček, *Sarajevo under Siege: Anthropology in Wartime* (Philadelphia: University of Pennsylvania Press, 2009), p. 63.
8 Antonius C. G. M. Robben and Carolyn Nordstrom, 'The Anthropology and Ethnography of Violence and Sociopolitical Conflict', in *Fieldwork under Fire: Contemporary Studies of Violence and Survival*, ed. Antonius C. G. M. Robben and Carolyn Nordstrom (Berkeley: University of California Press, 1995), p. 3.
9 Andras Riedlmayer, 'The War on People and the War on Culture', *The New Combat: A Journal of Reason and Resistance*, no. 3 (Autumn 1994), p. 16.
10 Coward, 'Urbicide in Bosnia', p. 161.
11 Said Makdisi, *Beirut Fragments*, p. 54.
12 Aseel Sawalha, 'Healing the Wounds of the War: Placing the War-Displaced in Postwar Beirut', in *Wounded Cities: Destruction and Reconstruction in a Globalized World*, ed. Jane Schneider and Ida Susser (Oxford: Berg, 2003), p. 271.
13 Sarah Rogers, 'Postwar Art and the Historical Roots of Beirut's Cosmopolitanism' (PhD diss., MIT, 2008), p. 164.
14 Dušan Babić, 'Journalism in Post-Dayton Bosnia: How to Make the Media More Responsible', in *Reconstructing Multiethnic Societies: The Case of Bosnia-Herzegovina*, ed. Džemal Sokolović and Florian Bieber (Aldershot: Ashgate, 2001), p. 157. Bougarel et al. give other figures, speaking of an estimated 100,000–150,000 casualties and the displacement of 2.1 million people. Xavier Bougarel, Elissa Helms and Ger Duijzings, 'Introduction', in *The New Bosnian Mosaic: Identities, Memories and Moral Claims in a Post-War Society* (Aldershot: Ashgate Publishing Limited, 2007), p. 5.
15 Anders Stefansson, 'Urban Exile: Locals, Newcomers and the Cultural Transformation of Sarajevo', in *The New Bosnian Mosaic: Identities, Memories and Moral Claims in a Post-War Society*, ed. Xavier Bougarel, Elissa Helms and Ger Duijzings (Aldershot: Ashgate, 2007), p. 59.
16 Andreas, *Blue Helmets and Black Markets*, p. 1.

17 Rada Iveković, 'Postcommunism and the Rewriting of (Art)History', *Art Press* 192 (1994), p. 43. Emphasis in original.

18 Samir Makdisi, *The Lessons of Lebanon: The Economics of War and Development* (London: I.B. Tauris, 2004), p. 35.

19 Bassam Fatthouh and Joachim Kolb, 'The Outlook for Economic Reconstruction in Lebanon after the 2006 War', *The MIT Electronic Journal for Middle East Studies* 6 (2006), p. 97.

20 The Lebanese Ministry of the Displaced defined displacement as follows: 'The displaced person is any individual, Lebanese or non-Lebanese national who lives on the Lebanese soil and has been affected by the war and hindered by its consequences from enjoying his or her full legal and civil rights to the house and properties from which he or she was displaced' (Ministry of the Displaced, Lebanon, 1996, p. 5). Drawing from this definition, I would then rather suggest that most Beirutis might indeed qualify as displaced.

21 The Ministry of the Displaced, Lebanon, 1996, p. 9. Cited by Sawalha, 'Healing the Wounds of the War', p. 276.

22 Cited in Craig Mitchell Zelizer, 'The Role of Artistic Processes in Peacebuilding in Bosnia-Herzegovina' (PhD diss., George Mason University, 2004), p. 79.

23 Boutros Labaki, 'The Postwar Economy: A Miracle That Didn't Happen', in *Lebanon in Limbo: Postwar Society and State in an Uncertain Regional Environment*, ed. Theodor Hanf and Nawaf Salam (Baden-Baden: Nomos Verlagsgesellschaft, 2003), p. 182.

24 The two-pages agreement was completed by eleven annexes, providing various mechanisms to promote democratization, protect human rights and aid the economic development in the region.

25 It counted more than 50,000 armed troops from the NATO countries and 18 other states and was a cross between a peacekeeping and a peace-making force. IFOR also assisted the OSCE insuring logistics and transportation capability for the elections held on 14 September 1996.

26 Between December 1995 and today, seven High Representatives – Carl Bildt (December 1995–June 1997), Carlos Westendorp (June 1997–July 1999), Wolfgand Petritsch (August 1999–May 2002), Paddy Ashdown (May 2002–January 2006), Christian Schwarz-Schilling (January 2006–July 2007), Miroslav Lajcak (July 2007–March 2009), Valentin Inzko (March 2009–July 2021), Christian Schmidt (August 2021–present)– took office in Bosnia and Herzegovina; the last four were consequently announced as the last one. In 2009, IFOR was expected to withdraw its last remaining troops still active in Bosnia, representing 200 peacekeepers. As Francine Friedman remarks, 'The success of the OHR in implementing the civilian portion of the DPA has been erratic. The fact that the HR and SFOR each controlled implementation of diff erent parts of the DPA meant that no one agency was fully responsible for its success. The result was

that conflicting objectives were pursued by the various actors, making it apparent that the international community had no clear overall strategy for achieving a vibrant civil society in Bosnia.' Francine Friedman, *Bosnia and Herzegovina: A Polity on the Brink* (London and New York: Routledge, 2004), p. 72.

27 Laurel E. Fletcher and Harvey M. Weinstein, 'A World unto Itself? The Application of International Justice in the Former Yugoslavia', in *My Neighbor, My Enemy: Justice and Community in the Aftermath of Mass Atrocity*, ed. Eric Stover and Harvey M. Weinstein (Cambridge: Cambridge University Press, 2004), p. 41.

28 Matthew Preston, *Ending Civil War: Rhodesia and Lebanon in Perspective* (London: Tauris Academic Studies, 2004), p. 27.

29 Youssef M. Choueiri, *Breaking the Cycle: Civil Wars in Lebanon* (London: Stacey International, 2007), p. 44.

30 The first part focused on general principles and internal reform; the second on aspects of Lebanese sovereignty, its re-establishment and its relations to Syria; the third one on the relations between Lebanon and Israel; the fourth one on future relations between Lebanon and Syria. Christoph Gerhard Klarmann, 'The Taif Agreement: A Historical Perspective' (Master Thesis, Beirut: American University of Beirut, 2006), p. 87.

31 Nawaf Salam, 'Taif Revisited', in *Lebanon in Limbo: Postwar Society and State in an Uncertain Regional Environment*, ed. Theodor Hanf and Nawaf Salam (Baden-Baden: Nomos Verlagsgesellschaft, 2003), p. 43.

32 Makdisi, *The Lessons of Lebanon*, p. 80.

33 Preston, *Ending Civil War*, p. 43.

34 Harvey M. Weinstein and Eric Stover, 'Introduction: Conflict, Justice and Reclamation', in *My Neighbor, My Enemy: Justice and Community in the Aftermath of Mass Atrocity*, (Cambridge: Cambridge University Press, 2004), p. 13.

35 Fouad Siniora cited by Muhamad Mugraby, 'The Syndrome of One-Time Exceptions and the Drive to Establish the Proposed Hariri Court', in *The Politics of Violence, Truth and Reconciliation in the Arab Middle East*, ed. Sune Haugbolle and Anders Hastrup (New York: Routledge, 2009), p. 24.

36 Tom Gjelten, *Sarajevo Daily: A City and Its Newspaper Under Siege* (New York: Harper Collins Publisher, 1995), p. 4.

37 Coal mining, for example, continued throughout the war, although its output fell from over 18 million tons in 1990 to around 1 million in 1994. Friedman, *Bosnia and Herzegovina*, p. 93.

38 Robert J. Donia, *Sarajevo: A Biography* (London: Hurst & Company, 2006), p. 347.

39 See Vamik D. Volkan, 'Ancient Fuel for a Modern Inferno: Time Collapse in Bosnia-Herzegovina', in *Bloodlines: From Ethnic Pride to Ethnic Terrorism*, ed. Vamik D. Volkan (Boulder: Westview Press, 1997), pp. 50–81.

40 Weinstein and Stover, 'Introduction: Conflict, Justice and Reclamation', p. 1.

41 Saree Makdisi, 'Beirut/ *Beirut*', in *Tamáss: Contemporary Arab Representations, Beirut / Lebanon*, ed. Catherine David (Barcelona: Fundació Antoni Tàpies, 2002), p. 34.
42 In 2004, Solidere launched an international competition to reconfigure Martyrs' Square. This call was responded by 400 participants from 46 countries. Samir Khalaf, *Heart of Beirut: Reclaiming the Bourj* (London: Saqi, 2006), p. 9.
43 Khalaf, *Heart of Beirut*, p. 20.
44 Robert Saliba, 'The Mental Image of Downtown Beirut, 1990', in *Beyrouth: Regards Croisés*, ed. Michael F. Davie (Tours: Université François Rabelais, 1996), pp. 305–49.
45 Jalal Toufic, 'Ruins', in *Tamáss: Contemporary Arab Representations. Beirut / Lebanon 1*, ed. Catherine David (Barcelona, Fundació Antoni Tàpies, 2002), p. 21.
46 Jens-Peter Hanssen and Daniel Genberg, 'Beirut in Memoriam. A kaleidoscopic space out of focus', in *Crisis and Memory in Islamic Societies*, ed. Angelika Neuwirth and Andreas Pflitsch (Beirut: Ergon Verlag Würzburg in Kommission, 2001), p. 233. Hanssen and Genberg add about the origins of the term: 'It was suggested as an antonym to amnesia, the loss of memory and anamnesia, the inaccessible, passive "other" memory that is triggered inadvertently, to denote a situation where memory is constantly present, multiple and celebrated.' Ibid.
47 In 2001, new history textbooks were delivered to schools for grades 3 to 6. They were shortly recalled by the Ministry of Education. Textbooks for grades 7 to 9, already under press at the time, were never delivered. Saree Makdisi, 'Beirut, a City without History?', in *Memory and Violence in the Middle East and North Africa*, ed. Ussama Makdisi and Paul A. Silverstein (Bloomington: Indiana University Press, 2006), p. 201.
48 See Albert Farid Henry Naccache, 'Beirut's Memorycide: Hear No Evil, See No Evil', in *Archaeology Under Fire*, ed. Lynn Meskell (London: Routledge, 1997), pp. 140–58.
49 Ibid., p. 146.
50 Ibid., p. 148.
51 Maček, *Sarajevo under Siege*, p. 55.
52 Zelizer, 'The Role of Artistic Processes', p. 134.
53 The actual existent Yugoslavia did not have right to take part in the Biennale given its role recognized by the international community as initiating war. In the pavilion bearing the name Yugoslavia, an exhibition entitled *Machines of Peace* was displayed. See Pejić, 'Postcommunism and the Rewriting of (Art) History', p. 38.
54 UNHCR did not grant permission for the transport of the artists and their works, despite Oliva's official invitation to the Venice Biennale. Enver Hadžiomerspahić, 'From a Hole in the Fence to the Venice Biennale', in *Artefacts: Bosnia and Herzegovina at the Venice Biennale 1993–2003* (Sarajevo: Ars Aevi, 2007), p. 238.

55 Jamey Gambrell, 'Sarajevo: Art in Extremis', *Art in America* (May 1994), p. 102.

56 Miroslav Bilać, 'Paintings Exhibited in the Lobby', in *The Siege of Sarajevo 1992–1996*, ed. Suada Kapić (Sarajevo: FAMA, 2000), p. 213.

57 Zelizer, 'Role of Artistic Processes', pp. 142–3.

58 Sontag became a honorary citizen of Sarajevo. Haris Pašović, the director of International Theatre and Film Festival – MES, recalls the impact of the premiere on 17 August 1993: 'It was the first time that a cultural event in Sarajevo made page one of the Washington Post and also the first time that the news got out that something else not just dying was happening in Sarajevo.' Haris Pašović, 'Susan Sontag in Sarajevo', in *The Siege of Sarajevo 1992–1996*, ed. Suada Kapić (Sarajevo: FAMA, 2000), p. 431. Despite much praise, Sontag was criticized for her action by many members of the Sarajevo cultural scene. Sontag describes her primary motivation in directing the play in these terms: 'I went to Sarajevo in mid-July 1993 to stage a production of *Waiting for Godot* not so much because I'd always wanted to direct Beckett's play (although I had) as because it gave me a practical reason to return to Sarajevo and stay for a month or more. I had spent two weeks there in April, and had come to care intensively about the battered city and what it stands for; some of its citizens had become friends. But I couldn't again be just a witness: that is, meet and visit, tremble with fear, feel brave, feel depressed, have heart-breaking conversations, grow ever more indignant, lose weight. If I went back, it would be to pitch in and do something. [. . .] It would be a small contribution. But it was the only one of the three things I do – write, make films, and direct in the theatre – which yields something that would exist only in Sarajevo, that would be made and consumed there.' Susan Sontag, 'Waiting for Godot in Sarajevo', in *Where the Stress Falls* (London: Vintage, 2003), pp. 299–300. Also see in the same volume her essay '"There" and "Here"', pp. 323–9.

59 Meliha Husedžinović, 'Aspects and Positions of Art from Bosnia-Herzegovina', in *Organising & Curating the Transition, Conference Reader* (Conference held in Sarajevo, 16–19 May 2007), p. 12.

60 See Zdravko Mlinar, *Globalisation and Territorial Identities* (London: Avebury, 1996) p. 80.

61 Donia, *Sarajevo: A Biography*, p. 314.

62 Hadžiomerspahić, 'From a Hole in the Fence to the Venice Biennale', pp. 240 and 242.

63 Edin Hajdarpašić, 'Museums, Multiculturalism, and the Remaking of Postwar Sarajevo', in *(Re)Visualising National History: Museums and National Identities in Europe in the New Millenium*, ed. Robin Ostow (Toronto: University of Toronto Press, 2008), p. 123.

64 Nicolas Guilhot, 'Reforming the World: George Soros, Global Capitalism and the Philanthropic Management of the Social Sciences', *Critical Sociology* 33 (2007), p. 468.

65 Between 1992 and 1999, the SCCA network functioned as part of the Soros Foundation Network, supporting the development and exposure of contemporary art in Eastern and Central Europe.

66 Nina Czegldedy and Andrea Szekeres, 'Agents for Change: The Contemporary Art Centres of the Soros Foundation and C[3]', *Third Text* 23, no. 3 (2009), p. 259.

67 Dunja Blažević, 'They Are Coming', in *Maxumim* (Sarajevo: Soros Center for Contemporary Art, 2000), p. 5.

68 'Outre une programmation ambitieuse, la présence de jeunes acteurs au sein de l'institution favorise d'une part l'émergence d'une nouvelle génération d'artistes, quoique relativement limitées; d'autre part, c'est de cette expérience qu'a discrètement émergé la figure aujourd'hui incontournable du curator.' Arnaud Chabrol, 'Le paysage théâtral libanais en sortie de guerre', in *Journées doctorales, Université de Provence* (blog.univ-provence.fr/gallery/41/ExposésJournéeDoctorale08.pdf), p. 7 (20 July 2020).

69 Catherine David, 'Contemporary Arab Representations', in *Dreams and Conflicts: The Dictatorship of the Viewer: La Biennale di Venezia, 50th international art exhibition*, ed. Francesco Bonami (Venezia: Marsilio, 2003), p. 294.

70 Paola Yacoub and Michel Lasserre, 'An Unprogrammed City', in *Dreams and Conflicts: The Dictatorship of the Viewer: La Biennale di Venezia, 50th international art exhibition*, ed. Francesco Bonami (Venezia: Marsilio, 2003), p. 295.

71 *Home Works* took place in 2002, 2003, 2005, 2008, 2010, 2013, 2015 and partially in 2019.

72 See www.fai.org.lb/Template.aspx?id=1 (20 July 2020).

73 See www.beirutartcenter.org/presentation.php (20 July 2020).

74 Dunja Blažević, 'Before After', in *Meeting Point. Sarajevo 1997: First Annual Exhibition of the Soros Center for Contemporary Art* (Sarajevo: Soros Center for Contemporary Art, 1997), pp. 8–9.

75 Ibid., p. 10.

76 Meliha Husedžinović, 'Meeting Point', in *Meeting Point: Sarajevo 1997* (Sarajevo: Soros Center for Contemporary Arts, 1997), p. 15.

77 Catherine David, 'Learning from Beirut: Contemporary Aesthetic Practices in Lebanon', in *Home Works: A Forum on Cultural Practices in the Region*, ed. Christine Tohme (Beirut: The Lebanese Association for Plastic Arts, Ashkal Alwan, 2003), p. 33. David previously attended the Ayloul Festival and thereafter included Beruti artists in the 1997 Documenta X. She later organized her own ongoing project *Tamàss: Contemporary Arab Representations*, launching its first volume on the Beiruti art scene in 2002.

78 David, 'Learning from Beirut', p. 33.

79 Rogers, 'Postwar Art', p. 157.

80 Ibid., p. 27.

81 Suzanne Cotter, 'Beirut Unbound', in *Out of Beirut*, ed. Suzanne Cotter (Oxford: Modern Art Oxford, 2006), p. 26.

82 Rogers, 'Postwar Art', p. 62.

83 Silvia Naef, *A la recherche d'une modernité arabe: l'évolution des arts plastiques en Egypte, au Liban et en Irak* (Genève: Editions Slatkine, 1996), pp. 183 and 184.

84 Abbas Baydoun, 'Culture and Arts', in *Home Works: A Forum on Cultural Practice in the Region*, ed. ChristineTohme (Beirut: The Lebanese Association for Plastic Arts, Ashkal Alwan, 2003), p. 24.

Chapter 2

1 On 13 May 1871, Rimbaud, at the time only seventeen, wrote this famous avowal in a letter addressed to his former rhetoric teacher, Georges Izambard.

2 Julia Kristeva, 'Strangers to Ourselves', in *The Portable Kristeva*, ed. Oliver Kelly (New York: Columbia University Press, 1997), p. 274.

3 Iain Chambers, *Migrancy, Culture, Identity* (London: Routledge, 1994), pp. 5–6.

4 Bojana Pejić stresses how, since abstract art had been established as Yugoslavia's official art in the 1950s, Yugoslav modernist painters were quite intolerant of those artists who cherished performance, conceptual art and video art. Unlike this official, visible art, an unofficial, underground dissident selection of artists were particularly attracted to Joseph Kosuth's and Joseph Beuys's work. See Bojana Pejić, *The Communist Body – Towards an Archaeology of Images: Politics of Representation and Spatialization of Power in the SFR Yugoslavia (1945–1991)* (PhD diss., Humboldt University, 2005), p. 33. Dakić's inspiration, therefore, inscribes itself in this artistic underground community in Yugoslavia. The artist recalls how she got her inspiration: 'When the SKC (Student Cultural Center) in Belgrade, headed by Dunja Blažević, initiated a festival of "extended media", Beuys accepted an invitation and delivered an eight-hour performance-lecture about his "social sculpture". I am a few years too young to have personal experience of all these things, but when I was a student in Sarajevo and Belgrade, the impulses of that era were still very palpable, and so they shaped my art. Even today I find the political and social force in Beuys' art very inspiring.' 'Ulrike Groos and Tihomir Milovac in conversation with Danica Dakić', in *Danica Dakić* (Köln: Verlag der Buchhandlung Walther König, 2009), p. 42.

5 Sketches drawn by Trogemann illustrate the choice to place the camera at a height of 1.20 metre and a distance of 2.3 metre, on a tripod.

6 Clement Greenberg, 'Collage', in *Collage: Critical Views*, ed. Katherine Hoffman (Ann Arbor: UMI Research Press, 1989), p. 68.

7 Gregory L. Ulmer, 'The Object of Post-Criticism', in *Collage: Critical Views*, ed. Katherine Hoffman (Ann Arbor: UMI Research Press, 1989), p. 385.

8 *Global Groove* was a project for the Television Laboratory at WNET in New York. It included performances by John Cage, Allen Ginsberg, Charlotte Moorman, Japanese commercials and go-go dances. Video images were electronic collages demonstrating the potential of this new form of art and challenging the boundaries of the tradition television broadcast. Max Almy, 'Electronic Collage', in *Collage: Critical Views*, ed. Katherine Hoffman (Ann Arbor: UMI Research Press, 1989), p. 356.

9 Donald B. Kuspit, 'Collage: The Organizing Principle of Art in the Age of the Relativity of Art', in *Collage: Critical Views*, ed. Katherine Hoffman (Ann Arbor: UMI Research Press, 1989), pp. 42 and 47.

10 Amelia Jones, *Self/Image: Technology, Representation and the Contemporary Subject* (London: Routledge, 2006), p. 23.

11 Ibid., p. 14. Jones also adds that 'The paradox is enacted: I feel in the work, seduced by it and immersed in it but I have to be outside the image world produced by the piece in order to construct it as something I can engage that is other from myself. Through this theoretical discourse between myself and the work, this is my way of producing distance. I disentangle myself from the image / sound complex,' p. 13.

12 Bojana Pejić, 'The Angel Effect', in *Danica Dakić: Voices and Images* (Frankfurt am Main: Revolver, 2004), p. 113. Until 2009, the piece has been exhibited under two names, *Autoportrait* and *Selfportrait*, after which the artist decided to name it *Autoportrait* in all languages.

13 'Danica Dakić in Conversation with Dunja Blažević: "Voices and Images"', in *Danica Dakić: Voices and Images* (Frankfurt am Main: Revolver, 2004), p. 25.

14 Adam Smith, 'Considerations Concerning the First Formation of Languages', in *Lectures on Rhetoric and Belles Lettres* (Oxford: The Clarendon Press, 1983), p. 219.

15 Roman Jakobson, 'Shifters, Verbal Categories, and the Russian Verb', in *Selected Writings. Vol. 2: Word and Language* (Paris: Mouton, 1971), p. 131.

16 Ibid., p. 132.

17 Jill Bennett, *Empathic Vision: Affect, Trauma and Contemporary Art* (Stanford: Stanford University Press, 2005), p. 2.

18 The population in Sarajevo decreased from 510,000 in 1991 to 360,000 in 1999 – 240,000 had left it, and a massive rural exodus of 90,000 people arrived in Sarajevo to occupy the homes of those who had fled or emigrated.

19 'Danica Dakić in Conversation with Dunja Blažević', p. 24. Dakić would later tell me that she was reading a novel while Egbert Trogemann was filming her.

20 Bennett, *Empathic Vision*, p. 3.

21 Didier Anzieu, *The Skin Ego* (New Haven: Yale University Press, 1989), p. 14.

22 Claudia Benthien, *Skin: On the Cultural Border Between Self and the World* (New York: Columbia University Press, 2002), p. 222.

23 Ibid., p. 187.

24 Ibid.
25 Irit Rogoff, 'Moving On: Migration and the Intertextuality of Trauma', in *Vera Frenkel . . . from the Transit Bar* (Toronto: Powerplant and Ottawa: National Gallery of Art, 1994), pp. 26–59; Griselda Pollock, 'Fictions of Fact: Memory in Transit in Vera Frenkel's Installations', *After-affects | After-images: Trauma and Aesthetic Transformation in the Virtual Feminist Museum* (Manchester: Manchester University Press, 2013), pp. 223–72; Sigrid Schade, 'Migration, Language and Memory in '. . . *from the Transit Bar*', in *Vera Frenkel*, ed. Sigrid Schade (Ostfinden: Hatje Cantz, 2013), pp. 155–83.
26 A. G. Stephens, 'The Read Page', *Bulletin 17* (1897), n.p, cited by Judith Johnston, 'The Genesis and Commodification of Katherine Langloh Parker's *Australian Legendary Tales* (1896)', *Jasal* 4 (2005), p. 160.
27 Johnston, 'The Genesis and Commodification of Katherine Langloh Parker's *Australian Legendary Tales* (1986)', p. 163.
28 Catherine Stow (Catherine Langloh Parker), *Woggheeguy* (Adelaide: Preece, 1930), p. viii.
29 Reinhard Spieler, 'Voices of Identity', in *Danica Dakić: Voices and Images* (Frankfurt am Main: Revolver, 2004), p. 61.
30 Judith Butler, *Precarious Life: The Powers of Mourning and Violence* (London: Verso, 2004), p. 49.
31 Kristeva, 'Strangers to Ourselves', p. 287.
32 Graham Tulloch, 'Stevenson and Islands: Scotland and the South Pacific', in *Robert Louis Stevenson Reconsidered: New Critical Perspectives*, ed. William B. Jones (Jefferson, NC: McFarland, 2003), p. 74.
33 Ibid., p. 78.
34 Roslyn Jolly, *Robert Louis Stevenson in the Pacific* (Burlington: Ashgate, 2009), p. 164.
35 Ann. C. Colley, *Robert Louis Stevenson and the Colonial Imagination* (Burlington: Ashgate, 2004), p. 5.
36 Robert Louis Stevenson, 'The Isle of Voices', in *The South Sea Tales* (Oxford: Oxford University Press, 1999), p. 102.
37 Danièle Klapproth Muazzin, 'Holding the World in Place: Narrative as Social Practice in Anglo-Western and Central Australian Aboriginal Culture' (PhD diss., University of Bern, 2001), p. 58.
38 Claude Lévi-Strauss, *Myth and Meaning* (London: Routledge, 1978), p. 18.
39 Ibid., p. 40.
40 Bob Hodge and Vijay Mishra, *Dark Side of the Dream: Australian Literature and the Postcolonial Mind* (Sydney: Allen and Unwin, 1990), p. 27.
41 Klapproth Muazzin, 'Holding the World', pp. 58–9.
42 W. E. H. Stanner, 'The Dreaming', in *Traditional Aboriginal Society*, ed. W. H. Edwards (Melbourne: Macmillan Australia, 1987), p. 229.

43 Klapproth Muazzin, 'Holding the World', p. 61.
44 Nicholas Evans, 'Aborigines Speak a Primitive Language', in *Language Myths*, ed. Laurie Bauer and Peter Trudgill (London: Penguin Books, 1998), p. 160.
45 To make matters more complicated, the book used by Dakić was a translation from Czech into German.
46 Trinh T. Minh-ha, 'Other than Myself/My Other Self', in *Traveller's Tales: Narrative of Home and Displacement*, ed. George Robertson et al. (London: Routledge, 1994), p. 10.
47 Walter Benjamin, 'The Task of the Translator: An Introduction to the Translation of Baudelaire's *Tableaux Parisiens*', in *Illuminations* (London: Pimlico, 1999), pp. 71–2.
48 Horst Bredekamp, 'Bodies of Language', in *Danica Dakić* (Köln: Verlag der Buchhandlung Walther König, 2009), p. 34.
49 Diane Amiel, 'Specifically Balkan Art', *Third Text* 21, no. 2 (2007), p. 137.
50 Ursula Biemann, 'Geography and the Politics of Mobility', in *Geography and the Politics of Mobility*, ed. Ursula Biemann (Vienna: Generali Foundation, 2003), p. 21 and p. 23.
51 Irit Rogoff, 'Engendering Terror', in *Geography and the Politics of Mobility*, ed. Ursula Biemann (Vienna: Generali Foundation, 2003), pp. 51–2.
52 Tassilo Herrschel, *Global Geographies of Post-Socialist Transition: Geographies, Societies, Policies* (London: Routledge, 2007), p. 20.
53 S. Slapsak, *Joegoslavie weet je nog?* (Amsterdam: Jan Mets, 1993), p. 43. Cited by Stef Jansen, 'Homeless at Home: Narrations of Post-Yugoslav Identities', in *Migrants of Identity: Perceptions of Home in a World Movement*, ed. Nigel Rapport and Andrew Dawson (Oxford: Berg, 1998), p. 92.
54 Maria Todorova, *Imagining the Balkans* (Oxford: Oxford University Press, 1997), p. 186.
55 Stuart Hall, 'Cultural Identity and Diaspora', in *Identity, Community, Culture, Difference*, ed. Jonathan Rutherford (London: Lawrence & Wishart Limited, 1990), p. 225.
56 Dubravka Ugrešić, *The Culture of Lies: Antipolitical Essays* (London: Phoenix House, 1998), p. 39.
57 'Ulrike Groos and Tihomir Milovac in Conversation with Danica Dakić', in *Danica Dakić* (Köln: Verlag der Buchhandlung Walther König, 2009), p. 43.
58 'The exile knows that in a secular and contingent world, homes are always provisional. Borders and barriers which enclose us within the safety of familiar territory can also become prisons, and are often defended beyond reason or necessity. Exiles cross borders, break barriers of thought and experience.' Edward Said, 'Reflections on Exile', in *Reflections on Exile and Other Literary and Cultural Essays* (London: Granta, 2000), p. 185.
59 'Seeing "the entire world as a foreign land" makes possible originality of vision. Most people are principally aware of one culture, one setting, one home; exiles

are aware of at least two, and this plurality of vision gives rise to awareness of simultaneous dimensions, an awareness that – to borrow a phrase from music – is *contrapuntal*.' Said, 'Reflections on Exile', p. 186. Emphasis in original.

Chapter 3

1 Ca. 8,000 Bosniak (Bosnian Muslim) men and boys aged between sixteen and sixty were killed by units of the Army of Republika Srpska, under the command of General Ratko Mladić. The rest of the Bosniak population living at the time in Srebrenica, forced to get on coaches, was expelled from the enclave.

2 United Nations Development Programme (UNDP), 'Rights-Based Municipal Assessment and Planning Project, Municipality of Srebrenica, Republika Srpska, Bosnia and Herzegovina, October 2003–February 2004', cited by Sarah Wagner, 'Tabulating Loss, Entombing Memory: The Srebrenica-Potočari Memorial Centre', in *Memory, Mourning, Landscape*, ed. Elizabeth Anderson, Avril Maddrell, Kate McLoughlin and Alana Vincent (Amsterdam: Rodopi, 2010), p. 63.

3 Slavenka Drakulić, 'One day in the Life of Dražen Erdemović', in *They Would Never Hurt a Fly: War Criminals on Trial in The Hague* (London: Time Warner Books, 2004), pp. 97–100.

4 Erdemović was held responsible for the death of 10 to 100 people. Sentenced to ten years of imprisonment, his initial sentence was reduced to five years. He was a witness for the prosecution in the Krstić case as well as the Karadžić-Mladić case, and lives today under a witness protection program. *Srebrenica: Erinnerung für die Zukunft* (Berlin: Heinrich-Böll-Stiftung, 2005), p. 18.

5 Amor Mašović recalls the case of 23-year-old Kadrija Musić, whose remains were found in five different locations, scattered up to 32 kilometres apart. 'Srebrenica 20 Years on: Every Year I Think This Is the Year I Will Bury My Son', *The Guardian*, 3 July 2015: http://www.theguardian.com/world/2015/jul/03/srebrenica-massacre-20-years-on (last consulted 21 July 2015).

6 Amor Mašović, cited by Sarah Wagner, *To Know Where He Lies: DNA Technology and the Search for Srebrenica's Missing* (Berkeley: University of California Press, 2008), p. 83.

7 Eelco Runia, 'Forget About It: Parallel Processing in the Srebrenica Report', *History and Theory* 43, no. 3 (October 2004), p. 295.

8 *Srebrenica, Erinnerung für die Zukunft*, p. 17.

9 International Commission for Missing Persons (ICMP).

10 Ibid.

11 See on this matter Anders Stefansson, 'Urban Exile: Locals, Newcomers and the Cultural Transformation of Sarajevo', in *The New Bosnian Mosaic: Identities, Memories and Moral Claims in a Post-War Society*, ed. Xavier Bougarel, Elissa Helms and Ger Duijzings (Aldershot: Ashgate, 2007), pp. 59–77.
12 Wagner, *To Know Where He Lies*, p. 67.
13 Dunja Blažević, 'Her Name Is Bajević, Maja Bajević', in *Maja Bajević: Women at Work* (Sarajevo: National Gallery of Bosnia and Herzegovina, 2002), p. 29. Emphasis in original.
14 'A Conversation between Angela Vettese and Maja Bajevic', in *Maja Bajevic*, ed. Angela Vettese (Vincenza: Edizioni Charta, 2008), p. 12.
15 Rozsika Parker, *The Subversive Stitch: Embroidery and the Making of the Feminine* (London: I.B. Tauris, 2010), p. 5. Emphasis in original.
16 'A Conversation between Angela Vettese and Maja Bajevic', p. 45.
17 Cited in Blažević, 'Her Name Is Bajević', p. 30.
18 Peter Biesboer, *Frans Hals und Haarlems Meister der Goldenen Zeit* (München: Hirmer Verlag, 2008), p. 112.
19 Seymour Slive, *Frans Hals* (Munich: Prestel-Verlag, 1989), p. 362.
20 Ibid., p. 366.
21 'A Conversation between Angela Vettese and Maja Bajevic', p. 9.
22 Bojana Pejić, 'Matrix of Memory', in *Maja Bajević: Women at Work* (Sarajevo: National Gallery of Bosnia and Herzegovina, 2002), p. 93.
23 Selma Leydesdorff, *Surviving the Bosnian Genocide: The Women of Srebrenica Speak* (Bloomington: Indiana University Press, 2011), p. 197.
24 Wagner, *To Know Where He Lies*, p. 73.
25 Dejan Jović, 'Yugoslavism and Yugoslav Communism: From Tito to Kardelj', in *Yugoslavism: Histories of a Failed Idea, 1918–1992*, ed. Dejan Djakić (London: Hurst & Co, 2003), p. 160.
26 Josip Broz Tito, 'No Compromise with Nationalism (1969)', in *The National Question* (Belgrade: Socialist Thought and Practice, 1983), p. 156.
27 Gallagher mitigates the importance of the common language arguing that 80 per cent of the population spoke Serbo-Croatian in the two literary forms when Tito came to power. Tom Gallagher, *Outcast Europe: The Balkans, 1789–1989: From the Ottomans to Milošević* (London: Routledge, 2001), p. 220.
28 'A Conversation between Angela Vettese and Maja Bajević', p. 9.
29 Gerhard Neweklowsky, *Die bosnisch-herzegowinischen Muslime: Geschichte, Bräuche, Alltagskultur* (Klagenfurt-Salzburg: Wieser Verlag, 1996), p. 180.
30 Both definitions are given by Abdula Škajlić, *Turcizmi u Sprskohravatskom-Hrvatskosrpskom Jeziku* (Sarajevo: Svjetlost, 1985), cited by Tone Bringa, *Being Muslim the Bosnian Way: Identity and Community in a Central Bosnian Village* (Princeton: Princeton University Press, 1995), p. 187.

31 Bringa, *Being Muslim the Bosnian Way*, p. 189.

32 Ibid., pp. 189–92.

33 Veena Das, 'Language and Body: Transactions in the Construction of Pain', in *Social Suffering*, ed. Arthur Kleinman, Veena Das and Margaret Lock (Berkeley: University of California Press, 1997), p. 68.

34 Ibid.

35 Ibid.

36 Jill Bennett, 'Dis/Identification: Art, Affect and the "Bad Death": Strategies for Communicating the Sense Memory of Loss', *Signs* 28, no. 1 (Autumn 2002), pp. 335–7.

37 Parker, *Subversive Stitch*, p. 11.

38 Ibid., p. 2.

39 Iva Popovicova, *New Body Politic: Czech and Polish Women's Art of the 1990s* (Saarbrücken: VDM Verlag, 2008), pp. 61–2.

40 Martina Pachmanová, 'In? Out? In Between? Some Notes on the Invisibility of a Nascent Eastern European Feminist and Gender Discourse in Contemporary Art Theory (2009)', in *Gender Check: A Reader. Art and Theory in Eastern Europe*, ed. Bojana Pejić (Cologne: Walther König, 2010), pp. 37–8.

41 Ibid., p. 38.

42 Nanette Funk and Magda Mueller, 'Introduction', in *Gender Politics and Post-Communism: Reflections from Eastern Europe and the Former Soviet Union*, ed. Nanette Funk and Magda Mueller (New York and London: Routledge, 1993), p. 8.

43 Bojana Pejić, 'The Morning After: Plavi Radion, Abstract Art, and Bananas (2002)', in *Gender Check: A Reader. Art and Theory in Eastern Europe*, ed. Bojana Pejić (Köln: Walther König, 2010), p. 98.

44 Daša Duhaček, 'Women's Time in the Former Yugoslavia', in *Gender Politics and Post-Communism*, pp. 135–6.

45 Slavenka Drakulić, 'Women and the New Democracy in the Former Yugoslavia', in *Gender Politics and Post-Communism: Reflections from Eastern Europe and the Former Soviet Union*, ed. Nanette Funk and Magda Mueller (New York and London: Routledge, 1993), p. 123.

46 Ibid., p. 129.

47 Ibid., p. 130.

48 Azra Hromadžić, 'Kriegsvergewaltigungen in Bosnien: Alte und neue Erklärungsansätze', in *Gender Identität und kriegerischer Konflikt: das Beispiel des ehemaligen Jugoslawien*, ed. Ruth Seifert (Münster: LIT Verlag, 2004), p. 114.

49 Popovicova, *New Body Politic*, pp. 17–18. Emphasis in original.

50 Ibid., p. 58.

51 Marina Gržinić, *Re-politicizing Art, Theory, Representation and New Media Technology* (Vienna: Schriften der Akademie der Bildenden Künste Wien, 2008), p. 089.

52 Ibid., p. 110.
53 'A Conversation between Angela Vettese and Maja Bajevic', p. 9.

Chapter 4

1 Lamia Joreige, *A Journey*, 2006, video documentary, 0'36"–0'54".
2 Marianne Hirsch, 'The Generation of Postmemory', *Poetics Today* 29, no. 1 (Spring 2008), pp. 103–28.
3 Joreige, *A Journey*, 0'00".
4 Joreige, *A Journey*, 1'01"–01'14".
5 The British Mandate for Palestine was put in place at the end of the First World War, after the collapse of the Ottoman Empire. This British administration lasted until the creation of the state of Israel in 1948.
6 Joreige, *A Journey*, 06'06"–06'13".
7 David Lowenthal, 'Nostalgia Tells It like It Wasn't', in *The Imagined Past: History and Nostalgia*, ed. Christopher Shaw and Malcolm Chase (Manchester: Manchester University Press, 1989), p. 21.
8 Malcolm Chase and Christopher Shaw, 'The Dimensions of Nostalgia', in *The Imagined Past: History and Nostalgia*, ed. Christopher Shaw and Malcolm Chase (Manchester: Manchester University Press, 1989), p. 4.
9 Pam Cook, *Screening the Past: Memory and Nostalgia in Cinema* (London: Routledge, 2005), p. 3.
10 Ibid.
11 Lamia Joreige, 'Here and Perhaps Elsewhere', in *Out of Beirut*, ed. Suzanne Cotter (Oxford: Modern Art Oxford, 2006), p. 18.
12 Joreige, *A Journey*, 14'35"–14'49".
13 Joreige, *A Journey*, 15'30"–15'58".
14 Joreige, *A Journey*, 9'31"–9'35".
15 Both quotes from Marianne Hirsch, *Family Frames: Photography, Narrative and Postmemory* (Cambridge, MA: Harvard University Press, 1997), p. 22.
16 Ibid.
17 See Hirsch, 'The Generation of Postmemory', pp. 103–28.
18 Tina Wasserman, 'Constructing the Image of Postmemory', in *The Image and the Witness: Trauma, Memory and Visual Culture*, ed. Frances Guerin and Roger Hallas (London: Wallflower Press, 2007), p. 160.
19 Ibid.
20 Kaelen Wilson-Goldie, 'Digging for Fire: Contemporary Art Practices in Postwar Lebanon' (Master Thesis, American University of Beirut, 2005), p. 119.
21 Rogers, 'Postwar Art', p. 56.

22 Joreige, *A Journey,* 10'27"–11'40".
23 Dietrich Jung, 'Global Conditions and Global Constraints: The International Paternity of the Palestine Conflict', in *The Middle East and Palestine: Global Politics and Regional Conflict*, ed. Dietrich Jung (New York: Palgrave Macmillan, 2004), p. 10.
24 Mark LeVine, *Overthrowing Geography: Jaffa, Tel Aviv, and the Struggle for Palestine, 1880–1948* (Berkeley: University of California Press, 2005), p. 28.
25 Ibid., p. 215.
26 Lili Galili and Ori Nir, 'Jaffa: City of Strangers', *Journal of Palestine Studies* 30, no. 3 (Spring 2001), p. 101.
27 André Masawi, 'Film Production and Jaffa's Predicament', *Jaffa Diaries* (9 February 1998), www.jaffacity.com (24 July 2020).
28 LeVine, *Overthrowing Geography*, p. 221.
29 Sharon Rotbard, *White City Black City: Architecture and War in Tel Aviv and Jaffa* (Cambridge: MIT Press, 2015), p. 265.
30 Salim Tamari and Rema Hammami, 'Virtual Returns to Jaffa', *Journal of Palestine Studies* 27, no. 4 (Summer 1998), p. 67.
31 Although this figure is commonly accepted as accurate, an ongoing ICRC investigation states that, in many cases, family of the disappeared declared them missing in more than one place in Lebanon; therefore, the figure is being re-evaluated downwards. Personal communication with ICRC members, Beirut, March 2015.
32 Joreige, *A Journey*, 17'56"–19'26".
33 Hadjithomas and Joreige, 'Latency', p. 47.
34 Ibid, p. 48.
35 Kaelen Wilson-Goldie, 'Contemporary Art Practices in Post-war Lebanon: An Introduction', in *Out of Beirut*, ed. Suzanne Cotter (Oxford: Modern Art Oxford, 2006), p. 83.
36 The Dziga Vertov Group was conceived as a partnership between Godard and another person: with Jean-Henri Regon first, then with Jean-Pierre Morin. *A Film like All the Others* on the May 1968 riots in France was the first film by the Dziga Vertov Group. Each film of the group involved various militant groups, and a lengthy collaboration with them in the planning and the discussions around each film. See James Roy MacBean, 'Godard and the Dziga Vertov Group: Film and Dialectics', *Film Quarterly* 26, no. 1 (Autumn 1972), pp. 30–44.
37 John Drabinski, 'Separation, Difference, and Time in Godard's *Ici et ailleurs*', *SubStance* 37, no. 1 (2008), p. 152.
38 Rogers, 'Postwar Art', p. 56.
39 Ibid.
40 Allan Sekula, 'Dismantling Modernism, Reinventing Documentary (Notes on the Politics of Representation)', *The Massachusetts Review* 19, no. 4, Photography (Winter 1978), pp. 862–3.

41 Linda Nochlin, 'Documented Success', *Artforum International*, September 2002, pp. 161 and 162.
42 Okwui Enwezor, 'Documentary/Vérité: Biopolitics, Human Rights, and the Figure of the Truth in Contemporary Art', in *Experiments with Truth*, ed. Mark Nash (Pennsauken: FWM, 2005), p. 101.
43 'Herein lies my own distinction: rather than accepting exclusively the term 'documentary' as a way to understand the manner in which the exhibition purportedly privileged the documentation of the real world on the analysis of social reality, I wish to address the documentary versus art issue by inserting into the field of Documenta 11 the concept of *vérité*'. Enwezor, p. 101.
44 Vit Havránek, 'The Documentary: Ontology of Forms in Transforming Countries', in *The Green Room: Reconsidering the Documentary and Contemporary Art*, ed. Maria Lind and Hito Steyerl (Berlin: Sternberg Press, 2008), pp. 130–1.
45 Mark Ryan Westmoreland, 'Crisis of Representation: Experimental Documentary in Postwar Lebanon' (PhD diss., The University of Texas, 2008), p. 3.
46 Ibid., pp. 12–13.
47 Hannah Feldman and Akram Zaatari, 'Mining War: Fragments from a Conversation Already Passed', *Art Journal* 66 (2007), p. 51.
48 T. J. Demos, *The Migrant Image: The Art and Politics of Documentary during Global Crisis* (Durham: Duke University Press, 2013), p. 190.
49 Ibid., p. 191.
50 See Jalal Toufic, *Vampires: An Uneasy Essay on the Undead in Film* (St. Saulito, CA: The Post-Apollo Press, 2003), p. 379.
51 Stuart Liebman, 'Introduction', in *Claude Lanzmann's Shoah: Key Essays*, ed. Stuart Liebman (Oxford: Oxford University Press, 2007), p. 5.
52 Lamia Joreige, 'Object Lessons', *ArtForum* (October 2006), p. 241. Emphasis in original.
53 Demos, *The Migrant Image*, p. 182.

Chapter 5

1 Edward S. Casey, *The Fate of Place: A Philosophical History* (Berkeley: University of California Press, 1997), p. xiii.
2 See David Eshel, 'The Israel-Lebanon Border Enigma', *IBRU Boundary and Security Bulletin* (Winter 2000–1), pp. 72–83.
3 See Paul Virilio, *Bunker Archeology*, trans. George Collins (New York: Princeton Architectural Press, 1994).
4 Walter Benjamin, 'Short History of Photography', *Artforum* 15 (February 1977), pp. 50 and 51, respectively.

5 Andreas Huyssen, 'World Cultures, World Cities', in *Other Cities, Other Worlds: Urban Imaginaries in a Globalizing Age*, ed. Andreas Huyssen (Durham and London: Duke University Press, 2008), p. 3.

6 Ibid., p. 3. Emphasis mine.

7 See Ibid., and Ulrich Baer, *Spectral Evidence: The Photography of Trauma* (Cambridge: The MIT Press, 2002).

8 See Ludwig Wittgenstein, *Tractatus Logico-Philosophicus*, trans. D. F. Pears and B. F. McGuiness (London: Routledge, 2010); Stanley Cavell, *The Claim of Reason: Wittgenstein, Skepticism, Morality, and Tragedy* (Oxford: Oxford University Press, 1979).

9 Paul Virilio and Sylvère Lotringer, *Pure War: Twenty-Five Years Later* (Los Angeles: Semiotexte, 2008), pp. 17–18.

10 Paola Yacoub, 'The Holiday Inn Cycle', in *Conflict and Memory: Bridging Past and Future in (South East) Europe*, ed. Wolfgang Petritsch and Verdan Džihić (Baden-Baden: Nomos, 2010), pp. 143–5.

11 Paola Yacoub and Michel Lasserre, 'An Unprogrammed City', in *Dreams and Conflicts: The Dictatorship of the Viewer*, ed. Francesco Bonami (Venezia: Marsilio, 2003), p. 297.

12 Walid Sadek cited by Kaelen Wilson-Goldie, 'Witness to Loss: Group Tuesday', *Bidoun: Arts and Culture from the Middle East* 1 (2007) p. 27. The 'we' used by Sadek refers to the think tank Group Tuesday, consisting of Walid Sadek, Bilal Khbeiz and Fadi Abdallah.

13 Paul Virilio, *Negative Horizon: An Essay in Dromoscopy*, trans. Michael Degener (London: Continuum, 2005), pp. 37–8.

14 Stanley Cavell, *The Claim of Reason: Wittgenstein, Skepticism, Morality, and Tragedy* (Oxford: Oxford University Press, 1979), p. 241.

15 Cavell's full quotation reads, 'It [The camera] does all and only what it is made to do. It tells no lies, any more than a typewriter tells lies; not because it is perfectly honest but because it is perfectly dumb. Unlike your use of a typewriter, however, you cannot know what you have made the camera do, what is revealed to it, until its results have appeared.' Stanley Cavell, *The World Viewed, Enlarged Edition* (Cambridge: Harvard University Press, 1979), p. 185.

16 'C'est basic, mais essentiel. Quand je trace une ligne avec une règle, je m'attends à ce que je vais voir. La surprise s'il y a lieu sera infine. Dans le tracement du trait, une chaîne causale relie parfaitement le geste au résultat. Quand je prends une photographie analogique, j'attends avec impatience le tirage. C'est tout le charme de la chambre noire. Aujourd'hui je jette un coup d'oeil sur l'écran de contrôle. Je ne sais pas ce que je vais obtenir, quelle que soit ma maîtrise.' Paola Yacoub, 'Text given at a conference at Bal' (working paper, December 2011), p. 2. Translation mine.

17 Paola Yacoub and Michel Lasserre, 'Exposed Villages', in *Beirut is a Magnificent City: Synoptic Pictures* (Barcelona: Fundació Antoni Tàpies, 2003), pp. 96–7.

18 Baer, *Spectral Evidence*, 2002.

19 Nicholas Green, 'Looking at the Landscape: Class Formation and the Visual', in *The Anthropology of Landscape: Perspectives on Place and Space*, ed. Eric Hirsch and Michael O'Hanlon (Oxford: Clarendon Press, 1995), p. 32.

20 See W. J. T. Mitchell, ed., *Landscape and Power* (Chicago and London: The University of Chicago Press, 2002).

21 W. J. T. Mitchell, 'Preface to the Second Edition', in *Landscape and Power*, ed. Mitchell, p. x.

22 Paola Yacoub and Michel Lasserre, 'An Unprogrammed City', in *The Remembrance of a City, the History of a Space: An International Symposium on Alternative Space* (Seoul: The Korean Culture & Arts Foundation, INSA, 2002), p. 27.

23 Ibid.

24 Ibid., p. 28.

25 Paola Yacoub and Michel Lasserre, 'The City of Beirut Is No Exception', in *Beirut Is a Magnificent City: Synoptic Pictures* (Barcelona: Fundació Antoni Tàpies, 2003), p. 99.

26 Baer, *Spectral Evidence*, pp. 61–2.

27 Ibid., p. 66.

28 Ibid., p. 71.

29 Ibid., pp. 76–7.

30 Yacoub and Lasserre, 'The City of Beirut Is No Exception', p. 101.

31 Ibid., p. 101.

32 Alan R. H. Baker, 'Introduction: The Identifying of Spaces and Places', in *Space and Place: Mirrors of Social and Cultural Identities*, ed. Dominique Vanneste (Leuven: ACTA Geographica, 1996), p. 4.

33 Jala Makhzoumi, 'Marginal Landscapes, Marginalized Rural Communities: Sustainable Post-War Recovery in Southern Lebanon', in *Lessons in Post-War Reconstruction: Case Studies from Lebanon in the Aftermath of the 2006 War*, ed. Howayda Al-Harithy (London: Routledge, 2010), p. 128.

34 Yacoub and Lasserre, 'Exposed Villages', p. 97.

35 See Ludwig Wittgenstein, *Philosophical Remarks*, ed. Rush Rhees, trans. Raymond Hargreaves and Roger White (Chicago: Chicago University Press, 1975), VI, 64, p. 95.

36 Boris Cyrulnik is a French psychoanalyst of Jewish origins, who experienced his parent's deportation to a concentration camp as a child. Drawing from his own experience, Cyrulnik introduced in France the notion of resilience, or the way people, especially children, recover from the traumas they have experienced turning them into a positive, emotional strength rather than victimhood. See Boris Cyrulnik, *Resilience: How Your Inner Strength Can Set You Free From the Past*, trans. David Macey (London: Penguin, 2009).

37 In December 2005, Cronulla beach became the site of sectarian clashes and riots. It started when lifesavers were assaulted on the beach by a group of young people

of Middle Eastern appearance. On 11 December, a peaceful crowd gathering deteriorated, resulting in extended property damages and physical assaults.

38 David McNeill, 'Australia: An Unresolved Problem', in *The Resilient Landscape*, ed. Phillip George, David McNeill and Khaled Sabsabi (Paddington: Ivan Dougherty Gallery, 2007), pp. 7–8.

39 Malcolm Anderson, *Frontiers: Territory and State Formation in the Modern World* (Oxford: Politi, 1996), pp. 1–3.

40 United Nations Development Programme, *The South, A Story of Hardship: The Socio-Economic Characteristics of the Liberated Regions* (Internal Document, 2000), cited by Makhzoumi, 'Marginal Landscapes, Marginalized Communities', p. 131.

41 Paola Yacoub and Michel Lasserre, 'Playing On . . . A Synoptic Presentation of Southern Lebanon', in *Beirut is a Magnificent City: Synoptic Pictures* (Barcelona: Fundació Antoni Tàpies, 2003), p. 105.

42 Eshel, 'The Israel-Lebanon Border Enigma', p. 75.

43 Ibid., p. 79.

44 Allen Buchanan and Margaret Moore, 'Introduction: The Making and Unmaking of Boundaries', in *States, Nations, and Borders. The Ethics of Making Boundaries*, ed. Allen Buchanan and Margaret Moore (Cambridge: Cambridge University Press, 2003), p. 6.

45 Yacoub and Lasserre, 'Playing On . . .', p. 107.

46 Ibid.

47 Ibid.

48 Virilio, *Bunker Archeology*, p. 43.

49 Michael Moore, 'On the Signification of Walls in Verbal and Visual Art', *Leonardo* 12, no. 4 (Autumn, 1979), p. 311.

50 Paola Yacoub and Michel Lasserre, 'Southern Lebanon Is Not the Same', in *Beirut Is a Magnificent City: Synoptic Pictures* (Barcelona: Fundació Antoni Tàpies, 2003), p. 112.

51 Franz Kafka, *The Complete Short Stories* (London: Minerva, 1992), p. 65. Ibid., p. 114.

52 Rolf. J. Goebel, 'Constructing Chinese History: Kafka's and Dittmar's Orientalist Discourse', *PMLA* 108, no. 1 (January 1993), p. 65.

53 Rolf J. Goebel, *Constructing China: Kafka's Orientalist Discourse* (Columbia: Camden House, 1997), p. 2.

54 Ibid., p. 8.

55 Avrum Stoll, *Twentieth-Century Analytic Philosophy* (New York: Columbia University Press, 2000), p. 59.

56 'Le fait que les petits objets soient arrangés de telle ou telle manière montre ce qui *aurait pu* être le cas.' François Schmitz, *Wittgenstein* (Paris: Les Belles Lettres, 1999), p. 80. My translation. Emphasis in original.

57 'Quelque chose d'absolument simple ne peut être décrit, on ne peut que le *nommer.*' Schmitz, *Wittgenstein*, p. 84. Translation mine. Emphasis in original.

Concluding words

1 Samuel Hynes, 'Personal Narratives and Commemoration', in *War and Remembrance*, ed. Jay Winter and Emmanuel Sivan (Cambridge: Cambridge University Press, 1999), p. 206.

2 Pierre Nora, 'General Introduction: Between Memory and History', in *Rethinking the French Past: Realms of Memory, vol. 1: Conflicts and Divisions*, ed. Pierre Nora, trans. Arthur Goldhammer (New York: Columbia University Press, 1996), p. 1.

3 Ibid., p. 14.

4 Ibid., p. 16.

5 Aida Cerkez, 'Twenty Years on from Its Siege, Sarajevo Still Feels the Emptiness', *The Independent*, 7 April 2012, p. 33.

6 Mieke Bal, *Of What One Cannot Speak: Doris Salcedo's Political Art* (Chicago: University of Chicago Press, 2010), p. 200.

7 Larkin considers Marianne Hirsch's concept of postmemory in relation to the younger Lebanese generation, through interviews with Lebanese students he conducted in Beirut during his field research between June 2005 and June 2006. Craig Larkin, *Memory and Conflict in Lebanon: Remembering and Forgetting the Past* (London: Routledge, 2012).

8 Andreas Huyssen, 'Present Pasts: Media, Politics, Amnesia', *Public Culture* 12, no. 1 (2000), p. 26.

Bibliography

Alam, Johnny. 'Real Archive, Contested Memory, Fake History: Transnational Representations of Trauma by Lebanese War Generation Artist'. In *History, Memory, Performance*, edited by David Dean, Yana Meerzon and Kathryn Price (Basingstoke: Palgrave Macmillan, 2015), 169–86.

Almy, Max. 'Electronic Collage'. In *Collage: Critical Views*, edited by Katherine Hoffman (Ann Arbor: UMI Research Press, 1989), 355–71.

Alphen, Ernst van. *Caught by History: Holocaust Effects in Contemporary Art, Literature, and Theory* (Stanford: Stanford University Press, 1997).

American Psychiatric Association. *Diagnostic and Statistical Manual of Mental Disorders*, fourth edition (Washington, DC: American Psychiatric Association, 1994).

Amiel, Diane. 'Specifically Balkan Art'. *Third Text* 21, no. 2 (2007), 137–44.

Anderson, Malcolm. *Frontiers: Territory and State Formation in the Modern World* (Oxford: Politi, 1996).

Andreas, Peter. *Blue Helmets and Black Market: The Business of Survival in the Siege of Sarajevo* (Ithaca: Cornell University Press, 2008).

Anzieu, Didier. *The Skin Ego* (New Haven: Yale University Press, 1989).

Babić, Dušan. 'Journalism in Post-Dayton Bosnia: How to Make the Media More Responsible'. In *Reconstructing Multiethnic Societies: The Case of Bosnia-Herzegovina*, edited by Džemal Sokolović and Florian Bieber (Aldershot: Ashgate, 2001), 157–66.

Baer, Ulrich. *Spectral Evidence: The Photography of Trauma* (Cambridge: The MIT Press, 2005).

Baker, Alan R. H. 'Introduction: The Identifying of Spaces and Places'. In *Space and Place: Mirrors of Social and Cultural Identities*, edited by Dominique Vanneste (Leuven: ACTA Geographica, 1996), 1–2.

Bal, Mieke. *Of What One Cannot Speak: Doris Salcedo's Political Art* (Chicago: The University of Chicago Press, 2010).

Baudrillard, Jean. *The Gulf War Did Not Take Place*. Translated by Michael Howard and Peter Paret (Bloomington: Indiana University Press, 1995).

Baydoun, Abbas. 'Culture and Arts; Re: The Actual'. In *Home Works: A Forum on Cultural Practices in the Region*, edited by Christine Tohme (Beirut: The Lebanese Association for Plastic Arts, Ashkal Alwan, 2003), 22–31.

Benjamin, Walter. *Illumination's*. Translated by Harry Zorn (New York: Schocken, 1969).

Benjamin, Walter. 'Short History of Photography'. *Artforum International* 15, no. 6 (February 1977), 46–61.

Benjamin, Walter. *One-Way Street*. Translated by Edmund Jephcott and Kingsley Shorter (London: New Left Books, 1979).

Benjamin, Walter. 'The Task of the Translator: An Introduction to the Translation of Baudelaire's *Tableaux Parisiens*'. In *Illuminations*, edited by Hannah Arendt, translated by Harry Zorn (London: Pimlico, 1999), 70–82.

Bennett, Jill. 'Dis/Identification: Art, Affect, and the "Bad Death:" Strategies for Communicating the Sense Memory of Loss'. *Signs: Journal of Women in Culture and Society* 28 (2002), 333–51.

Bennett, Jill. *Empathic Vision: Affect, Trauma and Contemporary Art* (Stanford: Stanford University Press, 2005).

Benthien, Claudia. *Skin: On the Cultural Border between Self and the World* (New York: Columbia University Press, 2002).

Berg, Rosemary van den. *Nyoongar People of Australia: Perspectives on Racism and Multiculturalism* (Leiden: Brill, 2002).

Bieber, Florian. 'Bosnia-Herzegovina and Lebanon: Historical Lessons of Two Multireligious States'. *Third World Quarterly* 21 (2000), 269–81.

Biehl, João and Peter Locke. 'Deleuze and the Anthropology of Becoming'. *Current Antrhopology* 51, no. 3 (June 2010), 317–51.

Biemann, Ursula, ed. *Geography and the Politics of Mobility* (Vienna: Generali Foundation, 2003).

Biesboer, Pieter. *Frans Hals und Haarlems Meister der Goldenen Zeit* (München: Hirmer Verlag, 2008).

Bilać Miroslav. 'Paintings Exhibited in the Lobby'. In *The Siege of Sarajevo 1992–1996*, edited by Suada Kapić (Sarajevo: FAMA, 2000), 213.

Blažević, Dunja. 'Before After'. In *Meeting Point, Sarajevo 1997: First Annual Exhibition of the Soros Center for Contemporary Arts Sarajevo* (Sarajevo: Soros Center for Contemporary Art, 1997), 8–13.

Blažević, Dunja. 'They Are Coming'. In *Maxumim* (Sarajevo: Soros Center for Contemporary Art, 2000), 3–7.

Blažević, Dunja. 'Her Name Is Bajević, Maja Bajević'. In *Maja Bajević: Women at Work* (Sarajevo: National Gallery of Bosnia and Herzegovina, 2002), 25–35.

Bredekamp, Horst. 'Bodies of Language'. In *Danica Dakić* (Köln: Verlag der BuchhandlungWalther König, 2009), 33–8.

Bringa, Tone. *Being Muslim the Bosnian Way: Identity and Community in a Central Bosnian Village* (Princeton: Princeton University Press, 1995).

Buchanan, Allen and Margaret Moore, ed. *States, Nations, and Borders. The Ethics of Making Boundaries* (Cambridge: Cambridge University Press, 2003).

Butler, Judith. *Precarious Life: The Powers of Mourning and Violence* (London: Verso, 2004).

Caruth, Cathy. *Trauma: Explorations in Memory* (Baltimore: The Johns Hopkins University Press, 1995).

Caruth, Cathy. *Unclaimed Experience: Trauma, Narrative, History* (Baltimore: The Johns Hopkins University Press, 1996).

Casey, Edward S. *The Fate of Place: A Philosophical History* (Berkeley: The University of California Press, 1997).

Cavell, Stanley. *The Claim of Reason: Wittgenstein, Skepticism, Morality, and Tragedy* (Oxford: Oxford University Press, 1979).

Cavell, Stanley. *The World Viewed, Enlarged Vision* (Cambridge: Harvard University Press, 1979).

Cerkez, Aida. 'Twenty Years on from Its Siege, Sarajevo Still Feels the Emptiness'. *The Independent*, 7 April 2012, p. 33.

Chabrol, Arnaud. 'Le paysage théâtral libanais en sortie de guerre'. In *Journées doctorales*, Université de Provence [blog.univ/provence.fr/gallery/41/ExposésJournéeDoctorale08.pdf].

Chad, Elias. *Posthumous Images: Contemporary Art and Memory Politics in Post-Civil War Lebanon* (Durham and London: Duke University Press, 2018).

Chambers, Iain. *Migrancy, Culture, Identity* (London: Routledge, 1994).

Choueiri, Youssef M. *Breaking the Cycle: Civil Wars in Lebanon* (London: Stacey International, 2007).

Chase, Malcolm and Christopher Shaw, ed. *The Imagined Past: History and Nostalgia* (Manchester: Manchester University Press, 1989).

Clark, T. J. 'A Conversation with Dominique Abensour, Etel Adnan, Rabih Mroué, Jacques Rancière, Michèle Thiériault, Jalal Toufic, Anton Vidokle'. In *Joana Hadjithomas, Khalil Joreige*, edited by Clément Dirié and Michèle Thériault (Zurich: JRP Ringier, 2013), 97–111.

Clausewitz, Carl von. *On War*, edited and translated by Michael Howard and Peter Paret (London: Campbell, 1993).

Colley, Ann C. *Robert Louis Stevenson and the Colonial Imagination* (Burlington: Ashgate, 2004).

Cook, Pam. *Screening the Past: Memory and Nostalgia in Cinema* (London: Routledge, 2005).

Cotter, Suzanne, ed. *Out of Beirut* (Oxford: Modern Art Oxford, 2006).

Coward, Martin. 'Urbicide in Bosnia'. In *Cities, War and Terrorism: Towards an Urban Geopolitics*, edited by Stephen Graham (Oxford: Blackwell, 2004), 154–71.

Cyrulnik, Boris. *Resilience: How Your Inner Strength Can Set You Free from the Past*. Translated by David Macey (London: Penguin, 2009).

Czegldedy, Nina and Andreas Szekeres. 'Agents for Change: The Contemporary Art Centres of the Soros Foundation and C^3'. *Third Text* 23, no. 3 (2009), 251–9.

Dakić, Danica. *Autoportrait*, 1999. Video installation, 4 minutes.

Dakić, Danica, ed. *Danica Dakić: Voices and Images* (Berlin: Revolver, 2004).

Dakić, Danica, ed. *Danica Dakić* (Vienna: Verlag für Moderne Kunst, 2018).

Das, Veena. 'Language and Body: Transactions in the Construction of Pain'. In *Social Suffering*, edited by Arthur Kleinman, Veena Das and Margaret Lock (Berkeley: University of California Press, 1997), 67–91.

Das, Veena. *Life and Words: Violence and the Descent into the Ordinary* (Berkeley: University of California Press, 2007).

David, Catherine. 'Contemporary Arab Representations'. In *Dreams and Conflicts. The Dictatorship of the Viewer: La Biennale di Venezia, 50th International Art Exhibition*, edited by Francesco Bonami (Venezia: Marsilio, 2003), 292–3.

David, Catherine. 'Learning from Beirut: Contemporary Aesthetic Practices in Lebanon'. In *Home Works: A Forum on Cultural Practices in the Region*, edited by Christine Tohme (Beirut: The Lebanese Association for Plastic Arts, Ashkal Alwan, 2003), 32–9.

Demos, T. J. *The Migrant Image: The Art and Politics of Documentary during Global Crisis* (London: Duke University Press, 2013).

Donia, Robert J. *Sarajevo: A Biography* (London: Hurst, 2006).

Douglas, Wilfrid H. *Original Languages of the South-West of Australia* (Canberra: Australian Institute of Aboriginal Studies, 1976).

Drabinski, John. 'Separation, Difference, and Time in Godard's *Ici et ailleurs*'. *SubStance* 37, no. 1 (2008), 148–58.

Drakulić, Slavenka. 'Women and the New Democracy in the Former Yugoslavia'. In *Gender Politics and Post-Communism: Reflections from Eastern Europe and the Former Soviet Union*, edited by Nanette Funk and Magda Mueller (New York and London: Routledge, 1993), 123–30.

Drakulić, Slavenka. 'One Day in the Life of Dražen Erdemović'. In *They Would Never Hurt a Fly: War Criminals on Trial in the Hague* (London: Time Warner Books, 2004), 94–106.

Dugandžić, Daniela. 'Politics between Art and Space: Sarajevo after 1995'. *Research Cluster on Peace, Memory & Cultural Heritage*, July 2018.

Duhaček, Daša. 'Women's Time in the Former Yugoslavia'. In *Gender Politics and Post-Communism: Reflections from Eastern Europe and the Former Soviet Union*, edited by Nanette Funk and Magda Mueller (New York and London: Routledge, 1993), 131–7.

Eager, Charlotte. 'The War Is Over but Sarajevans Cannot Find the Peace They Seek'. *Daily Telegraph*, 6 September 2003.

Elkins, James, ed. *Is Art History Global?* (New York: Routledge, 2007).

Enwezor, Okwui. 'Documentary/Vérité: Bio-Politics, Human Rights, and the Figure of "Truth" in Contemporary Art'. In *Experiments with Truth*, edited by Mark Nash (Pennsauken: FWM, 2005), 97–104.

Eshel, David. 'The Israel-Lebanon Border Enigma'. *IBRU Boundary and Security Bulletin*, (Winter 2000–2001), 72–83.

Evans, Nicolas. 'Aborigines Speak a Primitive Language'. In *Language Myths*, edited by Laurie Bauer and Peter Trudgill (London: Penguin Books, 1998), 159–68.

Farrell, Kirby. *Post-Traumatic Culture: Injury and Interpretation in the Nineties* (Baltimore: The Johns Hopkins University Press, 1998).

Fatthouh, Bassam and Joachim Kolb. 'The Outlook for Economic Reconstruction in Lebanon after the 2006 War'. *The MIT Electronic Journal for Middle East Studies* 6 (2006), 96–114.

Feldman, Hannah and Akram Zaatari. 'Mining War: Fragment from a Conversation Already Passed'. *Art Journal* 66 (2007), 48–67.

Fletcher, Laurel L. and Harvey M. Weinstein. 'A World unto Itself? The Application of International Justice in the Former Yugoslavia'. In *My Neighbor, My Enemy: Justice and Community in the Aftermath of Mass Atrocity*, edited by Eric Stover and Harvey M. Weinstein (Cambridge: Cambridge University Press, 2004), 29–48.

Foucault, Michel. *Society Must Be Defended: Lectures at the Collège de France, 1975–1976*, edited by Mauro Bertani and Alessandro Fontana, translated by David Macey (London: Penguin Books, 2004).

Fregonese, Sara. 'The Urbicide of Beirut? Geopolitics and the Built Environment in the Lebanese Civil War (1975–1976)'. *Political Geography 28*, no 5 (2009), 309–18.

Friedman, Francine. *Bosnia and Herzegovina: A Polity on the Brink* (London and New York: Routledge, 2004).

Funk, Nanette and Magda Mueller, ed. *Gender Politics and Post-Communism: Reflections from Eastern Europe and the Former Soviet Union* (New York and London: Routledge, 1993).

Galili, Lili and Ori Nir. 'Jaffa: City of Strangers'. *Journal of Palestine Studies* 30, no. 3 (Spring 2001), 100–102.

Gallagher, Tom. *Outcast Europe: The Balkans, 1789–1989. From the Ottomans to Milošević* (London: Routledge, 2001).

Gambrell, Jamey. 'Sarajevo: Art in Extremis'. *Art in America* (May 1994), 100–105.

Gana, Nouri. 'Trauma Ties: Chiasmus and Community in Lebanese Civil War Literature'. In *The Future of Trauma Theory: Contemporary Literary and Cultural Criticim*, edited by Gert Buelens, Sam Durrant and Robert Eaglestone (London: Routledge, 2014), 77–90.

Gjelten, Tom. *Sarajevo Daily: A City and Its Newspaper Under Siege* (New York: Harper Collins Publisher, 1995).

Goebel, Rolf J. 'Constructing Chinese History: Kafka's and Dittmar's Orientalist Discourse'. *PMLA* 108, no. 1 (January 1993), 59–71.

Goebel, Rolf J. *Constructing China: Kafka's Orientalist Discourse* (Columbia: Camden House, 1997).

Green, Nicholas. 'Looking at the Landscape: Class Formation and the Visual'. In *The Anthropology of Landscape: Perspectives on Place and Space*, edited by Eric Hirsch and Michael O'Hanlon (Oxford: Clarendon Press, 1995), 31–42.

Greenberg, Clement. 'Collage'. In *Collage: Critical Views*, edited by Katherine Hoffman (Ann Arbor: UMI Research Press, 1989), 383–412.

Gržinić, Marina. *Re-Politicizing Art, Theory, Representation and New Media Technology* (Vienna: Schriften der Akademie der Bildenden Künste Wien, 2008).

Guilhot, Nicolas. 'Reforming the World: George Soros, Global Capitalism and the Philantropic Management of the Social Sciences'. *Critical Sociology* 33 (2007), 447–77.

Hadjithomas, Joana and Khalil Joreige. 'Latency'. In *Homeworks: A Forum on Cultural Practices in the Region*, edited by Christine Tohme (Beirut: The Lebanese Association for Plastic Arts, Ashkal Alwan, 2003), 41–9.

Hadžiomerspahić, Enver. 'From a Hole in the Fence to the Venice Biennale'. In *Artefacts: Bosnia and Herzegovina at the Venice Biennale 1993–2003* (Sarajevo: Ars Aevi Books, 2007), 218–89.

Hajdarpašić, Edin. 'Museums, Multiculturalism and the Remaking of Postwar Sarajevo'. In *(Re)Visualising National History, Museums and National Identities in Europe in the New Millenium*, edited by Robin Ostow (Toronto: University of Toronto Press, 2008), 109–38.

Hall, Stuart. 'Cultural Identity and Diaspora'. In *Identity, Community, Culture, Difference*, edited by Jonathan Rutherford (London: Lawrence & Wishard Limited, 1990), 222–37.

Hanhardt, John G. *The Worlds of Nam June Paik* (New York: Guggenheim Museum, 2000).

Hanssen, Jens-Peter and Daniel Genberg. 'Beirut in Memoriam: A Kaleidoscopic Space Out of Focus'. In *Crisis and Memory in Islamic Societies*, edited by Angelika Neuwirth and Andreas Pflitsch (Beirut: Ergon Verlag Würzburg in Kommission, 2001), 231–62.

Havránek, Vit. 'The Documentary: Ontology of Forms in Transforming Countries'. In *The Green Room: reconsidering the Documentary and Contemporary Art # 1*, edited by Maria Lind and Hito Steyerl (Berlin: Sternberg, 2008), 128–43.

Hayek, Ghenwa. *Beirut, Imagining the City: Space and Place in Lebanese Literature* (London: I.B. Tauris, 2014).

Hensbergen, Gijs van. *Guernica: The Biography of a Twentieth-Century Icon* (London: Bloomsbury, 2004).

Herrschel, Tassilo. *Global Geographies of Post-Socialist Transition: Geographies, Societies, Policies* (London: Routledge, 2007).

Hirsch, Joshua. *Afterimage: Film, Trauma and the Holocaust* (Philadelphia: Temple University Press, 2004).

Hirsch, Marianne. *Family Frames: Photography Narratives and Postmemory* (Cambridge: Harvard University Press, 1997).

Hirsch, Marianne. 'The Generation of Postmemory'. *Poetics Today* 29, no. 1 (Spring 2008), 103–28.

Hromadžić, Azra. 'Kriegsvergewaltigungen in Bosnien: Alte und neue Erklärungsansätze'. In *Gender Identität und kriegerischer Konflikt. Das Beispiel des ehemaligen Jugoslawien*, edited by Ruth Seifert (Münster: LIT Verlag, 2004), 112–30.

Husedžinović, Meliha. 'Aspects and Positions of Art from Bosnia-Herzegovina'. In *Organising & Curating the Transition* (Sarajevo: Conference Reader, May 1997), 10–13.

Husedžinović, Meliha. 'Meeting Point'. In *Meeting Point: Sarajevo 1997* (Sarajevo: Soros Centre for Contemporary Arts, 1997), 14–20.

Huyssen, Andreas. 'Present, Pasts: Media, Politics, Amnesia'. *Public Culture* 12, no. 1 (2000), 21–38.

Huyssen, Andreas, ed. *Other Cities, Other Worlds: Urban Imaginaries in a Globalizing Age* (Durham and London: Duke University Press, 2008).

Hynes, Samuel. 'Personal Narratives and Commemoration'. In *War and Remembrance*, edited by Jay Winter and Emmanuel Sivan (Cambrdige: Cambridge University Press, 1999), 205–20.

Iveković, Rada. 'The Intellectual and Artistic Diaspora'. *Art Press* 192 (1994), 42–5.

Jakobson, Roman. 'Shifters, Verbal Categories, and the Russian Verb'. In *Selected Writings. Vol. 2: Word and Language* (Paris: Mouton, 1971), 130–47.

Jansen, Stef. 'Homeless at Home: Narrations of Post-Yugoslav Identities'. In *Migrants of Identity: Perceptions of Home in a World Movement*, edited by Nigel Rapport and Andrew Dawson (Oxford: Berg, 1998), 85–109.

Johnston, Judith. 'The Genesis and Commodification of Katherine Langloh Parker's *Australian Legendery Tales* (1986)'. *Jasal* 4 (2005), 159–72.

Jones, Amelia. *Self/Image: Technology, Representation and the Contemporary Project* (London: Routledge, 2006).

Joreige, Lamia. *Houna Wa Roubbam Hounak* [Here and Perhaps Elsewhere], 2003. Video documentary, 54 minutes.

Joreige, Lamia. *A Journey*, 2006. Video documentary, 41 minutes.

Joreige, Lamia. 'Object Lessons', *Artforum* (October 2006), 241.

Joreige, Lamia. 'Disappearance and Memory of War'. In *Politics of Memory: Documentary and Archive*, edited by Mario Scotini and Elisabetta Galesso (Berlin: Archive Books, 2013), 81–91.

Jović, Dejan. 'Yugoslavism and Yugoslav Communism: From Tito to Kardelj'. In *Yugoslavism: Histories of a Failed Idea*, edited by Dejan Djakić (London: Hurst & Co, 2003), 157–81.

Jung, Dietrich, ed. *The Middle East and Palestine: Global Politics and Regional Conflict* (New York: Palgrave Macmillan, 2004).

Kafka, Franz. *The Complete Short Stories* (London: Minerva, 1992).

Kaldor, Mary. *New and Old Wars: Organized Violence in a Global Era* (Stanford: Stanford University Press, 2007).

Kapić, Suada, ed. *Sarajevo Survival Guide* (Sarajevo: FAMA, 1993).

Kapić, Suada. *The Siege of Sarajevo 1992–1996* (Sarajevo: FAMA, 2000).

Kathib, Lina. *Lebanese Cinema: Imagining the Civil War and beyond* (London: I.B. Tauris, 2008).

Khalaf, Samir. *Civil and Uncivil Violence in Lebanon: A History of the Internationalization of Communal Conflict* (New York: Columbia University Press, 2002).

Khalaf, Samir. *Heart of Beirut: Reclaiming the Bourj* (London: Saqi, 2006).

Klapproth Muazzin, Danièle. 'Holding the World in Place: Narrative as Social Practice in Anglo-Western and Central Australian Aboriginal Culture' (PhD diss., University of Bern, 2001).

Klarmann, Christoph Gerhard. 'The Taif Agreement: A Historical Perspective' (Master Thesis, American University of Beirut, 2006).

Kristeva, Julia. 'Strangers to Ourselves'. In *The Portable Kristeva*, edited by Oliver Kelly (New York: Columbia University Press, 1997), 264–94.

Kuspit, Donald B. 'Collage: The Organizing Principle of Art in the Age of the Relativity of Art'. in *Collage: Critical Views*, edited by Katherine Hoffman (Ann Arbor: UMI Research Press, 1989), 39–57.

Labaki, Boutros. 'The Postwar Economy: A Miracle That Didn't Happen'. In *Lebanon in Limbo: Postwar Society and State in an Uncertain Regional Environment*, edited by Theodor Hanf and Nawaf Salam (Baden-Baden: Nomos Verlagsgesellschaft, 2003), 181–96.

LaCapra, Dominick. *History and Memory after Auschwitz* (Ithaca and London: Cornell University Press, 1998).

LaCapra, Dominick. *Writing History, Writing Trauma* (Baltimore and London: The Johns Hopkins University Press, 2001).

Larkin, Craig. *Memory and Conflict in Lebanon: Remembering and Forgetting the Past* (London: Routledge, 2012).

Lasserre, Michel. 'The Reasons for These Photographs, or Moriyama's Dog'. In *Essays & Stories on Photography in Lebanon*, edited by Clémence Cottard Hachem and Nour Salamé (Beirut: Kaph Books, 2018), 101–9.

Leese, Peter. *Shell Shock: Traumatic Neurosis and the British Soldiers of the First World War* (Basingstoke: Palgrave Macmillan, 2002).

LeVine, Mark. *Overthrowing Geography: Jaffa, Tel Aviv, and the Struggle for Palestine, 1880–1948* (Berkeley: University of California Press, 2005).

Leydesdorff, Selma. *Surviving the Bosnian Genocide: The Women of Srebrenica Speak* (Bloomington: Indiana University Press, 2011).

Liebman, Stuart, ed. *Claude Lanzmann's Shoah: Key Essays* (Oxford: Oxford University Press, 2007).

Lofranco, Zaira Tiziana. 'Displace in the Native City: Movement and Locality in Post-War Sarajevo'. In *Moving Places: Relations, Return, and Belonging*, edited by Nataša Gregorić Bon and Jaka Repič (New York: Berghahn Books, 2016).

Lowenthal, David. 'Nostalgia Tells It Like It Wasn't'. In *The Imagined Past: History and Nostalgia*, edited by Christopher Shaw and Malcolm Chase (Manchester: Manchester University Press, 1989), 18–32.

Luckhurst, Roger. *The Trauma Question* (London: Routledge, 2008).

MacBean, James Roy. 'Godard and the Dziga Vertov Group: Film and Dialectics'. *Film Quarterly* 26, no. 1 (Autumn 1972), 30–44.

Maček, Ivana. *Sarajevo under Siege: Anthropology in Wartime* (Philadelphia: University of Pennsylvania Press, 2009).

Makdisi, Jean Said. *Beirut Fragments: A War Memoir* (New York: Persea Books, 1990).

Makdisi, Samir. *The Lessons of Lebanon: The Economics of War and Development* (London: I.B. Tauris, 2004).

Makdisi, Saree. 'Beirut / Beirut'. In *Tamáss: Contemporary Arab Representations, Beirut / Lebanon*, edited by Catherine David (Barcelona: Fundació Antoni Tàpies, 2002), 26–39.

Makdisi, Saree. 'Beirut, a City without History'. In *Memory and Violence and the Middle East and North Africa*, edited by Ussama Makdisi and Paul A. Silverstein (Bloomington: Indiana University Press, 2006), 201–14.

Makhzoumi, Jala. 'Marginal Landscapes, Marginalized Rural Communities: Sustainable Post-War Recovery in Southern Lebanon'. In *Lessons in Post-War Reconstruction: Case Studies from Lebanon in the Aftermath of the 2006* War, edited by Howayda Al-Harithy (London: Routledge, 2010), 127–57.

Masawi, André. 'Film Production and Jaffa's Predicament'. *Jaffa Diaries* (9 February 1998), www.jaffacity.com.

McNeill, David. 'Australia: An Unresolved Problem'. In *The Resilient Landscape*, edited by Phillip George, David McNeill and Khaled Sabsabi (Paddington: Ivan Dougherty Gallery, 2007), 6–11.

Minh-ha, Trihn T. 'Other than Myself/My Other Self'. In *Traveller's Tales: Narratives of Home and Displacement*, edited by Jon Bird, Barry Curtis, Melinda Mash, Tim Putnam, George Robertson and Lisa Tickner (London: Routledge, 1994), 9–26.

Mitchell, W. J. T., ed. *Landscape and Power* (Chicago and London: The University of Chicago Press, 2002).

Mlinar, Zdravko. *Globalisation and Territorial Identities* (London: Avebury, 1996).

Moore, Michael. 'On the Signification of Walls in Verbal and Visual Art'. *Leonardo* 12, no. 4 (Autumn 1979), 311–13.

Mugraby, Muhamad. 'The Syndrome of One-Time Exceptions and the Drive to Establish the Proposed Hariri Court'. In *The Politics of Violence, Truth and Reconciliation in the Arab Middle East*, edited by Sune Haugbolle and Anders Hastrup (New York: Routledge, 2009), 21–43.

Mumford, Lewis. 'What Is a City?'. In *The City Reader*, edited by Richard T. LeGates and Frederic Stout (London: Routledge, 2000), 92–6.

Munder, Heiked, and Raphael Gygax, ed. *Maja Bajevic: Power, Governance, Labor* (Zurich: Migros Museum, 2017).

Naccache, Albert Farid Henry. 'Beirut's Memorycide: Hear No Evil, See No Evil'. In *Archaeology under Fire*, edited by Lynn Meskell (London: Routledge, 1997), 140–58.

Naef, Silvia. *A la recherche d'une modernité arabe. L'évolution des arts plastiques en Egypte, au Liban et en Irak* (Genève: Editions Slatkine, 1996).

Neweklowsky, Gerhard. *Die bosnisch-herzegowinischen Muslime: Geschichte, Bräuche, Alltagskultur* (Klagenfurt-Salzburg: Wieser Verlag, 1996).

Nochlin, Linda. 'Documented Success'. *Artforum International* (September 2002), 159–63.

Nora, Pierre. 'General Introduction: Between Memory and History'. In *Rethinking the French Past: Realms of Memory, vol. 1: Conflicts and Divisions*, edited by Pierre Nora, translated by Arthur Goldhammer (New York: Columbia University Press, 1996), 1–23.

Pachmanová, Martina. 'In? Out? In Between? Some Notes on the Invisibility of a Nascent Eastern European Feminist and Gender Discourse in Contemporary Art Theory (2009)'. In *Gender Check: A Reader. Art and Theory in Eastern Europe*, edited by Bojana Pejić (Cologne: Walther König, 2010), 37–49.

Parker, Rozsika. *The Subversive Stitch: Embroidery and the Making of the Feminine* (New York: I.B. Tauris, 2010).

Pejić, Bojana. 'Maja Bajević: The Matrix of Memory'. In *Maja Bajević: Women at Work* (Sarajevo: National Gallery, 2002), 69–100.

Pejić, Bojana. 'The Angel Effect'. In *Danica Dakić: Voices and Images* (Frankfurt am Main: Revolver, 2004), 110–13.

Pejić, Bojana. 'The Communist Body. Towards an Archaeology of Images: Politics or Representation and Spatialization of Power in the SFR Yugoslavia (1945–1991)' (PhD diss., Berlin, Humboldt University, 2005).

Pejić, Bojana. 'The Morning After: Plavi Radion, Abstract Art, and Bananas (2002)'. In *Gender Check: A Reader. Art and Theory in Eastern Europe*, edited by Bojana Pejić (Cologne: Walther König, 2010), 97–110.

Popovicova, Iva. *New Body Politic: Czech and Polish Women's Art of the 1990s* (Saarbrücken: VDM Verlag, 2008).

Preston, Matthew. *Ending Civil War: Rhodesia and Lebanon in Perspective* (London: Tauris Academic Studies, 2004).

Riedlmayer, Andras. 'The War on People and the War on Culture'. *The New Combat: A Journal of Reason and Resistance* 3 (Autumn 1994), 16–19.

Rimbaud, Arthur. *Œuvres Complètes* (Paris: Gallimard, 1972).

Robben, Antonius C. G. M. and Carolyn Nordstrom. 'The Anthropology and Ethnography of Violence and Sociopolitical Conflict'. In *Fieldwork under Fire: Contemporary Studies of Violence and Survival*, edited by Antonius C. G. M. Robben and Carolyn Nordstrom (Berkeley: University of California Press, 1995), 1–24.

Rogers, Sarah. 'Forging History, Performing Memory: Walid Raad's the Atlas Group'. *Parachute* 108 (2002), 68–79.

Rogers, Sarah. 'Postwar Art and the Historical Roots of Beirut's Cosmopolitanism' (PhD diss., MIT, 2008).

Rogoff, Irit. 'Engendering Terror'. In *Geography and the Politics of Mobility*, edited by Ursula Biemann (Vienna: Generali Foundation, 2003), 48–63.

Rotbard, Sharon. *White City Black City: Architecture and War in Tel Aviv and Jaffa* (Cambridge: MIT Press, 2015).

Runia, Eelco. 'Forget About It: Parallel Processing in the Srebrenica Report'. *History and Theory* 43, no. 3 (October 2004), 295–320.

Said, Edward. 'Reflections on Exile'. In *Reflections on Exile and Other Literary and Cultural Essays* (London: Granta, 2000), 173–86.

Salam, Nawaf. 'Taif Revisited'. In *Lebanon in Limbo: Postwar Society and State in an Uncertain Regional Environment*, edited by Theodor Hanf and Nawaf Salam (Baden-Baden: Nomos, 2003), 39–41.

Saliba, Robert. 'The Mental Image of Downtown Beirut, 1990'. In *Beyrouth: Regards Croisés*, edited by Michael F. Davie (Tours: Université François Rabelais, 1996), 305–49.

Sawalha, Aseel. 'Healing the Wounds of the War: Placing the War-Displaced in Postwar Beirut'. In *Wounded Cities*, edited by Jane Schneider and Ida Susser (Oxford: Berg, 2003), 271–90.

Schmitz, François. *Wittgenstein* (Paris: Les Belles Lettres, 1999).

Schreiber Thomas. 'Karl Bühler, Sein Leben und Werk' (PhD diss., Universität Würzburg, 2009).

Schröder, Ingo W. and Bettina E. Schmidt, ed. *Anthropology of Violence and Conflict* (London: Routledge, 2001).

Sekula, Allan. 'Dismantling Modernism, Reinventing Documentary (Notes on the Politics of Representation)'. *The Massachusetts Review* 19, no. 4, Photography (Winter 1978), 859–83.

Sekulić, Dusko, Garth Massey and Randy Hodson. 'Who Were the Yugoslavs? Failed Sources of Common Identity in the Former Yugoslavia'. *American Sociological Review* 59, no. 1 (February 1994), 83–97.

Simmons, Cynthia. 'Women Engaged/Engaged Art in Postwar Bosnia: Reconciliation, Recovery, and Civil Society'. *The Carl Beck Papers in Russian & East European Studies* (2005), 2010.

Slive, Seymour. *Frans Hals* (Munich: Prestel-Verlag, 1989).

Smith, Adam. 'Consideration Concerning the First Formation of Languages'. In *Lectures on Rhetoric and Belles Lettres* (Oxford: The Clarendon Press, 1983), 203–26.

Spieler, Reinhard. 'Voices of Identity'. In *Danica Dakić: Voices and Images* (Frankfurt am Main: Revolver, 2004), 60–5.

Srebrenica: Errinerung für die Zukunft (Berlin: Heinrich-Böll-Stiftung, 2005).

Stanner, W. E. H. 'The Dreaming'. In *Traditional Aboriginal Society*, edited by W. H. Edwards (Melbourne: Macmillan Australia, 1987), 225–36.

Stefansson, Anders. 'Urban Exile: Locals, Newcomers and the Cultural Transformation of Sarajevo'. In *The New Bosnian Mosaic: Identities, Memories and Moral Claims in a Post-War Society*, edited by Xavier Bougarel, Elissa Helms and Ger Duijzings (Aldershot: Ashgate, 2007), 59–77.

Stevenson, Robert Louis. 'The Isle of Voices'. In *The South Sea Tales* (Oxford: Oxford University Press, 1999), 103–22.

Stoll, Avrum. *Twentieth-Century Analytic Philosophy* (New York: Columbia University Press, 2000).

Stow, Catherine [Catherine Langloh Parker]. *Woggheeguy* (Adelaide: Preece, 1930).

Susser, Ida and Jane Schneider, ed. *Wounded Cities: Destruction and Reconstruction in a Globalized World* (Oxford: Berg, 2003).

Tamari, Salim and Rema Hammami. 'Virtual Returns to Jaffa'. *Journal of Palestine Studies* 27, no. 4 (Summer 1998), 65–79.

Tito, Josip Broz. *The National Question* (Belgrade: Socialist Thought and Practice, 1983).

Todorova, Maria. *Imagining the Balkans* (Oxford: Oxford University Press, 1997).

Tohme, Christine, ed. *Missing Links: Art Practices from Lebanon* (Cairo: Townhouse Gallery of Contemporary Art, 2001).

Tohme, Christine, ed. *Home Works II. A Forum on Cultural Practices* (Beirut: The Lebanese Association for Plastic Arts, Ashkal Alwan, 2003).

Toufic, Jalal. 'Ruins'. In *Tamáss: Contemporary Arab Representations. Beirut / Lebanon 1*, edited by Catherine David (Barcelona: Fundació Antoni Tàpies, 2002), 19–25.

Tulloch, Graham. 'Stevenson and Islands: Scotland and the South Pacific'. In *Robert Louis Stevenson Reconsidered: New Critical Perspectives*, edited by William B. Jones (Jefferson, NC: McFarland, 2003), 68–82.

Ugrešić, Dubravka. *The Culture of Lies: Antipolitical Essays* (London: Phoenix House, 1998).

Ulmer, Gregory L. 'The Object of Post-Criticism'. In *Collage: Critical Views*, edited by Katherine Hoffman (Ann Arbor: UMI Research Press, 1989), 383–412.

Virilio, Paul. *Bunker Archeology*. Translated by George Collins (New York: Princeton Architectural Press, 1994).

Virilio, Paul. *Negative Horizon: An Essay in Dromoscopy*. Translated by Michael Degener (London: Continuum, 2005).

Virilio, Paul and Sylvère Lotringer. *Pure War: Twenty-Five Years Later* (Los Angeles: Semiotexte, 2008).

Volkan, Vamik D. 'Ancient Fuel for a Modern Inferno: Time Collapse in Bosnia-Herzegovina'. In *Bloodlines: From Ethnic Pride to Ethnic Terrorism* (Boulder: Westview Press, 1997), 50–81.

Volkic, Zala, Karmen Erjavec and Mallory Peak. 'Branding Post-War Sarajevo'. *Journalism Studies* 15, no. 6 (2014), 726–42.

Wagner, Sarah. *To Know Where He Lies: DNA Technology and the Search for Srebrenica's Missing* (Berkeley: University of California Press, 2008).

Wagner, Sarah. 'Tabulating Loss, Entombing Memory: The Srebrenica-Potočari Memorial Centre'. In *Memory, Mourning, Landscape*, edited by Elizabeth Anderson, Avril Maddrell, Kate McLoughlin and Alana Vincent (Amsterdam: Rodopi, 2010), 61–78.

Wasserman, Tina. 'Constructing the Image of Postmemory'. In *The Image and the Witness. Trauma, Memory and Visual Culture*, edited by Frances Guerin and Roger Hallas (London: Wallflower Press, 2007), 159–72.

Weinstein, Harvey M. and Eric Stover, ed. *My Neighbor, My Enemy: Justice and Community in the Aftermath of Mass Atrocity* (Cambridge: Cambridge University Press, 2004).

Westmoreland, Mark Ryan. 'Crisis of Representation: Experimental Documentary in Postwar Lebanon' (PhD diss., The University of Texas, 2008).

Wilson-Goldie, Kaelen. 'Digging for Fire: Contemporary Art Practices in Postwar Lebanon' (Master thesis, American University of Beirut, 2005).

Wilson-Goldie, Kaelen. 'Contemporary Practices in Post-War Lebanon'. In *Out of Beirut*, edited by Suzanne Cotter (Oxford: Modern Art Oxford, 2006), 81–89.

Wilson-Goldie, Kaelen. 'Witness to Loss: Group Tuesday'. *Bidoun: Arts and Culture from the Middle East* 1 (2007), 27.

Wittgenstein, Ludwig. *Tractatus Logico-Philosophicus*, translated by D. F. Pears and B. F. McGuiness (London: Routledge, 2010).

Wittgenstein, Ludwig. *Philosophical Remarks*. Edited by Rush Rhees, translated by Raymond Hargreaves and Roger White (Chicago: Chicago University Press, 1975).

Yacoub, Paola. 'The Holiday Inn Cycle'. In *Conflict and Memory: Bridging Past and Future in [South East] Europe*, edited by Wolfgang Petritsch and Verdan Džihić (Baden-Baden: Nomos, 2010), 143–51.

Yacoub, Paola. 'Text Given at a Conference at Bal, Paris'. (Working paper, December 2011).

Yacoub, Paola. 'Trust Us'. In *Home Beirut: Sounding the Neighbors*, edited by Hou Hanru and Giulia Ferracci (Rome: Maxxi Museo Nazionale delle Arti del XXI Secolo, 2017), 60–6.

Yacoub, Paola and Michel Lasserre. 'An Unprogrammed City'. In *The Remembrance of a City, the History of a Space: An International Symposium on Alternative Space* (Seoul: the Korean culture & arts foundation, INSA, 2002), 27–33.

Yacoub, Paola and Michel Lasserre. 'An Unprogrammed City'. In *Dreams and Conflicts. The Dictatorship of the Viewer, La Biennale di Venezia, 50th International Art Exhibition*, edited by Francesco Bonami (Venice: Marsilio, 2003), 294–7.

Yacoub, Paola and Michel Lasserre. *Beirut Is a Magnificent City: Synoptic Pictures* (Barcelona: Fundació Antoni Tàpies, 2003).

Yacoub, Paola and Michel Lasserre. 'A Brief Journey Towards Scepticism'. In *Out of Beirut*, edited by Suzanne Cotter (Oxford: Modern Art Oxford, 2006), 9.

Zelizer, Craig Mitchell. 'The Role of Artistic Processes in Peacebuilding in Bosnia-Herzegovina' (PhD diss., Fairfax: George Mason University, 2004).

Index